W9-CQO-696

25

snapshot

BY

HOWARD BLINDER

authorHOUSE®

Library Resource Center
Renton Technical College
3000 N.E. 4th Street
Renton, WA 98056

AuthorHouse™
1663 Liberty Drive
Bloomington, IN 47403
www.authorhouse.com
Phone: 1-800-839-8640

© *2011 Howard Blinder. All rights reserved.*

No part of this book may be reproduced, stored in a retrieval system, or transmitted by any means without the written permission of the author.

First published by AuthorHouse 10/13/2011

ISBN: 978-1-4567-6497-5 (ebk)
ISBN: 978-1-4567-6498-2 (hc)
ISBN: 978-1-4567-6499-9 (sc)

Library of Congress Control Number: 2011908105

Printed in the United States of America

Any people depicted in stock imagery provided by Thinkstock are models, and such images are being used for illustrative purposes only.
Certain stock imagery © Thinkstock.

This book is printed on acid-free paper.

Because of the dynamic nature of the Internet, any web addresses or links contained in this book may have changed since publication and may no longer be valid. The views expressed in this work are solely those of the author and do not necessarily reflect the views of the publisher, and the publisher hereby disclaims any responsibility for them.

828.979 BLINDER 2011

Blinder, Howard

Snapshot

Snapshot Detection

This book is dedicated to Bernice Blinder my mother, my mentor, my best friend. Without her continued encouragement and support these small segments of my life would not have reached the following pages.

Acknowledgments

The writing of this book has provided a truly unique and unexpected pleasure in my life. The actual task of committing these memories into print has given me an opportunity to relive many experiences that were fun or at least unusual the first time around.

The Snapshot stories collection could not have been transcribed without the help and encouragement from family members. I would like to give special thanks to my mother Bernice, my sister Nancy, my father Sidney, now passed on, and to my children Felicia, Aimee, James and Chrystal.

Many of the accounts in this book are based on my long and happy association with the Harrison family of Wheatland, CA, my dear friends Dave & Pam Hunt who introduced me to Ben & Mary, Bill & Pauline, Rick & Sherri, Anita, Winnie, Jack & Louise, Amy & Bill, Bernard, Stevie, David, Brian & Karen, Mike, Carrie, Debby, Ralph, Peewee, Bob Harrison, and not to ignore all of the extended family, children, and close friends.

Through the years many of my friends have remained near and dear while others have drifted away. I apologize in advance for leaving someone out, but here is a special thanks to Kenny & Val, Paul & Lizz, Jay & Mickey, Bill & Linda, Crag & Gail, Don B, Don W, Myron & Judy, Jim & Bev, Butch & Barbara, Bobby & Kath, Kenny K, The Dove, John & Annette, JA & Dotty, Freeman & Kathy, Al, Mickey, Jim & Sandy, Cherryl, Angie, and Susie.

I certainly do not want to neglect my best friend and soul mate, my wife Carol who has learned to back up a trailer and has patiently listened to most of my stories way too many times.

All of the illustrations that accompany the Snapshot stories were drawn by my good friend Phil Armstrong. Copy editing was skillfully done at the hands of Hazel Barnes and then fine tuned and perfected by Sue Newton. Original book design and tolerant mentoring were by Joe Menkin.

Thank you all,

Howard Blinder

Contents

snapshot

BY
HOWARD BLINDER

Introduction

When I tell one of my stories at a party or at some kind of gathering, it is usually followed by laughter. Then occasionally someone in the group will ask me if the story is true. "Well, of course it's true," I respond without hesitation. "I'm surprised that you would even ask," I typically answer their question in mock defense with a smile on my face. But in reality as I myself read through the subject matter it is easy to see why some of the stories may sound as if they were made up; so this question of veracity does not really hurt my feelings. I freely admit that I will occasionally embellish the facts; however most of the Snapshot stories are taken from real events in my life. Two or three stories in this collection were told to me by close friends. I have transcribed their words from memory and I take them to be true as well.

Some of my friends are a bit shy, so I found the need to change a name or two in this writing. These name changes were done to avoid unnecessary embarrassment, but you know who you are.

Many of my near friends will read this collection in print for the first time and think back on events they shared with me. They will probably laugh when reliving their story; however I realize that most readers are not acquainted with the Harrison family of Wheatland, California, the local folklore in Sandpoint, Idaho, the residents of Budlong Avenue in Torrance, California, or the trials and tribulations associated with owning an antique locker plant and bait route in Oroville, California.

For you I simply hope that you get pleasure in the reading of these snapshots from my life. I can honestly say that I have enjoyed every minute of living these experiences and am very pleased to be sharing them with you now.

Thank you for choosing to read the Snapshot series of stories.

Enjoy the reading,
Howard Blinder

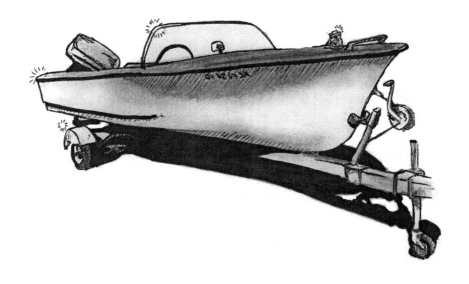

No Strings Attached

*N*o strings attached. That is what my dad said. I still can't quite believe this is true as I finish buffing a third coat of paste wax on my beautiful new fourteen-foot ski boat.

I turned sixteen this year. I am just an average student and enjoy some of the high school sports. Last year I went out for football as a halfback. I was really too small and got to sit on the bench a lot. About half way into the season I broke my nose during scrimmage. This gave me a real good reason to quit football without looking bad, and I actually had a good time the rest of the year watching the game from the stands. Track is where I excelled, especially the sprints. There is something about running without someone chasing you that has always appealed to me.

School sports don't come close to my favorite sporting activity—water skiing. My parents own a boat shop in Marina Del Rey, California. They sell small eight-foot dinghies that are used as tenders for larger boats. They also sell—my favorite—a fourteen-foot runabout type ski boat. As a kid growing up, having a boat available was never a problem. Almost all of our family vacations included some kind of water activity. My friends were always welcome on the weekend outings and most of them were introduced to water skiing, as I was, around the age of twelve or thirteen.

When I was fourteen, I started working in the boat shop. I don't remember if it was voluntary or mandatory but it happened. Nowadays, I am a two-year veteran; even have my own set of keys. My working schedule is a couple of hours every day after school and at least one weekend day each week. I enjoy installing hardware on the boats and talking to customers. It's easy to talk about something you love to do. Sometimes I get to go out on the demonstration rides with my dad and potential customers. On nice days Dad will let me ski. That is really a good way to show off how the boat performs. With all modesty, I am a good skier; I only weigh 110 pounds so I get up easy and I can probably make any small ski-boat look better than it really is.

Yesterday my dad gave me my own boat.

"You're giving it to me? Why?" I asked.

"Because you like skiing, and I know you'll take good care of it."

His explanation seemed plausible, but did not exactly answer the "why" question. My dad wasn't cheap; he paid me for working in the boat shop, but excluding birthdays and Christmas, I wasn't usually blessed with unexpected presents; especially gifts of this magnitude. So cautiously I pressed.

"You're giving me this brand-new boat, no strings attached. How many years will I have to work for free?"

"Son, I can't believe how hard you're making this for me. Why can't you understand that the boat is yours? All I'm asking you to do is take care of it. Keep it clean and shiny. You don't have to pay me anything, or work it off. We'll keep it here at the shop for show. The only thing that I might ask you to do is take an occasional customer out for a demo ride."

Now we have it, the two small words, "demo ride." My dad is a good businessman, and also an excellent salesman. Even though he enjoys boating himself and would love to go out on a demonstration ride, he knows that his time is better spent working in the shop as a salesman. He can usually sell two or three boats on an average weekend. So if he takes off for a three-hour demonstration ride it might cost him two sales. The other thing is that I don't have a driver's license, yet. As far as my dad is concerned, I will keep the boat polished up like a new dime and the only way that I will get to use it is when I give demonstrations to customers. They will pull the boat with their own vehicle and I will go along and show them how to use it. Then I will clean it up again when we get home. It will probably require more weekend work than I usually do; if you can call that work. Even knowing all of this, having my own boat is way too good of a deal for me to pass up. I stopped arguing and thanked my dad for the boat, promising to keep it looking beautiful.

Today is Sunday and I've been at the shop since seven a.m. My best friend, David, should be here in a couple of minutes to see if I was telling him the truth. Maybe I will have time for just one more coat of wax.

"So, Dave, what do you think? I'm sure this clamp-on hitch won't hurt the bumper on your mom's car. They're made to go on cars. Let's do it!"

"Are you positive this is all right with your dad?" Dave asked for about the tenth time.

"Yeah, I'm sure. It's my boat and I can do anything I want with it. He told me so, just as long as I keep it clean."

"Tighten those bolts some more. I think the bumper will probably straighten back out after we take it off."

After getting the trailer hitch secured we went to work on the lights. I was wishing that we had done the lights first because I kept hitting my head and back on the long bolts that stuck down from the rented trailer hitch. My knuckles were cut some from when the wrench slipped, but most of the blood on my T-shirt was from my forehead. I had a pair of water skis that I made in wood shop last semester and a brand-new towrope with double handles. We were going skiing.

Dave got behind the wheel and cautiously pulled out into traffic. He did seem a bit nervous but once we got going he settled down. The boat pulled like a dream. I couldn't help looking back as it followed us, still not quite believing that it was actually mine. About one hour later we arrived at the water. It was a beautiful sunny day, with just a slight breeze. David and I were both so excited that it could have been raining and we wouldn't have noticed. There was only one car way down on the end of the ramp so we had the place pretty much to ourselves.

"OK, Dave, back her in."

For the past couple of minutes we had been sitting in the car facing the water, almost daydreaming. Now Dave pulled forward and started a turn, which took us across the road where other cars and trailers all seemed to be parking. Then we began to back up but the boat and trailer didn't want to go the way that Dave intended. The car was backing in the right direction toward the water, but the boat was heading back down the road we came in on. This did not seem like a good plan to me.

"Dave, the boat is going the wrong way."

"You don't think I can see that!"

David continued backing until the noise started. We stopped, really quick, and I jumped out. The boat and car were at right angles to each other. I found out later that this is called a jackknife. It's a good thing that we were going slowly, because nothing bad happened, except for bending the bumper a little and scraping some paint off of the boat-trailer tongue. There was also a small dent about the size of my fist in the car fender that I think must have been there before. So I got back in the car and didn't see any reason to mention the little dent to Dave.

"We're OK, pull ahead and try her again."

Dave pulled ahead, now blocking the road with the boat, and just our luck, two cars pulled up close to us, one coming from each direction. The other drivers didn't honk or anything, they just sat there looking at us while Dave started backing up again. The trailer went the right way this time and the cars drove away. Pretty soon the trailer began turning away from the water all by itself. I glanced over at Dave, but didn't say anything because he was way turned around in the seat looking through the back window so hard that his face was getting red, and I wasn't exactly sure how he was managing to keep his feet on the pedals.

Now our car and trailer were both heading crossways on the ramp. We went for a while that way, not getting any closer to the water, but we were getting pretty close to the car at the far end of the ramp. Dave stopped our car and looked over at me. Usually I would have said something but somehow this time I didn't. About that time the guy who was at the end of the ramp drove away. At first I thought he was pulling forward to give us more room, but then I realized that his boat was loaded up and he was probably heading home. Dave turned the wheel and started backing up again. The boat began heading up the ramp. We stopped. He turned the wheel the other way as far as it would go; I can hear a squealing noise from the car that didn't sound good. We start backing up again. The boat keeps going uphill for a second or two, then like it got the idea, starts turning toward the water. Dave smiles at me and we keep backing up. Pretty soon the trailer is in the water and the tongue hasn't hit the car again. Dave turned off the car engine and we both got out to push the boat into the water. To my amazement, the boat's outboard motor is almost submerged and ocean water is running over the back end of the boat.

We both run to the back of the boat to see what's wrong, getting our pants, shirts and shoes wet, as we haven't changed yet. I had forgotten to take the tie down straps off of the back end of the boat. Once we see that, Dave runs back to the car, jumps in and pulls forward. I'm still back with my boat watching the gas tank float around like a beach ball in a small wading pool. When the boat is out of the water far enough I holler at Dave and he stops really fast.

We were starting to get a system going. I wish I had thought to get out of the car earlier. We got the straps unhooked, then Dave goes to put the straps into the trunk so that we won't lose them. He put a big gouge in the paint when the trunk lid hit on the trailer winch handle. I pulled the drain plug and watched as water began running out, then walked around to the front of the boat. Dave was rubbing the trunk with his T-shirt when I walked up, but the new scratch didn't seem to be going away.

While the water drained out we took off our wet clothes and started getting ready to ski. We both had our bathing suits on under our clothes and I couldn't think of a reason that we didn't take off our pants and shoes sooner but we didn't. The car seat should dry out OK because it's a nice warm day.

Water was just barely dripping out of the hole now so I replaced the drain plug and walked to the side of the boat. We were just eight or ten feet away from the water's edge, now stripped down to our trunks and barefooted. I smiled over at my best friend and he looked back at me from his position at the wheel. We both knew that everything was going to be OK. This was starting to feel like a real water-skiing trip.

Backing in the second time was real easy. Now we were getting the hang of it! I stayed back alongside of the boat up to my knees in the water, watching as both trailer and boat entered the water. When the time was right I hollered at Dave to stop. The boat was just bobbing around a little and all that I had to do was wade over to the front and unhook the winch snap. I climbed on to the trailer and walked the boat backwards, holding on to the bow eye. Once she cleared the trailer I stepped into the water and found myself actually swimming because the water was kind of deep this far down on the ramp. I didn't mind getting wet because the water was pretty warm, but if I had simply jumped onto the deck of the boat I could have easily postponed this early-morning swim.

Dave parked the car and trailer across the street with the other people and I messed with the engine. Luckily it started on the first pull and we were off on our first solo skiing trip without any mishap. Once we motored away from shore everything got pretty easy. Dave and I both knew how to drive the boat and even though this was our first trailer-launching experience we were actually very comfortable on the water.

After a short harbor cruise it was time to get down to the serious business of water skiing. We motored to a nice sandy beach so that we could practice our favorite shore-starts and shore-landings. Dave and I took turns being driver or skier all afternoon. Finally it started to get dark and we headed back for the ramp. We were both so happy to have our own boat that we didn't even realize that we were tired. Of course we were pretty hungry because we forgot to bring food or anything to drink on this first outing.

I sat on the bow with my feet dangling in the water as Dave headed for the parking area to get the car and trailer. Neither of us had given a thought to backing up the trailer in the dark and then loading the boat onto the trailer until the time came to do it.

After all, how hard could it be?

Country Music

*E*arly afternoon sun heated my already warm bare shoulders as ten or fifteen more cars entered the freeway on my right. Traffic volume was beginning to build, which was not at all unusual for this time of day. I was really happy to be driving this time. All of my past visits during the last four years were made by airplane. Somehow arriving by plane at LAX always made the trip seem like exactly what it was, a visit. The simple act of guiding a car through traffic made me feel like I was coming home to stay. Unconsciously I added pressure to the worn gas pedal, easily cruising at 75 mph, holding my two-car-length spot in the left lane of this semi-busy Los Angeles freeway.

My old convertible was a wreck, with worn tires, a faded white paint job dented and rusted out in spots, but it had served me pretty well for the past two years as a back-and-forth ride from the ship to town. This beat-up old '55 Chevy had lived its whole life in Hawaii. The fact that it did continue running for this the entire seven hour drive through the center of California kind of surprised me. It had handled the drive from San Francisco to Los Angeles without too much trouble, just one tank of gas and four quarts of oil. The dashboard temperature light stayed red and the oil light blinked on and off for the whole trip, but the car never did actually boil over and the radio worked. Who could complain? When you are in the service and stationed aboard ship, it is not a good idea to leave high-dollar cars sitting in the base parking lot for months at a time. So I kept this old beater. I had intended to sell this car, or just give it away when I got discharged, but the US Coast Guard offered to ship my old Chevy from Honolulu to San Francisco as a part of my household goods. Go figure. I thought, what the heck, it would save me the expense of a plane ticket, and once back in Los Angeles I would need a car to get around anyway. *I can't wait to see the folks, just one more exit.*

The Chevy eased to a stop, two tires slightly up on the curb, and the engine resting over years of old oil stains left in the street from numerous cars of my high school years. This was a familiar parking spot centered in front of my parent's house, my childhood home. The walls were beige now with a cream colored trim, different than the light green and white accent that I remembered from my last visit two years ago. I smiled at the short, stiff yellow grass that adorned the front yard. No amount of water could coax Southern California Devil-grass to stay green in the summertime. The old neighborhood always looked the same; nice wide streets and well cared for homes, with a few kids playing in some of the yards. The kids would grow up and move away to be replaced by new families with new kids, but the neighborhood never really changed much over the years. This was home.

Mom and Dad greeted me with a flood of conversation, hardly interrupted by the continuous flow of sandwiches, fruit, chips, cookies, and drinks that seemed to magically appear at arm's reach on the small round coffee table as we all talked. My younger brother and sister were still living at home, though at this moment they were both attending classes in college. Mom led me to the bedroom that I had shared with my brother. It was now his room, and I would be a guest this time, but I could see that he had done his best to make me feel welcome. I found a couple of drawers cleared in the dresser, and there was even some familiar looking clothes hanging in the closet. The shower felt wonderful as the hard steady spray washed seven hours of driving and seemingly the past four years away from my body. As I pulled the T-shirt over my head, the bathroom mirror looked back at me as it had done a hundred times before, just like I had never left. *I wonder what Dave is up to?*

Cigarette smoke and the familiar aroma of stale beer greeted me as my eyes attempted to adjust in the dim light of the Airport Bar. This old bar had been here, next door and semi-attached to the bowling alley for as long as I could remember. However, this was the first time that I had the opportunity to go inside. As a kid I spent many enjoyable days at the bowling alley but you had to be twenty-one to gain entrance into the bar and this was the first time I qualified for that privilege. Dave was hands-down my best friend and I couldn't wait to see him. My thoughts drifted as I tried to imagine a married David, with a new baby no less. Feeling a little sad for being so far away and missing his wedding last year, I took another cautious step inside and dim figures began swimming into view.

I saw the back of a head with dark hair. This was hair that I knew. It could never be controlled because of a stubborn patch that stuck up in back, and here was my pal Dave sitting comfortably at the bar. His features were exactly as I remembered; the same familiar flush on his pleasant face that would always betray his mood. I took the barstool at his right and we just smiled at each other for a second. It had been a long time. The two of us then launched into overzealous hellos and much back pounding, as the bartender came over for a cursory ID inspection. I produced my military identification card, and

Library Resource Center
Renton Technical College
3000 N.E. 4th Street
Renton, WA 98056

then pointed to the drink Dave was holding and ordered two more of the same.

We moved from the bar to a booth and took turns catching up. The years melted away as we talked. Dave was now married to Pam, his high school sweetheart. There was never any doubt about this marriage coming to pass, and he seemed happy and comfortable in this role. They had just produced a baby girl and Dave tried his best to macho away the deep feelings he held for this new addition to his life. He was working in a trade that he enjoyed, and was still getting in some water skiing on weekends. My side of the conversation revolved around the past tour of military service, which included almost four years of sea duty with ports of call in places like Japan, the Philippines, Hong Kong, Hawaii, and a number of islands with unpronounceable names. It seemed like we had just sat down when the bartender announced last call. David and I walked outside and took a long time saying goodbye, finally heading for our separate vehicles and promising to get back together soon.

The following evening Dave surprised me by calling and suggesting that I go out with him again. We met once more at the Airport Bar and launched into another round of drinks, immediately resuming the conversation that had been cut short the night before. Several more rounds were consumed as the night when on. At some point in the evening I felt compelled to ask if it was all right with Pam that he was out drinking with me. He said that she was fine with him going out drinking. After all, he had just turned twenty-one and was sure entitled to "sow some wild oats." Dave and I were nearly the same age, with him just two months older than I was. The only difference was that due to my military duty stations overseas I had basically been of legal drinking age for the past four years, while Dave had only been legal in our home town for the past several months. In my view, drinking while off duty in the military was kind of a recreational sport. I was somewhat doubtful that this logic would hold true for the civilian population. I pondered the "wild oats theory" but didn't comment further.

A couple of nights later I called Dave and asked if he would like to go out. After a short pause he said, "Sure, why don't you pick up a six-pack and come on over."

"I'll be there in twenty minutes. Leave the porch light on so I can find the place." I smiled into the phone. Apparently his wild oats had been sufficiently sown.

Sweat beaded on my forehead and I shrugged it off against the sleeve of my T-shirt, not wanting to drip on the freshly waxed Triumph convertible. I tossed the old polish rags into the trash barrel, collected the paste wax, and assorted cleaners, and returned them to the garage. My small upstairs apartment had a long covered porch that always caught a nice breeze. I stood there leaning on the railing for a couple of minutes admiring my fresh wax job on TR-4 before going in for a shower. This little red sports car got a lot of my attention, being the newest addition to the family. The apartment has a chair, a TV set, coffee table and a lamp, but still needs more furniture. I have been living here for about six months. For just a brief second I considered going shopping for a couch. *Na, the sun is shining and the little convertible was beckoning for a drive.*

With no particular destination in mind, I found myself on the Pacific Coast Highway; I then made a quick right turn to follow the coast through the hills of Palos Verdes. The car was made for this kind of road with steep hills, quick hairpin turns, and short straight-aways. I accelerated through the turns, shifting as the tachometer reached 5,500. She hugged the road like it was on rails. I kept one eye on my rearview mirror to assure myself that my fun afternoon drive wasn't producing any uninvited attention. After a while I slowed down a bit and just enjoyed the ride. The little car took me about fifty or sixty miles down the coast before my stomach told me it was time for lunch. Parking with a good view of the ocean I took my time with the hamburger and vanilla malt. I watched a skinny red headed boy playing in the gentle waves with a thin blond girl. Somehow the kids reminded me that I hadn't seen Dave and Pam for a while. They just had a second child, a baby girl and moved to a new, slightly larger house in Torrance.

Without another thought I turned around and went in search of them. Once in Torrance I found a small convenience store and stopped to make a quick purchase; then resumed my search. Dave had shown me the house just before they bought it. That was one night about two months ago; I slowed down and began checking street names. *I know it's around here somewhere.*

The street was named Budlong. It was a short cul-de-sac just the other side of Torrance Boulevard. I turned into the street, driving slowly. Several small to medium sized kids were playing in various front yards. I spotted Dave about six houses down on the right, working on his small front yard with a push-me style lawnmower.

I parked in front, got out and opened a beer, closing the car door with my hip. "Can I help?" I asked, walking toward Dave and offering an open can of Coors.

"You always show up at the right time to help," said Dave, accepting the beer.

The front door opened and Pam stepped onto the small covered porch. "Hi, stranger," she said smiling at me.

"Grab your swimming suit, beautiful; Dave and I were just talking about going to Mexico. Want a beer?"

One of the good things about push-me lawnmowers is that when you stop pushing they stop also. You don't have to embarrass yourself by reaching over and turning them off. Dave and I walked to the porch and sat down with Pam. We spent several minutes catching up and enjoying the sunshine.

I finished my beer and reached into the brown paper sack for another.

"Hey," Dave said, I want you to meet someone." He got up and started walking towards the street. "Come on, bring the beer."

"Ben!" Dave shouted from about midway in the street. He continued walking toward the house across the street. "Ben!"

The door on one of the houses opened and a large man in blue coveralls stepped onto the front porch. Dave walked up to the front steps and started the introductions using a voice loud enough to include the entire neighborhood.

"Ben, this is Howard. You guys will have a lot in common."

I stepped alongside of Dave to join in the conversation. If we were going to have a lot in common, I had better start by offering my new friend a beer, which I did.

"What do you know about decoys?" asked Ben, reaching for the beer.

"Decoys?"

"Yeah, duck decoys," smiled Ben.

I was already beginning to like this big guy, and knew that I was soon going to know a whole lot more about duck decoys than I had ever imagined.

We talked for a couple of minutes on the front porch, and then carried the conversation inside his house where Ben introduced me to a woman seated in the living room, his wife Mary. Ben stepped into the small kitchen that had a table lined with about eight or ten gray duck decoys. The kitchen itself looked clean, but seemed to emit a strange smell that I couldn't quite identify. I noticed several unusual canisters sitting on the stovetop. About that time a bell sounded. Ben turned, pulled on some large insulated gloves and then removed a strange pot-like contraption from the oven. Upon closer inspection, I saw that this pot also resembled a duck. Ben opened the pot, which had hinges on one side, and removed yet another gray duck decoy, which he added to the assortment on his kitchen table. Without comment he filled the duck-like pot from one of the canisters on the stovetop. He sort of rolled the pot around in his hands, then placed it back into the oven, closed door, and reset the timer. Ben was using these homemade duck molds and some kind of plastic to cook up decoys in his kitchen oven, just like making waffles.

I realized that the funny smell was coming from the cooking plastic that Ben was using to make these decoys.

Ben turned around, retrieved his beer from the table and lifted it for a long drink. He smiled at me around the beer can.

I had never seen anything like this before in my life. Dave was absolutely right; Ben and I did have a lot in common. We both love to build stuff, or as Ben would later say we both liked to tinker.

Introductions were far from over. The whole neighborhood turned out to be full of characters that were all willing helpers or contributors to new projects that typically began in Ben's garage-shop or in his back yard.

Ben Harrison was the natural leader of this happy band of shade-tree mechanic's. He was born and raised in the town of Wheatland, a small farming community slightly north and east of Sacramento, California. Ben and Mary came to Los Angeles about twenty years ago looking for work. Mary devoted herself to raising children, and also held down a factory assembly job. Ben found himself working for a vinyl plastic processing company and eventually gained the position of Senior Engineer and Shop Foreman. Over the years Ben had accumulated an astounding working knowledge of vinyl plastics, electronics, welding, assembly, and fabrication. His skills would easily surpass most college grad manufacturing engineers.

Several of Ben family members still reside in Wheatland and he visits or vacations there with Mary on every opportunity.

The hobby most dear to his heart was duck hunting. Ben is constantly looking for ways to produce inexpensive duck decoys that are used for hunting in the rice fields of Wheatland. Most of this hunting is done with his brothers, cousins, nephews, and friends during the mid-October to mid-January duck and goose hunting season.

Ben and Mary have three children: Karen, the eldest daughter, who had married and moved away, and the boys Mike and Brian, ages twelve and fifteen, who are both in high school.

Living next door to Ben are Jim and Beverly. They both enjoy water skiing, fishing, or just about any kind of social activity including hunting. Jim and Beverly have one daughter and one son living at home.

Their neighbors on the other side are Butch and Barbara, who also water ski. They own an18-foot inboard ski boat which has often proved to be the source of neighborhood projects. Their children were both girls still in grammar school.

Living directly across the street from Ben and next door to my pal Dave was a true character by the name of Myron Rick. Myron is married to Judy. They have two boys who could easily be classed as a Dennis the Menace variety. Myron works for a trucking company. He makes pickups and deliveries at a lot of commercial locations and it could be said that he never passed a dumpster that he didn't like. Myron's garage was home to a virtual cornucopia of items that he had liberated from years of dumpster-diving. His two-car garage had long ago overflowed into the backyard, which now contained three large odd shaped containers that held yet more treasure. In this neighborhood Myron's garage was absolutely the first place to go when searching out raw materials that may be needed for any new project.

From that day forward I spent many enjoyable weekends planning or tinkering on fishing, water skiing, or hunting related projects with the men, women and children who lived on that Budlong cul-de-sac.

I am back to work for my dad in his boat shop. The summer had passed in a blur with boat construction in full swing. Today is Thursday. This particular October morning found me working on the design for a new fiberglass sailboat, which was optimistically scheduled for production in the early spring. My desk, drafting board and surrounding surfaces are covered with a maze of schedules, budgets, and new designs, all in various stages of completion. I reached for the ringing phone, frowning at the interruption.

"Hello."

"Howard, this is Ben."

"Hi, Ben, how is everything in Decoy-vill?"

"I'm great. The ducks are in."

"Ducks?"

"Yeah, Bill just called from Wheatland. A new bunch came in last night. Do you want to go hunting?"

"Sure, when?"

"We'll fly out tomorrow night after work, then hunt the weekend and fly home on Sunday."

"I'm in, what will I need to bring?"

"Oh, you just need a hunting license and duck stamps. We have everything else. Don't forget to get a federal duck stamp as well, and bring warm clothes, it's going to be cold."

Weekends on Budlong always included duck hunting stories that I had been listening to for the past several months. I knew that Bill was Ben's youngest brother, though we had never actually met. Bill still lived in Wheatland and was working at a local saw mill. This was the phone call that Ben had been waiting for all year and I was sure happy to be included in the hunting party.

Walking into the sporting goods store that evening, I attempted an air of confidence that became very difficult to maintain as I surveyed this strange assortment of hunting gear and sportsman apparel on display. The truth of the matter was that to date my hunting experience was limited to my childhood BB-gun sparrow hunting safaris in the wilds of my Los Angeles back yard and several enjoyable hours at the shooting gallery on the Long Beach Pier.

After about thirty minutes of getting acquainted with this store, I selected a warm looking camo-colored hunting coat that the label described as waterproof. I then added gloves, and a hat that would also shed water. The store clerk was very helpful by providing me with my first hunting license which included two duck stamps, one federal, the other a state stamp. He pointed out that I needed to sign my name on each of the stamps, which of course I hadn't known.

Leaving the store with my purchases, I had a quick flash of what "cold" might actually mean. I returned to the counter and bought my first set of thermal underwear.

I left work early Friday afternoon and drove directly to Ben's house. My single bag was transferred to his car. Mary took us to the airport, dropped Ben and I in front of the departure terminal, and waved goodbye. We strolled into the terminal at LA International Airport without a reservation. It was exactly five-thirty p.m. when the two of us walked to the ticket counter, paid cash, $32.00 each, and were airborne at six p.m.; heading toward Sacramento.

As our plane pointed its nose upward toward our cruising elevation, a pretty blond stewardess emerged from a back compartment and began struggling with the heavy drink cart that she pushed uphill to start serving beverages at the front of the aircraft.

"This is a two-drink flight," Ben said, smiling at me as he shared a private joke.

He was right; before we had finished our second drink the plane was lowering its landing gear, and moments later we touched down at the Sacramento Airport. Total flight time was fifty-five minutes. I looked out of the window and was amazed to see several pheasants at the edge of the runway.

A smiling brother Bill met us at the gate as we cleared the telescoping ramp leading into the small one-building terminal. I noticed that the Harrison family members all seemed to share an easy welcoming smile that was warm and sincere.

Except for the fact that both men were tall, Bill didn't resemble Ben in any way. Ben was heavy boned, which made him appear fat, his face was round with full lips, and his coloring was very light, including a head of near-gray hair. Bill on the other hand was of dark complexion. He had a medium to thin build. His face was longer than Ben's and much thinner with sharper features. He also had dark brown, almost black hair. If we had not been introduced, I would never have guessed these two men were brothers.

As Bill's old Ford pickup cleared the last stoplight leading from Sacramento Airport, streetlights were left behind, a mere memory. The only light provided on these narrow country roads came from the dim headlights of our truck or from the occasional vehicle we met driving in the opposite direction. Bill maintained level speeds as he expertly navigated a series of right and left turns that would come up unexpectedly as we angled northward through tree-tangled orchards, open or fenced fields, with an occasional house or barn. There were small sign posts that would suddenly appear out of the darkness with names of places that I couldn't identify. The pickup slowed, and then made a left turn into an open parking spot at a dimly lit building that displayed a small pink-colored neon window sign that stated simply RED HILL.

Unfamiliar country music could be heard once the pickup engine was turned off. Bill led us across a wide wooden porch and opened the torn screen door. He then turned the handle on a solid white-painted wooden door. Bill swung the door open and the music got louder as we entered a different world.

Bill and Ben were greeted warmly and loudly with shouts of, "Hello, Bill! Hi, Ben!" As we joined twenty or so men and women seated or standing at the long U-shaped bar. Two bartenders were working in shirtsleeves. With practiced ease they mopped the bar top, scooped up money, and transported drinks two, three, or four at a time to the delight of their customers. Voices mixed as they tried to compete with the old-fashioned dime jukebox that belted out country music from its central location on a wall that opened at either end with small white doors leading into the bathrooms.

Two pool tables were in use, receiving due attention from several pool cue-wielding participants. At the far end of the room a large stone fireplace produced heat that could easily be felt from the doorway entrance. Couples were dancing on the far side of the bar, and a poker game in one corner of the large room seemed to be getting serious concentration from the six participants and several spectators. Beer came in two flavors, Bud or Olympia, light beer was not an option. I was introduced to the owner Wally, who gave me a warm hug like I was a long lost best friend. This was Red Hill Saloon on a typical Friday night.

Three beers later, Ben, Bill, and I crowded into the now cold Ford pickup. We were once more on the road for the last two mile stretch that led to Bill's house.

"See you boys in the morning," said Bill, and he was gone.

Two beds looked very inviting in the spare bedroom, so Ben and I didn't waste any time putting them to use. I vaguely remember my head hitting the pillow.

"It's that time!" The smell of morning coffee greeted me as I awoke to the bright overhead bedroom light and sound of Bill's voice.

Remembering to put on my long johns, I emerged from the bedroom fully clothed, including the new jacket and hat. Ben followed a few minutes later wearing not only a jacket but also a pair of chest-waders that looked like a combination of bib overalls and tall boots rolled into one. I looked at him for a moment, then at my own short brown boots, not having considered this extent of hunting attire.

Bill saw my concerned look and told me that he had an extra pair of hip boots in the truck. After coffee and some very sparse conversation, Bill opened the large gun cabinet and removed three shotguns. He then went to an open carton on the floor and began removing boxes of shells. We each took two boxes of ammunition and placed them unopened into the large pockets of our hunting coats.

Bill had taken time to start the pickup, which was now warmed up and idling quietly outside of the utility room door. On our drive from the airport, the previous evening, the small bench seat of the truck seemed to accommodate the three of us just fine. This morning however was a different story. We were all dressed in heavy hunting gear, shells bulging in our pockets. Ben weighed in at about 220, and Bill near 190, with my skinny butt adding another 150 pounds; not to ignore the three shotguns which were piled between our legs pointed muzzles' down at the pickup floor. It took Ben several attempts before he was able to slam the door shut. We were on our way, the smell of cigarette smoke and gun oil filled our little cocoon and I was just about too excited to talk.

The drive to our intended hunting spot was not far at all. Bill got out and opened a metal gate leading into a field. He asked me to pull the truck forward. I did and he then closed the gate behind us and returned to the truck. It was pitch black out there, yet Bill had the headlights off and we drove with parking lights only. We followed the tracks on this narrow path-like road, which had water and some kind of stubble growing on both sides. I was later to learn that we were driving on a rice check. The water that I saw on each side of the road was actually rice fields, the stubble being rice stalk left over from the fall harvest.

We parked Bills truck in a wide spot at the end of the small track we had been driving on, then sat on the tailgate of the pickup as Bill and I replaced our short boots with the long, cold hip boots. Ahead of us was a very narrow path that led out across the water. Speaking almost in a whisper, Bill told me to be careful because it was very slippery. We started walking slowly, single file, with Bill leading. I was in the middle and Ben followed. After just a few yards along this mud path there was a loud commotion of beating wings and squawking. The sudden noise scared the crap out of me. This was the sound of ducks taking flight. They had been resting on the pond and we had startled them by our entry into their territory.

Bill arrived at a wide spot on the path. He knelt down and began clanking around on something. This wide spot turned out to be the blind we were going to hunt out of. Bill removed the metal lids that covered the blind and tossed them into the water. I had visions of this spot being smaller than the pickup seat but found out that it was a lot bigger at the bottom than the top, and was actually very comfortable once the three of us were all inside. The blind contained three padded seats that allowed us to sit with our heads at about eye level with the top of the rice check.

As my eyes gradually adjusted to the darkness, I could see that there was water on both sides of our blind. We were in the middle of some kind of a lake. Patches of stubble broke through the water surface and I noticed an occasional mound of mud. Decoys are floating on the water in front of our blind and as I turned I could see that more decoys had been placed behind us. There is another small path across the water that looks just like the one we had walked in on. The decoys look amazingly real and seem almost alive as they slowly bobbed and moved in the gentle morning breeze.

All conversation is held in low tones and whispers as Bill and Ben seldom take their eyes away from the sky. We are smoking, each with cigarettes cupped in our hands to avoid the flash of light that could signal our presence. Daylight is creeping in as distant shadows begin to resemble fence posts and other known objects. I feel the pressure of Bill's hand on my shoulder, urging me deeper into the blind; at the same time hearing the unfamiliar sound of squeaking wings above us. The sound grew fainter. "Too high," whispered Bill, "next time."

The strange squeaking sound of wings was coming again, but this time from behind us. I didn't turn but watched Bill's eyes for direction. Suddenly he is standing, and his gun was spitting flashes of fire as the deafening sound of shotgun blast rang out. Ben was standing behind me, and seemed to be firing also, though I really couldn't hear anything at the moment. I stood up and attempted to wrestle the unfamiliar shotgun to my shoulder but fell short by a couple of inches. Birds were falling. I saw one splash down near the blind, and thought that at least two more had fallen farther out.

"Get back down," said Bill. Both Bill and Ben had resumed the low position in the blind and were again searching the sky.

Minutes passed, I didn't dare move, my heart took a long time to quiet down, and my ears continued to ring as I tried to listen with Ben and Bill for more birds.

Bill stood and stretched. "OK, Howard, you may as well go get those ducks."

I stood as well and looked questioningly at the water.

"Don't worry," said Ben, "it's just ten or twelve inches deep."

Who knew, I thought we were in the middle of a lake. I stepped gingerly into the shallow pond and began wading toward the closest duck. I brought it back to the blind and then started after the ducks that had fallen farther away.

"It might be a good idea for you to take your gun," said Bill.

All three of the shotguns had slings attached. I slung my shotgun barrel up over my shoulder and began the slow trek across the pond in search of the ducks that I saw fall earlier. Each clump of mud seemed to be a duck, until one of them actually was. As I reached down to pick it up another clump some distance away began to flop its wings. "**Shoot it**," came the shout from behind me.

Dropping the bird from my right hand, I un-slung the shotgun and successfully positioned it against my shoulder. Taking careful aim, I squeezed the trigger. . . then applied more pressure. . . then still more. *Nothing*.

"**The safety!**"

Taking a moment to examine the gun, I remembered the little red-ringed button near the trigger guard that Bill had pointed out to me earlier this morning. The button made a soft click as I pushed it into the gun. Looking once again for the duck, I realized it had gained several yards from its original position. *Bang!* The duck continued its escape. *Bang!* It stopped moving. I had killed my first duck.

We hunted until about nine a.m. that morning; killing twenty birds between us. I was sure of the six ducks that I had killed, as I was the only one in pursuit of them; however I seriously doubt that I had actually knocked any unimpaired birds from the sky.

The trip back to the house included a stop at a bar located in downtown Wheatland called Bill's Place, no relation. The barroom appeared very stark with sparsely adorned white walls holding several mismatched photographs, memories of long past hunting trips and special events. Some were pictures of distinguished, unsmiling, serious looking mustached men in outdated clothing. The room itself was long and narrow with an exceptionally high ceiling. There was a well-warn wooden bar-top that ran from the front entrance to the back wall with an uninterrupted brass foot rail being the only adornment. Six men were seated near the center of the long bar, each turned to give us their attention as we entered.

"How's the huntin', Bill? Hi Ben."

"Not so good this morning, Jack, maybe tomorrow." Hellos were exchanged and I was introduced to all of the men but my already overloaded brain cells could not accurately record their names at that moment. The six of them turned from us to quietly resume their private conversation.

We drank cups of strong black coffee laced with brandy. I didn't actually realize that I was cold until the warm liquid began to defrost me from the inside out. My fingers were blue and kind of numb and I realized that the new hunting gloves that I bought two days ago were probably nice and warm in my overnight bag or possibly still sitting on my bed at home.

After leaving the bar, Bill said something to Ben about the "military retarded." I was sure that I had misheard what he said, but Ben chuckled at the statement, apparently a private joke.

Once back at the house we removed our heavy clothing and sat down to relax in the living room. I just had to ask. "Bill, did you say *military retired* or *military retarded*?"

Bill seemed to light up at the question and sat back to explain away my confusion.

"Howard, the guys you met back there are all retired military. That is, all except for Jack, who's our older brother. Most of them are ex Air Force. They retired from Beale Air

Force Base which is a few miles east of town. All of them seemed to like Wheatland as they spent most of their military off-duty time with their elbows on the bar at Bill's Place, so after they retired they just kind of stayed on. You can find most of them at Bill's Place any time of day or night. I just call them the *Military Retarded* and they're usually too drunk to care."

Bill got up and went to the kitchen. A few moments later he returned with a beer for each of us. Somehow I knew that his story wasn't quite finished.

"Last year five of those guys were sitting in Bill's Place drinking. It was a weeknight around midnight and as you can imagine the town is pretty quiet at night. So the Bill's Place crew members were kind of taken by surprise when the front door bursts open and in walks a big guy wearing a red-plaid hunting jacket and a black ski mask on his face. He is holding a pistol, and demanding money. The guys look at him for a second and then start laughing. They're all sure that it's Jack Harrison playing a practical joke. Now the man in the ski mask is waving his gun around and keeps asking for money, but they just laugh louder, calling him Jack and asking him to sit down and have a drink, so the would-be robber fires off a shot. The Bill's Place crew now goes into hysterical laughter at the thought of Jack actually shooting off blanks in the bar. So at this point the robber apparently frustrated, turns and dashes out the door and drives off.

"When the guys eventually stop laughing one of them says, 'I wonder where Jack got that white car?'

"Another says, 'Is that a fresh hole in the floor?'

'Jack wouldn't have used real bullets, would he?'

"They took turns looking at the bullet hole in the floor."

'Are you sure that was Jack?'

'Maybe we should call a cop.'

"Fifteen minutes later, about six miles north of Wheatland the state police located an abandoned white Ford LTD. Keys were in the ignition; the vehicle was still warm and the police determined that the car was out of gas. A black ski mask was found lying on the front seat. Two miles north on the same road they came across a big man walking along the highway. This man was wearing a red-plaid hunting jacket. He didn't have money or any type of identification. He was arrested on suspicion of armed robbery. No gun was found, but this was not really surprising as the fields on both sides of the road were one or two feet deep in muddy water left from a week of rain. The following week at a court arraignment one of the Bill's Place crew was on the stand.

"The judge asked, 'Mister Moffet, can you identify this man?'

'Yes,' said Mr. Moffet, 'that's him, he looks just like Jack.'

'Mister Moffet, were you drunk at the time of the robbery?'

'No, I was drinking but I wasn't drunk.'

'Mister Moffet, the attempted robbery took place around midnight. What time did you first arrive at Bill's Place?'

'I got there at eight.'

'Mister Moffet, between eight and midnight is four hours. That is a lot of time for drinking. Are you sure that you weren't drunk?'

'I didn't get there at eight in the evening.'

'I'm sorry, Mister Moffet, I must have misunderstood. What time did you get to Bill's Place?'

'Eight in the morning; we all did, just like always.'

"The case was dropped. Now can you understand why I call them the Military Retarded?"

I was still laughing at the story as I followed Bill and Ben into the back yard. Bill started making preparations to clean the ducks. I was completely unprepared for the amount of equipment that was necessary for this single operation. The first thing Bill did was to start a burner under a large pot of water. He explained that they like to scald the ducks before attempting to remove any feathers. The idea was that the scalding process removed the natural body wax and loosened the feathers. The trick was not to get the water too hot. Bill had a thermometer in the water that he monitored carefully. The optimum temperature was between one hundred seventy and one hundred ninety degrees, "never above the one ninety or the skin will tear," Bill cautioned.

While the water was heating Bill began fooling with a length of rope that had several loops tied about one foot apart. Bill hooked these loops over the legs of about five or six ducks. Then he squirted a bit of liquid soap into the water and stirred it with a long handled wooden spoon. Now satisfied with the temperature, he dunked the ducks into the vat, taking time to push them under water with the big wood spoon. "Once they quit bobbing back up they're ready," he said.

The ducks soon stopped rising to the surface and Bill pulled them out to cool. He removed the rope from their legs and then fastened the rope to five more birds.

Ben picked up the duck closest to him and began rubbing off the feathers into a trash barrel. I watched him for a second, then picked up a duck of my own and soon got the hang of this process. The duck feathers kind of sluffed off with very little effort, almost like pealing an orange. Once the twenty ducks had been picked we moved into the shed to finish the cleaning process. Bill brought the birds to a cutting board and quickly went to work. When the wings, feet and heads were gone Bill made an incision and skillfully removed most of the entrails, which were placed in canning jars to be frozen for future use as catfish bait. We then flushed the inside of the bird with plenty of fresh water and used our fingers to remove anything that didn't look like it belonged. The cleaned birds were left to dry on an old dishwasher rack that seemed ideal for this purpose. The whole cleaning job didn't take much more than an hour.

Someone was calling us for breakfast. Bill dropped the duck that he was cleaning into the rack; turned without a word and headed out the door. Ben smiled at me, "Pauline doesn't like to be kept waiting."

I was about to be introduced to Bill's wife and a real country breakfast.

Once inside the house I found a seat at a crowded kitchen table and was introduced to Pauline and also several more of the Harrison family members who seemed to have magically appeared just in time for breakfast.

Ben and I ignored the drink cart on the two-drink flight home. We were both too focused on the scraps of paper that covered our small seat-back trays. Each of us were each eagerly drawing and sharing the crude sketches of decoys spread out in front of us. Ben said that he had built most of the decoys that we had hunted over. The current decoy count was about five hundred but Bill figured that they needed at least twice that many more. Now that I had seen the decoys in action I was pretty confident that we could find a way to produce another 1,000 decoys before the next hunting season.

Little Paul

My name is Paul Andrew Martin. I will be twelve years old in two weeks. All of my school friends call me Paul, even my teacher Mrs. Evens calls me Paul, or Paul Martin when she is taking role, but here at home my mom, and dad, and my uncle Alex call me Little Paul. I often wonder when I will stop being little.

The hay is soft against my back and I am comfortable just lying here. I love this old barn. It is cool in the summer; the wind finds openings and creates soft sounds and breezes that always make me feel welcome and safe. The barn always smells like old hay and I never worry about making the floor dirty. Lots of times I come up here after chores and just kind of let my mind run free.

Now my eyes take in a big coil of rope hanging high on the wall. It must have been there for years yet I can't remember actually seeing it before, nor can I remember any one using it for anything around the farm. It just seems funny that I never noticed it there before now. I wonder how long that rope is. It looks pretty long. I doubt if my dad or Uncle Alex even remembers that it's hanging up there.

My dad would say that I spend too much of my time daydreaming, but that isn't what I do exactly, not really daydreaming, I'm just thinking about stuff. Like the time on the playground when Timmy told all of us at school about his new BB gun. He was sure excited. He pointed his arm and said how he lined up the cans on his back fence, and could hit one almost every time he shot. He told me that I could come over to his house, and maybe shoot it sometime.

Dad would never let me have a BB gun. Not that I have ever wanted to shoot at cans. In fact there aren't any cans lying around the farm for me to shoot at. Whenever my dog Rusty and I want to go hunting I take the .410 shotgun from the rack in the hallway, grab a few shells from the brown chest and go out back. The shotgun isn't really mine, but nobody except me uses it. My uncle Alex is dad's younger brother. He lives with us on the farm and works every day with my dad. Uncle Alex taught me how to aim and shoot the shotgun when I was seven. The gun was way too big for me then, but now my arms are longer and I can shoot it pretty good. I hunt for squirrels or rabbits, even quail sometimes. I can shoot the big twelve gauge shotgun when my uncle is with me, but it is really heavy and I don't like to carry it very far.

I didn't say anything at school about the .410 shotgun because Timmy is a good school friend and his feelings would have been hurt if I told everyone that I have a real gun.

None of my school friends have ever been to our farm. We live too far out for them to ride their bikes. Mrs. Donald drives me to school on the school bus. She lives in Mayland and drives the bus home every night. I am the very first one onboard every morning, and the last one off every night, then she drives on to Four Corners for gas, then on home to Mayland.

The farm has been in our family for eighty-five years since my granddad started it. Now it belongs to my dad, and mom, and Uncle Alex. It is my home and my only playground. We have 1,260 acres with pastures, a stream that feeds into a small lake, and hills with timber. I have probably walked on every foot of it. Dad and Uncle Alex always have a lot of work to do so they pretty much leave me be, as long as I get my chores done every day. Mom doesn't like me coming in and out of the house because she says that I track in too much dirt. Most of the time Rusty and I are just exploring in the woods, or fishing, or hanging around in the barn building stuff. We can almost always find something to do. Summer gets a little long some years, but school will be starting back up next week. Yesterday Mrs. Donald called my mom to remind me to be at the gate Monday morning. Mom invited Mrs. Donald and her husband over for Sunday dinner. She said that they would come after church. I like her husband Pete. He rides in on the bus sometimes and we talk about fishing.

There is an old black 1940 Ford pickup truck under the side shed that my uncle told me we could make run. He knows that I'm excited about the truck, but I won't say anything to him about it. If I'm good, pretty soon he will just fix it. That's the way Uncle Ales likes to do things.

Dad never smokes his pipe except like now, in the evening when he is sitting on the porch with my uncle. The pipe smoke must be heavy because it just hangs in the air and won't go up very fast like trash-barrel smoke. It smells sweet to me, not sharp and strong like the Chesterfields that my uncle smokes all the time. This is a nice time of day when the work is done. It is always cooler out here on the porch than it is in the house. Dad and Uncle Alex are talking about buying a new tractor, and my mom is rocking slowly back and forth on the porch swing. Rusty is sitting on the step with me. He likes to lay his head on my leg so that I can scratch behind his ears. He never licks at me or anything like some dogs will do. Rusty will just sit there as long as I do. Everything is quiet, even my dad and uncle are talking quietly, and the gentle hum of the crickets is almost putting me to sleep.

The barn is two stories high with a big hayloft all the way across the top. It looks so small from here on the porch. It is almost dark but I can still see the roof of the shed around the side where the old Ford truck is stored and the silver top of the water pump tower way back behind the barn on the hill.

I wonder if that rope would reach from the back of the barn to the water tower.

Drops of sweat run into my eyes as I struggle with the gray rope. I shrug the wet off my forehead onto the sleeve of my T-shirt and keep working. The rope is really heavy and doesn't uncoil as easily as I thought it would. I have one end tied to the old water pump handle in back of the barn. Two times I had to untie the rope so that I could pull out a knot. Then I tied it to the pump again. The water pump still works but we hardly ever use it anymore. Most of the water we use comes from the new well close to the house.

I have been looking at my silver watch with the red band that I got for a present last Christmas. It is almost noon when I finally get to the base of the water tower. For a while I thought that it might not reach, but there is still a lot of rope left over. I leave the rope lying on the ground and go up to the house to clean up for lunch before my mom needs to come looking for me.

The lunch is good. We have cold fried chicken and sweet corn still on the cob left over from supper last night. Mom even made fresh lemonade. My dad and uncle have gone to town today, so just my mom and I are here for lunch. The kitchen always smells like fresh bread. Mom keeps everything really clean. Mom and I don't usually talk much especially during meal times. Sometimes I think that she is mad at me about something even though I was good. Dad says that lunchtime is for eating and not for talking. Today I don't notice because I am still trying to figure out what to do with the rope now that I know it will reach the water pump tower.

Tools hang on the walls and some are scattered on the two big workbenches. There is always equipment of one kind or another being worked on by my dad or uncle. We call this the workshop, but it is really just another part of the barn. Some of the tools are left over from when my granddad owned the farm, but most of the tools are newer than that. My uncle has a big box of tools that he doesn't let me use. I have a small green toolbox with my own tools. I made the toolbox last year from a box that a pump came in from John Deere in Oklahoma City. Then I put in my wrenches and pliers and three screwdrivers that I got for my birthday. I walk around the shop and pick up two big nuts from the workbench. I don't want the nuts for anything special, but need to have something to distract my hands as I wander around looking at all of the stuff hanging on the walls. I have an idea in my head somewhere, but it just won't come out. Rusty is following me but he doesn't seem to have any ideas either.

My hands find a long bolt on the low workbench. The nuts that I was holding seem to fit, so I thread the big nuts onto the bolt. I raise the bolt in both hands with the nuts in the middle and turn the bolt in the air like it's a steering wheel, and then raise the bolt over my head. I leave the bolt and nuts together on the low bench and continue looking. I am standing at the far end of the workshop when I see exactly what I have been looking for. It is tied to a post, hanging high up on the wall. It was way too high up for me to reach so I went around to the main part of the barn and found the big ladder. When I got back into the workshop with the ladder I knew just what I needed to do. I had to use my knife to cut the old rope that was tied to the snatch-block pulley, and then carried it back to the work bench so that I could look it over real good.

Once I had the ladder back where I found it, standing against the barn wall, I had already been outside of the barn and untied the rope from the water pump. Then I climbed up on the ladder and pushed the end of the rope through the knothole that I had spotted when I got the ladder earlier.

The knothole was about fifteen feet up on the back wall of the barn. I just moved the ladder to the inside of the barn and tied the rope onto the top rung and I was done with this part. Now I can go out and work on the other end of the rope.

I have to be careful climbing this time. I have been up on the pump tower lots of times before but never with a heavy rope tied around my waist. The rope is gently tugging at my middle as I continue to climb. I don't wipe the sweat from my face because my hands will get slippery. The water pump tower has a pipe railing about chest-high that runs all the way around following the little walkway on the top. I wrap the rope around the pipe rail and start working out the slack. This is really hard to do because the rope is heavy, especially now that it is almost off the ground. There is a small hill about two thirds of the way to the barn. The rope is still on the ground there. I am trying to pull it up until I am sure that all of it is off of the hill. That will be my landing spot.

The rope is tied tight, with a good knot that I learned at 4-H. I look at the long, gray, curving rope stretching the one hundred or more yards from me to the barn. I am really pleased with my work. The view from here is beautiful. Looking over the barn, I can see my house, then the big front pasture and then the main road. It all looks so small from up here.

Climbing once more up the pump tower, the snatch-block pulley that I found tied to a beam in the barn is now hanging from my belt, which is wrapped around my neck, just like a big necklace. I am very excited as I reach the platform. It only

takes a second to remove the belt and snatch block from my
neck. I carefully unbuckle my belt and thread it back through
my pant loops. Now I open the snatch block and then clamp it
over the rope and snap it closed again.

It's time.

I reach under the pipe railing, put one hand on each side of
the big bolt that is now tightened in the eye of the snatch block,
and. . . step off of the pump tower.

I am going so fast.

Standing up in the back of my dad's moving pickup truck
was the only thing that even came close to the rush of air that
blew on every part of my body. This was the last thought I
had before sailing ten or twelve feet above the small hill, my
would-be landing zone. The rope had looked a lot closer to the
ground from the tower than it did now, besides I was going so
fast, and my fingers just wouldn't let go. Now I was flying up
and up, still higher off of the ground. I shifted my eyes from
the ground just in time to see the barn coming at ninety miles
an hour.

"Stop it, stop, Rusty!" He never licks.

I was lying on the ground. Maybe I fell asleep. Rusty was
looking at me, his big head just inches from my face. It took a
couple of minutes for me to figure out how I got here. I looked
at my cut, bloody fingers and slowly opened and closed them.
They worked OK. I reached for the burning place on my
forehead and decided that I still had a head. My legs took
another minute or so before they could get me standing; most
of my weight was supported against the barn. I sat back down
and thought about the ride from the tower. *Wow!*

My eyes went to the tower, then followed the rope from the
tower to the barn. I couldn't help smiling even though it hurt
my lips to do it. Hanging on the rope about thirty yards out was
the old wooden snatch-block pulley; a long bolt was fastened in
its eye with two big nuts. I really did it, wow, what a ride!

I worked the old hand pump and washed my face and hands. The cuts on my hands were not really bad; it was just that there were so many of them. I looked in the old mirror hanging on the barn wall. My face was bruised a little with lots of red scuff marks, my lips were both split and puffed up, and I had a cut on my right ear. I guess that I am really pretty much OK.

The important thing to do now is to get the rope down.

My legs were still a little weak, but climbing was a lot easier without the rope attached to my waist or the weight of the big snatch block around my neck. Once up on the tower platform I had the rope untied within five or ten minutes. Then I returned to the barn and untied the other end from the ladder. It took an hour or more to gather the bundle of rope and return it to the barn. Rusty and I decided to go to the lake for a swim.

At supper that night Dad asked what happened to me. I told him the truth that I fell down.

Later that evening I fell asleep on the front porch with Rusty lying next to me, his head across my lap.

Uncle Alex was gently squeezing my shoulder.

"Go to bed, Little Paul, tomorrow we'll have a look at that old pickup."

Bobby

"Five fives."　　　[JA]
"Five sixes."　　　[Admiral]
"Six sixes."　　　　[Bobby]
"Seven fives."　　　[Howard]
"Eight fives."　　　[Dove]
"Nine fives."　　　[John]

"Call, got you, ass hole!" JA smiled brightly at John. "I don't have any fives. How many you got?"

"Well, let's see how many I need," John grinned back. "You, Admiral?"

"None."

"Dove?"

"Two."

"Bobby?"

"One."

"Howard, you got to bale me out, buddy," John tried to keep a straight face.

"Just one John." I knew John too well; he already had it.

"I only have six fives myself," John says, showing his bill to JA. "That makes, let me see, ten? Thought I only needed nine? Buy, sucker. That was for two pitchers."

Liar's poker is an easy game. We use dollar bills instead of cards. The serial numbers on everyone's dollar bills make up a hand. The idea is to beat the previous call. If you think that you can make a better poker hand with everyone's combined serial numbers you say what you think you can make, or if you don't think that the previous hand can be made you call as JA just did. If you are wrong you lose.

I couldn't blame JA for calling John this time. He sure did his best to set him up. But nobody beats John at Liar's Poker. It's the same every Friday night.

These are my best friends. We all work in different parts of town now, but still manage somehow to make Friday night at the Launch Pad. How long has it been? Damn, must be at least two years now since JA got transferred to Hawthorne. And at least that long since Bobby and Admiral went to work at Parker Seal in Santa Monica, and John is at Paper Mate. Dove is working in Inglewood now. I'm the only one that hasn't changed jobs.

Bobby stands up and finishes his half glass of beer in one long swallow, then gently sets his glass upside-down on the table. "Got to go," he said.

"Where are you off to?" I asked. "You just got here."

"I'll be back," says Bobby. "Just got to run to the bank and cash my check."

John tried to get another Liar's Poker game started but couldn't find any takers. We got to shooting pool, and were just generally having a good time. At least an hour passed before someone thought to ask where Bobby had disappeared to. I said that I thought he went to the bank.

"Bank?" asked John. "Bobby uses my bank, Bank of America, and it's just across the street."

"I don't know about that, John. That's just what he said when he left."

Another hour passed. Dove and Admiral were gone. John was waving his arms, as he usually did when excited, still talking with JA, and I was getting my butt handed to me on the pool table by Kelly Roberts.

Bobby came in, ordered a glass of beer at the bar, paid for it and returned to our table. He quietly sat down in his previously vacated chair. Bobby leaned back and took a swallow from the glass like he had been there all night. I watched the eight ball disappear into the side pocket and fished a crumpled one-dollar bill out of my shirt, then returned to our table.

"Hi, Bobby, where you been?"

"I told you, I went to the bank," Bobby said, and took another small sip of beer.

"Don't you still bank across the street?" asked John.

"Yeah, B of A, same as you."

We all looked at Bobby for an explanation, but that seemed to be all he had to say about his long trip to the bank. I had to ask.

"What happened at the bank? That was over two hours ago."

Bobby leaned forward and filled his glass from the community pitcher. He took a small sip, mostly foam, then set his glass down.

"I started to walk across the street but there wasn't a break in the traffic. So I decided to take the bike. It was parked in front anyway. I rode to the corner and made a left and went behind the bank. Then I cashed my check and came back here." He picked up his glass and looked at it, then took a long swallow.

All of us were still looking at Bobby expectantly until JA just couldn't stand it. "How could it take you two hours to ride a 750-Honda across the street?"

Bobby looked at JA like he was a rude child.

"It didn't take me two hours to ride across the street. I started across the intersection and this dumb ass in a yellow Mustang left-turned me."

"Did you go down?"

Bobby looked straight at John. "No, I didn't go down. I locked it up and gave him the finger. Then he gave me the finger back and didn't stop."

We looked at each other.

"Stop?" I asked.

"Yeah, he just gave me the finger and drove off like nothing happened." Bobby explained quietly. "I swung the bike around and tried to get him to pull over, but he just kept on going. I ended up following him over thirty miles, clear to Redondo Beach before we finally got stopped at the same light. I parked my bike behind his car, and grabbed him through the window. When he finally did get out of the car, I knocked him on his ass. I was still mad so I reached in and broke off his turn indicator lever. He didn't use it anyway. Then I came back here."

Our eyes unconsciously looked at the fresh cut on the first knuckle of Bobby's right hand. We had been friends too long for anyone to doubt one word of what Bobby just told us.

My First 1,000 Decoys

*E*arly morning sun is warming my neck and the back of my arms as a cool breeze does its best to chill my front side. I am dressed in a pair of worn Levi's and a plain white T-shirt; this is pretty much my normal weekend attire.

I enjoy riding my motorcycle, and wasn't in a big hurry this morning. My body moved smoothly with the bike, unconsciously guiding it with a slight shift of weight as my left foot rocked gently through the gears.

Traffic is light to nonexistent this early in the day, so it only takes a few minutes to cover the three-mile drive between my house and Ben's. My Sunday morning visits are fairly regular, but not exactly planned. I just kind of got into a pattern of dropping over to have a cup of coffee and to say hi. This visit is no exception. I am always welcome to join in on any project that may be going on or just to sit at the kitchen table with Ben and talk about the first subject that comes to mind. It is really uncanny how much the two of us have in common.

I pulled into the driveway and parked the bike behind Ben's blue Chevy pickup, then walked around the back of his house and without knocking, entered through the back door.

"Hi, Ben!" I called as I rounded the corner of his kitchen.

He was dressed in blue coveralls. Ben would get up every day and pretty much dress for work. Coveralls are his typical weekend dress code as Ben was often called back to the job for one off shift emergency or another. This morning he is sitting at the small kitchen table reading an article in what appeared to be a trade magazine. Ben is a big man. His large frame was completely obscuring the white-padded-chrome dinette chair that supported his ample weight. I was surprised to see a stack of multicolored, irregular shaped, thin sheets of plastic laid out on the small kitchen tabletop in a haphazard array. There were so many of these plastic sheets that they actually covered most of the remaining table surface.

"Morning, Howard, pour yourself a cup of coffee," said Ben without looking up. Finishing the article, he pointed toward the pile of plastic sheets and asked, "Do you know anything about this kind of plastic?"

I opened the upper left cupboard door and selected a red coffee mug, then filled it from the big, well-used metal coffeepot on the stovetop. I couldn't help moving a couple of the plastic sheets as I sat down. Picking up the top piece of plastic I flexed it in my hands and said, "Yeah, this is styrene or something like that. What are you planning to do with it?"

"I'm not sure yet. Do you know how to form it?" asked Ben.

"Well, I think they vacuum form this kind of plastic," I said, "but I haven't ever seen it done, just read about it. Where did you get all of this stuff?"

Ben smiled his big smile. "Myron brought it over a couple of days ago. He says that he can fill my garage with this stuff. It's all scrap from one of the companies that he delivers to. You know how Myron likes to dig through the dumpsters," he laughed.

I took a closer look at the sheet still in my hands and noticed that it wasn't a solid color. At first glance it looked white, but on closer inspection I could see that it had some irregular light blue streaks running across the surface.

Ben picked up one of the sheets and pointed to the same striations that I had noticed. "I think that when they extrude this material they did a color change, and this batch of material becomes scrap because of the streaking. We have the same problem when we change colors on our vinyl boot processing line."

Ben worked at a company called Principle Plastics. They manufactured vinyl rain boots and other products that were also made from liquid Polyvinyl plastic. He had been there for over twenty years. During that time period, Ben had designed or actually built most of the equipment that his company was currently using in their production process. He knew a lot about vinyl plastic molding and was a genius when it came to design, or assembly of any electrical or mechanical system.

My company made composite products that included boats, car parts, airplane parts, and a host of other fiberglass components. I worked with epoxies, urethane foam, and polyester resins. Some of the materials that I worked with overlapped with the products that Ben used, as we both formed or molded plastic parts; however, as a rule our companies processed the raw material in very different ways.

"So, tell me about vacuum forming," Ben said, leaning back in his chair. "How does it work?"

It only took me about five minutes to convey my limited knowledge of the vacuum forming process. This was basically heating the plastic sheet to a soft state, then moving it over some sort of mold that is a vacuum box. Once the plastic is sealed against the mold, you use vacuum to remove any air that has been trapped between the plastic, and the mold surface. The mold has a series of small holes in it that air can pass through, but not the plastic itself. As the vacuum removes the air, the soft hot plastic is pulled down over or into the mold. The plastic will then cool in place on the mold surface and will retain the shape of the mold. You then release the vacuum and lift off the finished part.

Ben sat watching me, quietly listening to my words but his mind was way ahead of my explanation as he was already planning a way through the mechanical process of forming this thin plastic sheet. When I had finished talking he asked, "I wonder how hot it needs to be for forming."

"No idea," I said.

"Well, let's find out," said Ben, rising from the table. He walked over to the kitchen stove and turned a dial. "We'll try it at three hundred degrees and see what happens."

I sat and watched quietly, always amazed by Ben's direct approach to any question or problem. He let the oven warm up for a couple of minutes then opened the oven door and placed one of the plastic sheets inside. He closed the oven. "Let's give it one minute," he said while looking at the big clock on the wall above my head.

I swiveled in my chair to watch the second hand slowly sweep around the dial. That was a long minute. Ben was up and rummaging through a small kitchen drawer. When he returned to the table he had a wooden spoon in his hand. Ben opened the oven door and gently probed the plastic sheet with the spoon.

"Still pretty stiff," he said. "Let's give it another minute."

I swung around and once more watched the second hand on the clock. "Now," I said, as the minute was up.

Ben opened the door and again probed the plastic with his spoon. "It's starting to get soft, Howard, take a look," he said, offering me the spoon.

I gently pressed the spoon into the plastic. I could see and feel that it was indeed getting soft.

"Another minute?" Ben asked, including me in this experiment.

"OK," I said, closing the oven door and immediately looking at the wall clock.

At the next one-minute interval, Ben opened the oven door to find that the plastic had now become very soft and pliable. We took turns pressing at it with the wooden spoon and could easily push the plastic down through the gaps in the oven tray. Ben turned off the oven and pulled the tray out to cool. We continued messing with the plastic but very soon it began to firm up and then became rigid again. When the plastic was cool to the touch Ben lifted it from the rack and inspected the grid pattern on the underside.

"Look at the detail on the back," Ben said. "It really formed nicely around the bars." He handed the sheet to me for my inspection.

Ben smiled his big smile at me. "Let's build us a vacuum former," he said.

I rolled my plastic sheet to look again at the front side and ran my fingers over the surface.

"Are you thinking decoys?" I asked, already knowing the answer.

"Howard, if Myron can come through like he thinks he can, I'm thinking lots of decoys."

We spent the remainder of the morning brainstorming and sketching at the kitchen table. When we were finished, we had designed a small oven with racks similar to his kitchen oven. We planned to build the oven out of plywood. We would then protect the inside with aluminum foil. Holding racks for the plastic would be made similar to window frames. They would also be made from plywood with a series of holes for screws around the perimeter. This open frame would hold the plastic sheet in place while it was being heating, and then we could hold the outside of the frame with our hands and press it down over a mold. Like most projects, once the basic plan was in place the details were easy. I began writing down our bill of materials. We needed plywood, a heating element of some kind, and a vacuum source, and of course a mold.

"I have a couple of old vacuum pumps at work," Ben said. "So that won't be a problem. What do you think we should use for a mold?"

We both kind of looked around the kitchen. Ben stood up and removed a small Plaster-of-Paris wall hanging decoration from one of the walls. It was a country store scene with a lot of fine detail.

"Do you think you can make a mold off of this?" he asked.

"No problem," I said, running my fingers over the intricate detail of the plaster casting. "I can make a fiberglass mold off of this easy enough, but I might mess up, or break it, Mary will kill me."

Ben laughed at that. "We'll ask Mary first."

Ben's wife, Mary, was the sweetest woman in the world. She would give me anything that she owned. I just didn't want to wreck any of her things and plaster parts are easy to break.

"OK, I said, if it's all right with Mary this will be our first mold. I have a toaster-oven at home that we don't ever use. I think that we can get the heating elements out of it."

We met again on Wednesday night to do a bit more planning. I told Ben that the mold was almost ready, and that I had rounded up the plywood for the oven and frames. Ben had retrieved the old vacuum pump and we were both excited to get started on the project. We decided to meet at my house the following Saturday.

I was up early using the table saw to cut pieces of plywood needed for the oven. Ben arrived about the time all of the oven parts were ready for assembly. He started hooking up the vacuum pump that would be plumbed into my vacuum mold while I finished building the oven.

When the oven was finished, we lined the inside with aluminum foil, and then installed cleats on the sides of the oven which will hold the picture frame wooden rack and the plastic sheet. The heating element from the old toaster was mounted in the bottom of the oven. Ben drilled a small hole in the side of our oven so that a thermometer could be inserted.

We went to work on the fiberglass mold using a very small drill to make holes through the face of my mold. Once we were happy with the amount of holes that we had drilled into the mold face we attached the vacuum pump to the mold-box. Ben turned on the vacuum pump and we tested the mold by covering it with a piece of clear PVC plastic sheet to visualize how the heavier plastic might pull down when heated. We noticed right off that this thin plastic was not pulling down evenly into all parts of the mold, but we were on the right track. From that point we simply drilled a couple of dozen more holes and tested it again until it looked like the PVC was pulling into all of the small crevices. By around noon we were ready for our first real test.

We had selected some very thin material that Myron provided, thanks to his scavenging the previous week. The plastic sheet was bolted into the frames with small machine screws and we put the first sheet into the oven. Ben turned on the oven heater and we both watched the thermometer rise rapidly as the seconds ticked off on our stopwatch. At the first one-minute interval, Ben opened the oven door to check the progress. The plastic was very hot but still stiff. We closed the door quickly and waited another minute, then checked again. This time the plastic was sagging in the frame. I pulled it out of the oven and pressed the frame over our mold as Ben activated the vacuum pump. The plastic sheet immediately sucked down and took on the intricate shape of our mold.

We were amazed at how easy it had been to form this first part. I inspected the formed shape and decided that some of the detail was not quite complete. We needed to drill more holes. Once this was done a second piece of plastic was placed in the oven, heated for two minutes, pulled out and sucked down. This time we produced a perfect replica. Two hours later we had about ten or fifteen more country store scenes piled on my workbench.

"Howard, this works better than I could have hoped for," Ben said. "I'm going to ask Myron to bring home all of the plastic that he can get his hands on."

"So what do you think, Ben, should we build a real vacuum form machine?"

"Yeah, let's have us a beer and talk about it," said Ben.

The following day Ben called to tell me that he read about a plastic processing class that was starting in a couple of weeks at one of the trade schools. He asked if I would like to go.

"Sure," I said without any hesitation. We signed up for the class the following evening and soon started a class that would meet two nights a week for the next five weeks. This class turned out to be one of the most enjoyable and informative night school courses that I have ever attended. We found ourselves in a small class of about seven students and the instructor.

It happened to be one of those rare occasions where each of the students was a specialist in his own unique field. Each student was in the class to learn about a different plastic process or discipline. It was almost like each of us could teach one week of the course. The instructor was sharp enough to pick up on this talent that his students had. He used the student's expertise as part of the course program. It was a win/win situation for all of us.

For the next couple of weeks Ben and I spent all of the evenings that were not taken up by the plastics class at his kitchen table working out the design details for our vacuum form machine.

We had decided to build a machine that would form up to a three-foot by three-foot shape. The thought was that we could always make something smaller, but it would be nice to have the ability to make a big part if we ever wanted to. Who knew? While our design process was going on, Ben's neighbor Myron was doing his part by adding more and more pieces of plastic to a growing pile on the floor of Ben's garage.

Within about two weeks we had our design. The oven came first. Ben and I met at his house on a Saturday morning, and then drove to his shop. We spent the entire day cutting and forming sheet metal that we had purchased the previous week. This metal was then moved to my garage where we would do the assembly. Our oven consisted of an inner and outer sheet metal wall. Fiberglass insulation was sandwiched between the metal wall sections. It took a whole weekend to build the oven. When it was completed, I began welding the main frame. It took several weeks for me to finish this metal work. After this rough structure was ready I got started on the cylinder mechanism that would pull the tray from the oven, and yet another cylinder that would raise and lower the mold.

As I worked on my part of the project, Ben designed and assembled all of the electronics that would be used to make our machine completely automatic. He built the entire electronic console on his kitchen table. Ben set up multicolored lights to check the various electrical components. He used the five or six lights to simulate the various modules that I was installing. Ben and I spent a couple of weeks working on our individual projects. Once we were both ready, we met in my garage and for the first time plugged Ben's controls into my hardware.

Ben walked over to the control box, smiled at me and pushed the start button. The conveyor tray moved into the oven...a timer ran through its cycle... the tray moved out of the oven. When the tray reached its stop, a cylinder raised the mold station. At the top of the cylinder stroke, our vacuum pump started. Several seconds later a fan came on...another timer started...the vacuum pump stopped ... the fan stopped ... and the mold station cylinder retracted. The cycle was completed. I was amazed!

Now for some decoy molds; this was my job. I was very familiar with making fiberglass molds. It was a simple process for me to build three duck molds which were replicas taken from a factory decoy that we had selected as our model.

Two weeks later we were ready for our first real test. The newly made molds were secured to the lifting platform. Ben and I adjusted the frames in the vacuum form machine and inserted three sheets of plastic. Our oven temperature was set for three hundred degrees.

"Let's give her a rip," Ben said, and calmly pushed the start button.

It only took a couple of tries to get our controls adjusted properly. After a few minor adjustments we could make three decoy shells every four minutes. While the vacuum former was working we used a bandsaw to trim the decoy shells from the unwanted plastic sheet. Ben and I worked through the next two weekends forming decoy shells. We were now ready for the next step in our process.

The plan was to cast polyurethane foam into the decoy shells. I used a two-part urethane foam at my job making our small boats and was certain that the same basic process could be used to fill the decoy shells.

We went to work. Thanks to Ben's neighbors we had plenty of help. Our assembly line consisted of Ben and his next-door neighbor Jim, the *mixing crew*. They would mix and pour foam into the shells, then clamp on a metal backing plate. Trevor, Myron's youngest boy, *the conveyor*, would carry the filled shells away to cure. Next was Bruce, our *trim operator*, who would use a bandsaw to trim the flange from the decoy. Now Mike, another *conveyer;* would place the trimmed decoy on a table, ready to be painted. Myron, our *painter,* began painting the three colors on the decoys. He worked with his oldest son Little Myron, and a neighbor boy Scott, another of our team *conveyors,* who moved the painted decoy out to the *drying area,* which was Ben's back yard.

My job was to keep the parts coming by restocking Ben and Jim, unclamping the metal plates from the formed decoys, and removing the clutter of trimmed scrap that Bruce was generating. Trash barrels began to overflow.

The back yard soon became filled with neat rows of painted gray and white, black-trimmed decoys drying in the sun.

One case of beer and a box of ice cream bars later, our little crew had built 1,000 decoys for a unit cost of two and one half-cents each. We were ready for this year's hunting season.

The Hunting Cow

The shotgun was too cold for me to actually hold but I managed to cradle it at my side with an arm draped across the stock. That way even though it was very dark, I still knew where my gun was located. Bill was on my right with Ben lying down at his other side. Rick was on my left. The four of us had been lying down in this position for almost an hour and the thin canvas tarp offered very little cushion or insulation from the frozen ground. A small flock of geese passed over our spread of decoys, but they were way too high, out of shotgun range.

"Turn," whispered Ben, offering a spoken wish.

Bill and Rick cut loose with a spontaneous cadence from their goose calls, but the birds were not interested, as they winged slowly but steadily west until the flock was out of sight.

The sun was making a weak appearance on the horizon and I knew that it would be warming up soon. I tried to wiggle my toes but couldn't actually feel anything much below my knees.

"I'm about frozen solid," said Ben. "How about a stretch?"

The brown-camo netting was thrown aside and the four of us rolled to a kneeling position, then cautiously tested our unsteady legs, before actually standing upright. Rick poured a cup of coffee from the big thermos. He took a sip, then offered the cup to Ben. The cup traveled between the four of us, was refilled and passed again. We each milled around in close circles, stomping our feet as circulation slowly returned to our legs. This small amount of movement did wonders. I was still cold, but could now feel my feet and maybe even some of my toes.

A hazy smudge was forming on the horizon just to our east.

"Those birds will be coming our way," said Bill. "Let's get down."

We each dove towards our previous positions on the tarp, pulling the netting over us like a blanket. The birds came our way. This was a large flock of geese maybe two or three hundred birds, but they were way too high, and soon became small specks in the gray morning sky.

After another hour Bill threw off the netting and rolled to his knees. "Well, boys, I'm about frozen out."

"You won't get any argument from me," said Rick, already heading toward our spread of decoys.

I helped Rick gather the plastic shell decoys and we stuffed them into three canvas gunny-sacks. Once this was done, I went back to help Bill stuff our netting into another canvas bag. I attempted to lift one corner of the canvas ground cover but it was frozen solid.

"Leave it," said Bill. "We can come back this afternoon when it's thawed out."

The four of us started the half-mile walk across the field, toward Bill's van. Ben had the netting, Rick and I shared the bags of decoys and Bill was carrying all four shotguns slung over one shoulder.

"You know, Bill, the birds seemed to be working south of us this morning," Ben said.

Bill studied the sky before answering. "On a clear day like today they could be anywhere. It's just plain luck if they happen to decide on your spot."

On the drive home Bill slowed the van, and then stopped without any comment. He reached across Ben and opened the glove compartment, fishing out an old worn set of binoculars. Bill steadied his elbows on the window frame and studied the field on our left. We all followed his lead and looked at the field as well. I could see the flock of geese that had attracted his attention. They were on the ground about one-quarter mile away. The birds were smack-dab in the middle of the hay field, in plain view of the road.

"They know that they're safe out there," said Bill, handing the glasses over his shoulder to me. "No one could get close enough for a shot."

I refocused the glasses and watched what appeared to be at least one hundred geese. So close, I thought. Cows milled in the field, their movement not bothering the geese at all.

"The cows don't seem to have any trouble sneaking up on them," I said jokingly.

"No, the pasture belongs to the cows," Ben answered. "The geese are just visitors."

"Yeah, and cows don't shoot at them," added Rick, laughing.

Bill pushed the floor shift into first gear and started us rolling again. We left the geese and cows behind.

Several weeks later, Saturday morning found me en route to Ben's house. I had planned to stop by for a cup of coffee and to say hi. It was only about seven a.m. but I wasn't worried about waking anyone, as Ben and his household were all early risers.

Walking through the open back door, I went into the kitchen and helped myself to a cup of coffee. The kitchen was empty, so I went back outside and wandered toward the garage/workshop looking for Ben. There was never an end to the projects that were conceived and built in this small workshop. I was always happy to participate in the fabrication of these back-yard creations.

Ben was sitting on the workshop floor, surrounded by bent shapes of metal conduit. He had used chalk to draw a large oval shape on the floor and was in the process of bending the tubing to match this shape.

"Morning, Ben, what are we making?"

"Oh, hi, Howard, we need three of these hoop shapes," he said, not exactly answering my question.

I watched him work for a minute, and then reached over to help him with the assembly of this second hoop. We worked together for another half-hour or so, finishing the second hoop, then making a third.

Retrieving my coffee cup, I took a sip of the now cold brew.

"So, what are we building?" I asked again.

Ben smiled at me. "You haven't guessed yet?" he asked.

"World's ugliest hula-hoop?" I asked.

Ignoring my attempt at humor, Ben simply said, "No, it's a cow."

I took a fresh look at the three metal hoops, then at Ben.

"A cow?"

"Yes, a cow. You gave me the idea last time we were hunting." He met my puzzled expression.

"Don't you remember watching the geese in the big field? You said the cows didn't seem to bother them much. Well, now we'll build us an imitation cow and test your theory."

So, just like that, our Hunting Cow was born. Ben had a roll of heavy mesh hog wire that was about three feet wide.

We used the hog wire to make the sides of the cow. Ben and I attached the wire mesh to two hoops binding it in place with bailing wire. One hoop was fastened to the top and the other on the bottom creating an open oval shape. Now we cut another piece of the hog wire that was about six inches wider than our third hoop. We used the bailing wire again to attach one side, then bent the hog wire so that it went into a curve when the other side was attached. This curved shape would eventually become the cow's back.

About this time, Ben's neighbor, Myron, from across the street came over to see what we were doing. Myron immediately joined the fun by fashioning the cow's head using small pieces of hog wire. When the head was finished we wired it to the body. Now we had a complete wire skeleton. The three of us covered all of the surfaces with burlap. The back was intended to be a hinged lid. We attached the back to the sides using two short lengths of leather belt. Myron had the idea to add a length of hemp rope for a tail. We fastened the rope and un-braided the strands.

By noon our masterpiece was just about finished. We took a short lunch break eating sandwiches in the shop and admiring our work. After wolfing down the sandwiches, a bag of chips and a couple of beers, we moved the cow across the street to Myron's garage for painting.

Black paint was applied to the burlap, and believe it or not, this thing was really beginning to look like a big black cow. Or possibly we had just been looking at it too long, but we were all happy with the result.

"Let's take it for a test drive," I suggested, already lifting the back end and crawling into the hollow center of the cow.

"OK," said Ben. "Why don't you and Myron walk it around a little? I want to see how it looks."

"Cool," Myron said, lifting the back end of the cow and crawling in behind me. "Let's go."

Myron and I grabbed the bottom rail lifted the cow off of the ground. Holding the metal rail with my hands turned outward was a bit hard on the fingers, but the cow wasn't really very heavy. "Ready, Myron?"

"I'm right behind you, H, start walking."

We walked slowly around the yard.

"Bring it back across the street to my house," said Ben.

So we walked down the driveway and headed in the general direction of Ben's house.

"Can you see anything?" Myron asked.

"Not a damn thing," I answered, now somewhere in the middle of the street.

"This wire is killing my hands," Myron said. "Let's put it down for a second and get another grip."

"Good idea," I answered, stopping and setting my end on the street. We opened the hinged back to get a look around and I was sure surprised to see that two cars were stopped in the middle of the street and waiting for us to cross. Ben and his next-door neighbor Jim were standing on Ben's front lawn, laughing. "We better move a bit, Myron."

"Oh, yeah," said Myron, lifting his end of the cow. We left the back lid of the cow open so that we could see better and walked into Ben's yard.

Ben and Jim were still laughing.

"Damn, Ben, why didn't you tell us there was a car coming?"

"What did you want me to say?" he asked. "No one in their right mind would run into a cow with their car."

Now we were ready for some refinements. We added two shoulder straps that attached to the lower hoop. Then we removed some of the burlap from the front of the cow in the brisket area so we could see where we were going. The hole was covered with a thin piece of camo netting that we could see through.

"I have an idea," said Myron, "be right back," he added, heading toward his house. He returned with a set of window-mount gun racks. "No sense carrying your shotguns."

"Perfect," I said. We mounted these light racks to the inside of the cow so that we wouldn't need to carry our shotguns when walking into the field.

Myron and I got back inside and gave the cow another test run. This time we used the shoulder straps and it was a lot easier to carry; and thanks to the camo netting I could actually see where we were going.

"Can you see, H?" Myron asked.

"I can see that Ben brought us a beer," I answered, stopping and placing my end on the ground, then lifting the lid.

"Thanks, Ben," I said, hoisting my beer in a mock toast.

The following Friday, Ben and I both took the day off to deliver the Hunting Cow up north. Our hunting area in Wheatland, California, is about four hundred and fifty miles north of our homes in Los Angeles. We made the drive in eight hours, arriving at Ben's brother Bill's house at about four in the afternoon. The news of our arrival had traveled fast. Our hunting partners, Ben's younger brother Bill, his nephew Rick, and our good friend Kenny had all turned out to check out this masterpiece. Rick and Ken helped us unload the cow into Bill's back yard, and then took it for a walk around. We planned to have our first real hunting test the following morning.

Rick was planning to be married the following month. His future father-in-law managed a five hundred-acre cattle ranch located a few miles east of town. We had permission to hunt on this private land and figured it would be a great place to try out our cow.

At about six a.m. on Saturday we unloaded her in a back pasture. Ben, Rick, Bill, Kenny and I stood quietly and watched a large flock of geese land in the field about a half mile from where we were standing.

"Well, girls," said Bill, "who's going first?"

"You mean, who's going with me?" said Rick, as he began walking toward the cow.

"I'll get in back," said Kenny.

They both climbed into the cow and began adjusting the carrying straps. Bill handed in two shotguns, which were placed in the racks.

"It looks like you have enough room in there for me," I said.

We all looked at each other for a second. "Why not?" said Rick. "Come on, H."

I handed my shotgun to Rick, then crawled under the side of the cow to take a position in the middle. Bill closed the lid.

"Good luck, boys."

We had only walked about fifty yards when it started. "Who ever heard of a six-legged cow?" asked Kenny.

Rick turned right without warning, causing me to bang my head against one of the shotguns.

"Where are you going?" I asked, rubbing my bruised head.

"There's a nice patch of clover, and I'm going to eat it," said Rick.

Laughter erupted all around me.

"Hey, Kenny, you won't be laughing so hard when it gets to your end."

"Ha, ha, ha—"

"Shush," said Rick, "there's a bunch of ducks in that little puddle up ahead."

"What are you doing back there?" whispered Rick.

"Passing grass, ha, ha, ha—"

"Shut up."

We were working hard to keep our laughter under control as we walked to within twenty yards of the ducks.

"Well, let's give them a broadside," whispered Rick.

Rick and Kenny set the cow down. We each retrieved shotguns from the rack.

"Now!" said Rick, standing and raising the lid.

We all stood, picked birds and shot. It was hard for me to pick out a single bird. We were so close. After shooting, we got out of the cow and gathered the five ducks that we had killed.

"Well, ducks don't seem bothered by six-legged cows," I said as the three of us prepared to move again.

We were walking toward the center of the field.

"Brace yourself, Kenny," said Rick.

"What?"

"Here comes a bull, be brave," Rick laughed.

"Ha, ha, ha. . . ." On we walked, finally cresting a small rise, still laughing.

Rick stopped.

"Damn." he set his end of the cow on the ground and raised the lid.

We all watched as about one hundred geese took flight well out of our range.

"Well, they might not be able to count, but there is sure nothing wrong with their hearing."

About one hour later, we came on another small bunch of geese. By this time we were pretty much laughed out. We approached slowly and quietly. The geese didn't fly until we raised the lid, stood up and shot. Birds fell.

As we headed back towards the truck a couple of hours later, we were walking inside of the fence line that had a road on the opposite side of the fence. We could see a blue pickup coming toward us. As it got closer, we recognized the truck. It belonged to Ted, the foreman of this ranch, and soon to be Rick's new father-in-law.

"Wonder what Ted will say when he gets a look at us," Kenny said. We stopped walking and watched the truck as it came closer, closer still, then passed by without even slowing down.

"Damn," said Kenny. "Ted can't count either."

"I don't think it would be wise to repeat that one," Rick answered.

By the time we got back to the fence corner, we had worked out a pretty good hunting plan for the following day. We decided to leave the hunting cow in the fence corner so that it would be ready for an early morning hunt, and also to avoid hauling it around town.

Back at Bill's house, Ben and Bill both got a big kick out of the retelling of our day in the Hunting Cow.

"Well, do you boys think you got all of the laughing out of that cow today?" Bill asked.

"I'm sure we did," Rick answered.

"Well, good, because tomorrow we can make it an eight-legged cow," said Bill.

At about five a.m. the next morning, we drove to the field. As we approached the fence corner, I could see that several real cows were gathered near the fence. Bill parked his van and we walked toward the fence, startling the cows away.

Our hunting cow was gone. At first I thought that someone must have stolen it. I climbed the fence and walked around in the dim light, starting to get pretty mad, when my boot caught on something. I reached down to find a large piece of hog wire covered with burlap. It didn't take much to figure out that the real cows had trampled our hunting cow flat.

Later that afternoon when retelling our hunting adventure at the local bar, one of our audience said, "It's a good thing the game warden didn't catch you boys walking around in that hunting cow of yours."

"Why?" I asked. "It was just kind of a portable hunting blind."

"Well," he said, "it's against the law to hunt behind a cow, or a horse, or anything that looks like one of them."

"No way!" Kenny put in.

"Well, son, you best check the law before you try it again," was all our friend had to say on the subject.

It turned out that he was right and none of us much wanted to get arrested, no matter how good the hunting was. We told this story many times over the years but never did get up the nerve to build another hunting cow.

The Honeymoon Is Over

*C*lear traffic—cool. I kick the motorcycle shift lever down into third. Just a quarter turn of my wrist snaps the bike forward like an angry cat waking from a nap. Traffic has been dogging along stop-and-go for half an hour; this is more like it. The big 650-Triumph leaps past a green Ford Pinto as we enter the open lane. It feels great to be moving again. I sense more than feel a gentle click as the shift lever moves against my boot. The bike changes gears as I sharply tap the lever upward, now finding fourth. I adjust my position on the seat a little and in seconds I am cruising at 70 mph, perfectly centered in the far-left hand lane. The warm afternoon wind feels good on my face. It's whooshing in around my sunglasses, and I blink my eyes a couple of times to clear the tears. This isn't a long open stretch; I can already see brake lights a quarter of a mile ahead. *Damn this traffic, it's getting terrible.*

We've been living in Torrance four years now. I drive this same twenty-five mile stretch of freeway every day. When we first moved to Torrance from Culver City, it only took about twenty minutes to get to work; now it's more like forty-five. I always shave some time with the bike because I can split traffic.

But it's still slow going, and these heading-home ass-holes are the worst. In the morning I can maintain an easy forty-five or fifty even hold thirty-mph when splitting traffic. Everyone is cool, sipping at their coffee or shaving as they roll along. But these going-home guys, damn, it's hard to believe these are the same people. Some of them actually try to cut you off; like who gives a shit if a bike gets ahead of you. It's getting hard for me to enjoy the ride—if I don't keep my eyes open I'm dead. Maybe tomorrow I'll drive the Dodge.

I ease the bike one lane over to the right, slowing down to fifty-five as I get behind a red Ford pickup truck. Then up to sixty-five as I pull around him on the right hand side, slowing again as I pass the gray van on his left. Now I drop in front of the van to make my off-ramp for Western Avenue. Bikes are cool.

There are a lot of cars parked in front of TeaTime. This is a favorite local beer bar. All of the locals just call it The "T". I'm not going to stop today; the lawn mower is still in pieces on my workbench at home and I plan to get it back together.

I am nearly past The T when I see the familiar green Chevrolet pickup. It looks like Bobby's and I wonder what he's doing here. Bobby is one of my best friends. I haven't seen him in almost a month. *Funny he isn't riding his bike.* Almost without bidding, the Triumph spins up the drive and stops in a convenient spot near the front door. *Maybe just one quick beer.*

It wasn't Bobby. I didn't think he would be in The T on a Tuesday. But once I was inside I got talking with John Mitchell, and we shot a couple of games of pool. So it worked out OK. Damn, my pool game is getting weak. I'm really missing the practice hours I used to put in every day before I got married. Last year I would have eaten John for lunch. How many games did he beat me today? Three, four? Yeah, probably at least four; damn, I really need to work on my game.

It's a lot cooler now. I love to ride on these seventy degree L.A. nights. I kick the Triumph down into second gear and just touch the front hand brake, slowing for a red light on Torrance Boulevard, then crack the throttle and snap the bike up into third as the light changes back to green. Not a long ride from here, I'll be home in five minutes.

The big single headlight pans the front lawn of our place as I slow the bike and slalom around Angie's Volkswagen. I stop in front of the garage and hit the kill button. It's quiet in this neighborhood. All I can hear is the gentle ping of my exhaust pipes as they cool, and maybe a distant TV set. This is definitely not a big party neighborhood. The oldest kid on the block isn't over six. That's the thing though, we should be having parties, but how do you party with two kids asleep in the back bedroom? Even when we go somewhere for the night, like maybe to a movie, it always seems to be some big deal.

I unlock the garage door and pull it open, smiling up at the overhead florescent lights as they blink on, then sputter to a steady glow. I hooked up a little circuit two weeks ago that makes the lights turn on when the garage door opens. It works great; I smile upwards again, as if the lights were responsible; then I walk back and grab the handlebars on my bike. As I roll the Triumph to rest in the garage, I look across at the mess on my workbench. This weekend I have to get that lawn mower together. If I borrow Dave's mower one more time I'll be overhauling it, too. Maybe tomorrow night I'll get started. I could have it done by Saturday, and then we might even catch a little water skiing on Sunday. I reach over and pick up the lawnmower carburetor, slowly rolling it around, like I could really see what was going on inside. The carb should be rebuilt also, or else I'll be back into this mower again next month. Damn, the to-do-list is really getting pretty long around here. I could sure use a vacation.

I shut off the light, then pull the garage door closed and lock it from the outside. The circuit I built only turns the light on; it doesn't turn it off when the door closes. Lots of nights I work in the garage with the door shut and need the light on.

A white flicker is playing with the shadows on our front drapes. It must have been our TV I heard from the driveway. You never know these days. Sometimes Angie goes to bed at eight, sometimes not until two in the morning, when nothing is on the tube but the black and white movies. I turn the handle on the front door and start in, then remembering what the lawn looked like; I bend down on one knee and open the valve for the sprinkler system.

"Hi," I say quietly, not wanting to interrupt *Leave It to Beaver.*

"Hi. There's some dinner in the oven, if you want it." Angie doesn't look up.

She hasn't moved her eyes from the TV, but I know she isn't watching it. I walk between her and the television, then down the hall to the front bathroom. I run the water in the sink to let it get cool, then splash my face a couple of times. The bathroom fan runs all the time that the light is on. I will have to figure out a way to rewire that some day. My hand is still playing with the water and it feels cooler now. I cup my hands and let the water run over, and then bring it to my face again.

I know that she was crying; I could see the shine on her cheeks. Damn, I don't want to do this movie again tonight. I splash my face once again then pull one of the yellow hand towels from the chrome bar. The towels are always clean, always the same color, yellow, or light green, or pink, never mixed. Three were hanging today. Some days there are just two, but today there were three. *What the Hell could it be this time?*

I pat my face dry and carefully refold the yellow towel, then hang it back on the bar. It doesn't matter how neatly I hang the towel, tomorrow it will be gone. All three of them will be changed. I reach behind me to fish the broken comb out of my Levi's back pocket, and then run it through my hair. *I sure need a haircut.*

Maybe we both need a break. I think a road trip might be just the ticket.

A Family Business

*H*ere I am, your basic city boy, a normal five-days-a-week working guy. After the four-year Coast Guard tour was behind me, I followed it with eight years of steady employment that has turned into a successful job. My life now includes a perfectly good four-year-old marriage that has produced two babies. Our oldest daughter is three, and the second daughter will be one next July. At thirty I should be a bit young for midlife crisis but maybe not; my wife and I are actually discussing the possibility of leaving all the city of Los Angeles has to offer and moving to a smaller country town. *Back to the good life*, as the wife likes to say.

My dear, young wife Angie says that she will follow me anywhere. This is stated without reservation, as long as I continue to provide food, shelter, cars, and money. Armed with this bit of knowledge, we embarked on a two-week driving vacation through Northern California. Our plan was to stop at various small towns, off of the beaten path, and check out the atmosphere. As our trip unfolded we developed a kind of pattern. Upon entering a new town we would stop at the first real estate company that we found and ask about home prices. This technique would usually give us some idea of property values, and also a bit of local insight about the various neighborhoods, schools, shopping centers, and a general lay of the land.

In the third town that we visited the real estate agent asked a very pertinent question: "Just what kind of work do you do?"

Sheepishly I made reference to my various qualifications, which did not include an actual job within four hundred miles of this particular city.

"Well," said the salesman, "it seems to me that what you two need is a business to get into, not a house. And you happen to be in luck, because I've just listed an excellent business opportunity—worms."

"Worms?" Angie and I questioned in unison.

"Yes, worms for fishing. Bait. . . this is a bait route; a family business."

He went on to describe a wonderful ten-year-old established business that was currently owned by a dear old man with failing health; finally ending his narration with, "All you have to do is to drive around town and deliver bait to happy fishermen."

What a Godsend, to actually purchase our own business, an established business that included a fifty-year-old meat locker plant, which was already rented. We could immediately see the magic in it. Angie and I would be landlords, we both knew how to drive, and the rest couldn't be all that difficult.

The following morning, after signing papers and writing a check for the earnest money deposit, we headed back to the city. Upon our return to Los Angeles I gave notice at my job and got our house on the market. We were hoping for a quick sale. The money that we anticipated from selling our house would be needed to cover the down payment for our new business.

More good luck—the real estate market was red hot. We had a full price offer, and the escrow started within thirty days. Leaving my wife Angie and the children to finish packing, I headed back up north to close on the bait business and to find housing for our family.

This would be my first solo business venture, but I knew that we should anticipate start-up expenses. My calculations told me that after closing on our house and making the down payment on the business, we would enter into our new enterprise with almost two thousand dollars in reserve. I did not spend a lot of time pondering this particular line of thought; however to make matters a bit more complicated, the two-thou seed money did not factor in moving expenses or housing, which was proving to be elusive.

I was amazed to find that the local paper did not offer *one* house for rent. It took several days of beating the streets before I found a slightly rundown two-bedroom house that could be rented for a comfortable $65.00 per month. My little woman sat in the cab and cried when I eased the U-Haul to the curb in front of this gray-shingled beauty. Fortunately we had friends to help with this move. It took some real imagination attempting to pack the furnishings from our previous three-bedroom, 1,500 square foot home into this tiny 800 square foot two-bedroom. It can be done. Things that did not quite fit into the house were stored in the garage, a one-car dirt floor structure behind the house, or the-shack-out-back, as my wife preferred to call it.

My bait route vehicle was a late model Dodge one-ton truck that had been fitted with a frame mounted five-door refrigerated storage unit. As per our contract, Mel, the prior owner of the bait business, would work with me for a couple of weeks and "show me the ropes." We started early each day, first loading the truck and then heading out on the various daily routes.

Mel was friendly and very sincere about this business. His failing health turned out to be the beginnings of emphysema, complicated by an over fondness for straight Kentucky bourbon. The steady alcohol intake did in fact cause him to be less than alert in the evenings.

Mel and I traveled around the countryside driving from town to town, servicing the bait route customers. The complete five-day tour covered some twelve hundred miles of highway. I drove while trying to master the spider web of county roads, alleyways, highways, quick right turns, customer names and obscure locations.

As we drove Mel talked constantly in his raspy voice, which was generally loud, but at other times could be very soft. He would respond to my questions by first touching his hearing-aid-ear and would often supply very strange answers. The hearing aid proved to be an asset, however. We would go into each place of business and check stock that was leftover from the previous week. After a quick inspection of the live bait, checking the worms, we would determine how much bait to restock.

"Going to bring in four dozen night crawlers," Mel would say. The shopkeeper would voice approval, or he might say something like, "I think that *two dozen* will be enough this week, Mel." In either case, Mel would nod, touch his hearing-aid-ear and say, "Fine, be right back." We would return with the four dozen that Mel had initially proposed and write up a bill. I could never determine if Mel actually heard the request for a change of quantity or not, but the shopkeeper did not seem bothered by the overstock, and promptly paid with cash from the register. *Neat trick,* I thought making a mental note to find an old hearing aid somewhere for myself.

Most evenings the drive home was quietly capped off with me at the wheel pondering my own thoughts about the day as Mel relaxed against the passenger door, his hands folded gently around a half-pint of Jim Beam bourbon whiskey. At the end of my first week, we had serviced most of the bait route customers. I had been introduced to about eighty or ninety shop owners. Some were friendly, some were remote and others seemed kind of gruff.

Saturday morning was the time for us to restock our supplies and to get ready for the following week. Mel and I met early to do what he called "pa-ken." As I drove into the parking lot on that gray Saturday morning, I took a serious look at this second phase of my business, my fifty-year-old locker plant. This place was home base for the bait route. The half acre piece of property was located in downtown Oroville just behind the post office. It included the locker plant itself, which was a one-story rectangular building about fifty feet wide and one hundred and fifty feet long. In this building was a butcher shop, a chill room for hanging and aging farmer killed meat, and a deep-freeze locker room including about five hundred lockers that were available for customer rental. There was also a 1,600 square foot ice room with an ice maker and a monstrous ice crushing and sorting machine. In one small corner of the building there was a refrigeration compressor room, which hopefully would continue to keep everything cold.

A long, wide loading dock fronted all of the rooms and was accessible from the L-shaped parking lot. There was one small building on the corner of the property that had been an office of some kind in its prior life. It was now vacant. This office building also provided the only bathroom facilities on the premises. The south end of the property was bounded by a long row of garages that stood door-less, gaping open into the main asphalt parking area.

The white paint on the locker plant seemed to be quite faded and I noticed peeling that I did not remember from my first tour. The open garages were not painted at all and I quickly dismissed the unbidden thought that included a future necessity of fitting doors of some type to these garages and the associated costs for this upgrade.

We started our morning pa-ken in one of the garage outbuildings. I was quick to learn that *pa-ken,* in Mel-speak, actually means packing night crawlers. This was done by hand mixing dry, dusty paper bedding with water, then placing a small handful of the now wet bedding into individual white-foam cups which Mel directed me to arrange two deep on the pa-ken table. Once the long table was covered with all the cups it could hold Mel brought out a shallow Styrofoam box that contained one thousand bulk night crawlers which were in a brown bedding of some kind, and dumped them unceremoniously into a well-used wooden tray. He then began picking the large worms out of the bedding in batches of twelve. The counted night crawlers were placed in individual cups and covered with snap-on plastic lids. Our bulk night crawlers were stored on a shelf in the gut-room.

This evil smelling, dimly lit room was about twelve-foot square and refrigerated. The gut-room was not built-in but was a self-contained wooden unit that had been placed inside of the open storage garage. The door of the gut-room opened to the parking lot. I noticed that besides the night crawlers the gut-room was also home for about five or six open 55-gallon drums of, that's right guts. This was an assortment of heads, hides, and internal organs from farmer-killed beef and hogs which would later be picked up by a rendering plant. I was initially surprised by the sight of these waste products, but was very glad to learn that the smell escaping from this nasty little room did not come from the worms.

After three or four hours the packing was finished and our big truck was loaded with fresh bait. We now walked over to the locker plant for a look at the frozen bait. Sardines, anchovies, clams and salmon roe was all stored in the main freezer room. The locker plant itself was leased as a separate business, but for some reason I had not grasped the idea that the maintenance of the facility was to become my responsibility. This refrigeration maintenance concept became apparent to me upon entering the compressor room.

The sound of running machinery could be heard at least one hundred feet from the closed compressor room door. When Mel opened the door, the equipment noise was almost forgotten as an initial blast of ammonia-scented air assaulted my eyes, nose, and lungs. I actually backed up a couple of steps and attempted to reprogram my respiratory system before following him into this hot, smelly, mini-maze of piping, gauges, and oil dripping machinery; all of which was powered by open belt motors and huge spinning flywheels.

Mel fondly patted the top of one compressor, much like a person would do with a favorite hunting dog; he then laid hands on a pipe or two and seemed to take mental note of the readings that were displayed on several of the gauge dials. Mel appeared to be satisfied with this inspection and looked across at me as if to ask "if it was OK with me as well." What the Hell did I know? I was more than happy to take two steps backward and exit this bad dream. Once my head had a chance to partially clear from the ammonia-rich air I realized that I was now the proud owner, soon-to-be caregiver for this antiquated equipment.

My head was a bit fuzzy but my feet seemed to be operating OK so I followed Mel; still cautiously inhaling shallow breaths of semi-clean air as our tour continued around the corner of the building up four cement steps and into the butcher shop. A large, round lady was seated on one of the two counter stools just inside the butcher shop door. My gaze drifted past the seated woman as a scene from the movie *Halloween* loomed on my right.

"How-do?" said the butcher, my new tenant as he moved towards me. Fortunately he did not reach out to shake my hand, as the long knife that was still firmly grasped in his right hand would have run me through.

It took me a long second to pull my eyes away from the bloody apron and menacing knife. I looked the tall man full in the face and amazingly found my voice.

"Hi, I'm Howard."

That evening the wife and I were reclining in our new digs. We had just finished our first dinner together since moving in. I felt relaxed and began to convey the past week's activities. After a few sentences Angie interrupted me with, "But didn't the salesman say that this was a family business?"

"Yes it is," I said, reaching under the coffee table. My hand came back with two beer flats containing a week's worth of customer invoices and cash receipts. These included multiple gas tank fill ups, miscellaneous business purchases, and about twenty-five hundred dollars in currency bound with two wide rubber bands.

"The way it works is, I drive, and you take care of the books. You may want to have a look at this stuff."

That first season Angie found a perfect union with her ever-present large, noisy, electric calculator, and the thick, red, leather-bound account book. I attempted to achieve a twenty-five hour workday, and our youngest said her first words, "Mommy," "Daddy," and "Bait Route."

Fresh Frozen

Store owners are by nature a very cautious group. Their buying practices and careful inventory control will often determine the actual success or failure of the business itself. Each of these owners will face the balancing act between too much or too little inventory. They know the pitfalls of overstocking as it applies to out of fashion, out of date, or spoiled merchandise. In all cases their final decisions are equal to dollars made or lost for the store.

The second concern for an owner is the painful consequence of running out of stock. This condition is possibly the worst scenario, as it will cause customer complaints and will be a direct loss in revenue due to the lack of merchandise on the shelf.

In an effort to ease these very real concerns, some of my predecessors proposed a very simple solution, which would address both of these problems. The concept that they developed was called "Guaranteed Sale." This is an agreement between the wholesaler and storeowner based on the premise that the delivery driver is responsible for all previously delivered merchandise until it is actually sold.

With this unique philosophy in mind, the bread man assures fresh rolls, as the dairyman restocks milk and cheeses, and the bait man inspects his white cartons of live worms, replacing any containers that may be doubtful.

This wonderful agreement between delivery driver and shop owner can assure fresh merchandise for the customer and help maintain a well-stocked store.

Being the new bait man, I embraced this concept keeping a watchful eye on all live bait left over from the previous delivery, often exchanging old containers for new ones. Dead worms did not make anyone overly happy.

My bait service also offered an assortment of frozen products, which included fresh-frozen sardines and anchovies. These small fish were caught off the California coast. They are processed by flash freezing and packaging into one-pound bags. The individual bags were neatly folded into fifty-pound cardboard boxes and sealed for delivery.

The frozen bait does not require any particular inspection because, well, it was already dead.

Today was Thursday, July 6[th,] my youngest daughter's birthday. Upon arriving at my first customer location at eight in the morning; I was forced into rethinking the entire Guaranteed Sale concept as it applied to fresh-frozen bait.

The small store was located in Butte City, just east of the Sacramento River. Striped bass, originating in the ocean, swim this far up river every year to the delight of thousands of local fisherman. The run can last anywhere from six weeks to two months, but seldom much longer than ten weeks. Lures of every description are used to catch these big fish that can weigh in at well over thirty pounds, and literally thousands of pounds of frozen fishing bait is expended each year during this event.

My customer had just asked me to pick up two cases of anchovies that were left over from this year's run. The striped bass season was essentially over on this part of the river, and his reasoning for returning the bait was sound. So without further thought, I wrote him a cash receipt, and then went to retrieve the two boxes of bait from his freezer. Being very familiar with the business practices at this grocery store, I removed the large brass key that was hanging on a nail near the side door. This key would give me access to the adjacent icehouse where the cases of fishing bait were stored along with clear plastic bags and blocks of ice. I located the anchovies on the floor toward the back of the small icehouse. Once I had moved the bags of ice covering them I was annoyed to find that the boxes of bait seemed to be kind of soft. This could only mean one thing. The bait had been allowed to thaw. The nature of my business caused me to be very aware of freezer and refrigerator operating temperatures. Besides owning the bait business I was also the owner of a freezer-locker-plant, and knew from experience that some of the older icehouses in this part of the country would not maintain particularly cold, sub-zero, temperatures.

I loaded the bait onto my truck without a word of complaint, honoring the long standing Guaranteed Sale agreement, but made a mental note that these boxes of anchovies would need to find a new home pretty fast. The outside temperature was already over one hundred degrees, and promising to get a lot hotter. My truck was insulated and did a good job keeping things cold, but it worked kind of like an ice chest; it wouldn't actually freeze anything, and my merchandise would gradually get warmer as the day progressed.

This particular route had twenty stops, all of them selling bait that would essentially be used for fishing in the same general area. For that reason it was not surprising when none of these customers had a requirement for anchovies today.

The two returned boxes of anchovies that I had picked up in Butte City at eight that morning were all that remained in the freezer compartment of my truck, as my engine pinged to a stop at Bob's Mini Mart, my last customer. It was exactly eight-thirty p.m.

I was sure glad that the day was almost over as I stepped from the cab of my truck. "Evening, Bob, what can I do for you today?"

"Hello, Howard, how about two flats of night crawlers, and do you have any anchovies?"

"Sure," I heard myself say, turning, already heading for my truck. I was completely worn out from the long hot day and found myself pretty much working on auto-pilot. I transferred a single box of anchovies from the front compartment of my bait truck to the light aluminum hand-truck with the practiced ease that thousands of repetitions will produce. My mind did not admit the fact that these little fish were probably spoiled from the warm icehouse temperature in Butte City, not to mention the long day that they had been driving around with me, as I slipped the case unopened into Bob's chest-style freezer, and gently re-latched the door. I then returned to my truck a second time for the four dozen cups of night crawlers that he had requested.

As I waited patiently, invoice in hand, a gas customer came into the station. Bob serviced the customer, politely checked under the hood and cleaned the windows. After depositing the money he received from his customer, Bob turned his attention to me.

"Hey, look at all those cats," he said, casting his eyes around the station.

I followed his gaze and watched in horror, as cats seemed to be everywhere. Some were hanging around my truck while others were tracing the invisible path just made by my small aluminum hand-cart.

"That's funny," I said as I offered my bill to Bob.

The ringing phone woke me up just before five a.m. the following morning.

Bob's angry voice pounded into my sleepy eardrum. "Get that junk out of my freezer!"

I swung immediately into action; driving first to the locker plant for a new box of anchovies and then to Bob's station.

We didn't exchange any actual words. The cats were still there.

I replaced the previous night's delivery with the new box of anchovies and then drove quietly away. On my way home I stopped at a river crossing and dumped the box of dead anchovies into the water.

Bob didn't buy any more anchovies from me. In fact, he never bought anything else from me.

I'm sure sorry about that, Bob. You know, at times I can just be incredibly stupid.

Jack

The Harrison clan have some interesting family members to be sure. The mold was broken after each new child was born. Harrison brothers and sisters are all unique and no one has ever been saddled with a derogatory name like "black sheep of the family." This being said, I will not break the longstanding tradition when describing Jack.

My friend Ben Harrison has an older brother by three years. This brother is a lifelong resident of Wheatland, California. He is known to everyone simply as Jack. Brother Jack and his wife Louise live in a small house on the outskirts of Wheatland; their home is just east of Ben's property and they share a fence line.

Growing up in this small farming community, Jack has done his share of labor-intensive work including all types of jobs for most of the local farmers, log mills, and factories as far away as Sacramento. He would often break into short periods of self-employment endeavors such as "market hunting" for ducks when this practice was still legal, cutting firewood, junk collecting, prospecting for aluminum cans, or working as a handyman. Jack is always on the lookout for a new opportunity as is true for many of the Harrison brothers and sisters. There are not many things that Jack cannot do.

I own a locker plant in Oroville, California, which is about forty miles north of Wheatland. The locker plant itself is ancient, having been built in the mid-twenties. It has several rooms for frozen food storage and meatpacking.

All of these rooms are made cold by an ammonia gas refrigeration system. There is also a freezer room that was used for making block and crushed ice. This ice room is about forty feet wide and forty feet deep with an eight-foot high ceiling. The ice making equipment is original and actually still works but has not been used for several years. My plan is to remove all of the old ice making equipment and the old ammonia freezer pipes. Then I would update the freezing equipment to a modern user-friendly Freon gas evaporator system.

The main thing that is holding this project back is the necessity to remove the freezer pipes from this room. The entire ceiling is covered with a maze of suspended pipes that run in an east and west direction. The pipes are attached at one end to a long six inch pipe manifold, which runs the full length of the west wall. The pipes are about two inches in diameter. They hang down about twelve inches and are suspended by hundreds of metal rods. These pipes are part of the ancient ammonia freezer system. When the system is turned on the pipes become cold and will make the room into a freezer. As they become extremely cold. The temperature change causes condensation to collect on the pipes; this moisture then freezes into ice. It takes about one month for an ice ball to grow to one foot in diameter. This unwanted build up of ice has to be removed which will prompt a need to defrost the pipes.

Defrosting the ice room is an all-day event requiring three or four men. Hot gas is pumped into the pipes which loosens the ice. Then with the help of some pounding the ice ball is broken up and falls to the floor. Now for the clean up; this cold labor intensive job includes shoveling many tons of ice into wheelbarrows and then transferring the pile of ice out of the room and leaving it to melt in the parking lot. I only participated in this backbreaking chore twice before deciding to upgrade the freezer system. The first obstacle that stands in the way of this revision is the need to remove the old piping.

I thought of Jack.

We stood in the middle of the ice room and discussed the job.

"So Jack, do you think you can get these pipes out of here?"

"Sure I can. It'll just take a cutting torch. I can have all of the pipes down in a day or two. I've got a buddy that can help me."

"OK, how much would you charge to do the job?"

"Well, how about a hundred and fifty bucks and let me keep the scrap pipe."

"That sounds fair, Jack, when can you start?"

"I'll call my buddy Stan and probably get started tomorrow or the next day."

"You got a deal, Jack. Thanks. Oh, do you need some up-front money for gas or anything?"

"Nah, you can pay me when we're done," Jack said, turning to leave. "See you in a day or so."

The following morning I arrived at the locker plant and saw an old brown Chevy pickup parked near the back of the lot. The ice room door was standing open, belching black smoke. As I walked up the stairs to the loading dock the foul smell of ammonia gas combined with burnt oil greeted me. Once at the ice room door I blinked my eyes into the smoky grey interior and eventually made out the forms of Jack and Stan. Jack is cutting a pipe with his torch. He is standing on a short wooden ladder, in an array of crisscrossed pipes that had been cut and now laid haphazard on the floor. Stan is straddling several of these pipes. He is standing near Jack holding the hose for the cutting torch. I cautiously entered the smoky room and can see that a steady stream of burning oil is leaking from the pipe that Jack was cutting. The oil ignited as it left the pipe and continued burning in a small puddle on the floor. Jack finished his cut and the long length of pipe fell to the floor with a loud clatter and a shower of burning sparks. My gaze was riveted on the small pool of oil that continued to burn on the ice room floor.

Stan looked up and saw me standing in the doorway.

"Don't worry, it'll only burn for a couple of minutes," he said.

As if on cue, the flame sputtered, died down, and then went completely out, leaving only a few tendrils of smoke coming from the black puddle. The room looked like something out of a bad science fiction movie. Jack noticed my concern.

"Don't worry Howard. Once we finish cutting we'll haul all the pipes out. Not much sense in moving them twice."

"How do you plan to carry the pipe, Jack? It looks like too much for your truck."

"We'll finish cutting today," Jack replied. "Then I'll bring a trailer tomorrow and haul the pipe home."

"I'm going into town," I said, "do you need me to get anything for you?"

"Yeah," said Jack, "a beer would go good."

"OK," I laughed, "I'll be right back; anything else?"

"Yeah," said Stan, "make it two beers."

Before leaving I hooked two lengths of garden hose together and ran it into the ice room.

"Just in case," I said and left for the beer run. After returning with two six packs of Bud I left Jack and Stan to their work and got busy with a project in my workshop. About or an hour or so later I heard my name being called.

"Howard," Jack shouted from outside of my little workshop, "I'm out of gas for the torch; we'll be back tomorrow."

I walked from my workbench to the shop door in time to see the back end of Jack's old brown Chevy pickup leaving the locker plant and making a left turn onto High Street. The ice room door was standing open so I wondered over to inspect the day's work. Once again the room was smoke filled; the air heavy with noxious fumes. I did not actually venture into the interior this time. Oily pipe covered the floor like big rusty pick-up-sticks in an ungodly mess. Twenty or thirty lengths of piping had been cut down as Jack had promised. However several lengths of pipe were still attached to the main manifold and jutted diagonally from the floor to their attachment point near the ceiling. From my vantage point at the doorway I could see several puddles of oil that had pooled under the pipes. I had a brief thought that the oil should be cleaned up before it had a chance to soak into the concrete floor. Most of the oil was under the piping. I could see that cleaning would be a very difficult job without first moving some of the crisscrossed obstacles. I quickly dismissed this thought as a bad idea, deciding that I could wait until Jack and Stan removed the pipes the following day. Leaving the ice room door standing open, I left the locker plant for the day.

The following morning I returned to the locker plant expecting to see Jack's pickup. It wasn't there. I walked to the open ice room door and glanced once more at the mess inside. I just shook my head at the disaster and pushed the big door closed. Jack and Stan did not return that day, or the next day, or the day after that. In fact it was a full three weeks later when I ran into Jack, seated comfortably on a bar stool at his favorite bar, Bill's Place in Wheatland. A glass of amber liquid was on the bar in front of him. I knew that when Jack drinks whiskey his personality takes on a big change. It converts him from mellow to obnoxious. One glance at his puffy complexion and blood shot eyes told me that this was not the best time to discuss business.

"Hi, Jack," I said quietly, not slowing down as I passed him to choose a seat at the far end of the long bar. Jack may have answered in my wake, but I did not plan to turn around in any event. I really tried my best to avoid Jack when he was drinking whiskey.

Two weeks later I was returning to Ben's house after a morning duck hunt. I noticed that Jack was wandering around in his back yard gathering sticks, and adding them to a smoldering burn pile. This was evidence that he had been doing some cleaning up around the place and I took that as a good sign. I went into Ben's house and poured two cups of coffee then walked diagonally across the damp back yard to the fence corner near the burn pile that Jack was now poking with a shovel.

"Like some coffee, Jack?" I offered a white mug over the wire fence.

Jack turned his attention away from the fire, noticing me for the first time.

"Best offer I've had all morning," he said, walking towards me. "Thanks."

I watched his face as he took a first cautious sip of the hot coffee, noticing that the puffy look was almost gone. His eyes were still more pink than white. They were crisscrossed with angry red lines, but the dazed, whiskey look was gone, and I was sure that mellow Jack was back. We sipped our coffee quietly for a couple of minutes before Jack spoke again.

"Stan and I have been pretty busy cutting wood for the past couple of weeks. We'll be back over to your place tomorrow or the next day."

"OK Jack, that'll be fine," I answered, knowing that the unfinished job was bothering him.

"I've actually been back to Oroville three times since I saw you last," he said.

"Oh, sorry I missed you; I must have been at home or working one of the routes."

"After we cut down the pipes at your locker plant," Jack continued, "Stan and I went for a cold beer at that little bar at the end of High Street. We started talking with one of the local guys at the bar and somehow the conversation got around to firewood. I told him that I had a bunch of black walnut back in Wheatland. Well, he got real interested and ended up giving me a hundred bucks for a cord. The next day I picked up Stan and we went over to the Watts farm and bucked a cord of walnut from the blow down trees that Doug Watts asked me to clean up. Then on Tuesday I was going to deliver the wood but I couldn't find the little slip of paper that the guy in Oroville wrote his address on. I decided to go back up to Oroville anyway, and thought that maybe I would remember what his name was on the way.

"So Stan and I go back to the little bar and had a couple of beers, but I still couldn't remember the guy's name, and I don't think that the bartender was the same one either. My truck was parked in front loaded with the black walnut firewood, and I was hoping that the guy might drive by and see it parked there. I kind of lost track of time, but I guess that Stan and I spent most of the day at that little bar. Some other guy in a red plaid jacket came over and asked me about the wood, saying that he wanted to buy it. I told him that the wood was already sold, but I couldn't find the guy that bought it, and I couldn't find his address either. So the guy in the red jacket asks why don't I sell the wood to him and then go get another cord for the guy that I can't find. Now that sounded like a good idea so I took the wood to his place and unloaded it. Now I was paid twice for one cord of wood and I was feeling kind of bad about selling the wood that was already paid for from the first guy. So Stan and I went back to the little bar again, but still didn't run into the first guy.

"My chain saw was kind of messed up and I worked on it for a couple of days, and then finally got together with Stan again and we drove over to the Watts farm to cut some more firewood. It got pretty warm that day so after we cut the wood we went over to the Four Corners Bar to get a cold beer and a bit of air conditioned air. Bill Terry asked me about the load of wood on my truck and I told him about the guy in Oroville and that I was going back there the next day to see if I can find him and deliver the wood. Well, Bill thought this was pretty funny; he bought Stan and me a couple of rounds of beer. Then Bill says why didn't I sell him this cord of wood and I could cut another one for the guy that I can't find or maybe sell another load to the guy with the red jacket. This sounds like a real good idea, so we go ahead and take the wood to Bill Terry's place.

"The next day Stan and I hooked up the trailer and were going to go on up to your locker plant to haul away the pipes, but I was still thinking about the guy that already paid for the first cord of wood. So Stan and I decide to cut one more load of firewood, and if we don't find the guy this time, at least we tried. When we get to the Watts farm Stan has an idea to load the wood into the trailer instead of the truck because the trailer is lower and is easier to load. We begin to load up the trailer and realize that it takes a lot more wood to load up the trailer then it does to load the truck. It actually took us a whole day to fill the trailer, and we probably had at least a cord and a half, maybe two cords of wood in there. Stan was pretty happy because we sure weren't having any problem selling the firewood and this big load would bring a lot more money.

"So the next day we got up early and headed on up to Oroville again. We went back to the little bar. This time the first bartender is working and we told him about the guy that we're looking for. Well, he says that he remembered us and he remembers the guy that Stan and I are talking about but doesn't know his name. We spend almost all day in that little bar and never did find the guy, or anyone else that is interested in buying the trailer load of firewood. Now Stan and I are stuck, because we can't load your pipe until we unload the wood. You know the damnedest thing is that it seems like it's a lot easier to sell wood when you have an empty truck than it is to sell it from a full trailer. Stan and I have no choice but to drive on back to Wheatland. It took us almost two weeks to sell that nice load of firewood but we finally managed to get her sold.

"You know, this pipe cutting job of yours is turning into quite a big project."

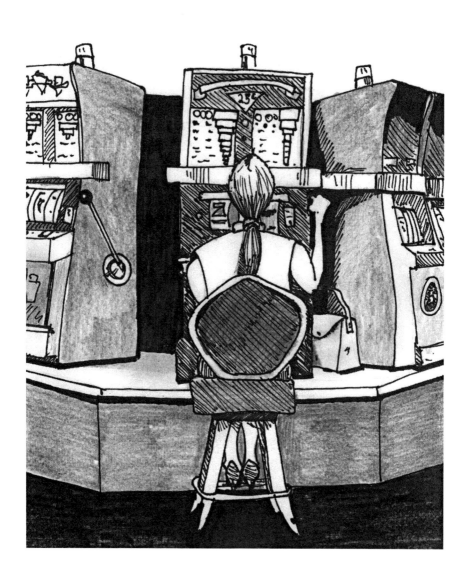

The Synchronizer

What a nice day. It is mid June. Most days are clear and sunny this time of year, although the weather can get a little warm in Northern California. We are in Wheatland. This is a small town about forty miles north and slightly east of Sacramento. Most Californians have never heard of Wheatland with its modest population of around five thousand people. This is a quiet farming community, kind of tucked into the foothills. There isn't a major freeway near us, so we are pretty much left alone. I guess you would describe this community as "laid back." All I know is that we like it here. My friends and I are all gathered at Bill's house on this particular Saturday afternoon. Today is probably in the low 100s but not hot like it will be next month or in August. August always seems to bring the really hot days. This is a good day to sit and swap stories with my best friends; a perfect beer-drinking day.

Bill is a square-built man, six foot something. The start of a belly softens his features but he is actually very fit. I think his fitness is due more from working outside every day on his job with the water district than to any personal care, but hey, whatever works. Bill has the kind of voice that can easily reach across a crowded room or will clearly carry to the other side of a twenty acre duck pond. Today he is relaxing in his own living room so he doesn't have any reason to talk very loud.

My other friend Rick works for the power company as an electrician. Rick is also a big man. He is not quite as tall as Bill, probably just under six foot, but he is quite stocky and solid. Rick is usually quiet, well, not exactly quiet, but soft-spoken and deliberate. His gentle ways sometimes make people underestimate his size and strength. I have never witnessed Rick actually "red faced" mad at anyone, and I wouldn't particularly I want to. The three of us do a lot of hunting and fishing together. When we are not engaging in these outdoor activities we usually get together and work on one project or another that relates in some way to hunting or fishing. Sometimes we plan the next event or simply hang out and have a few beers at Bill's house. Once in a while on a day like today we might spend a whole day working out ways to improve our equipment or simply take turns storytelling, talking about past or upcoming hunting trips.

Bill has picked a relatively cool spot in the room. He is sitting in a small chair by the open front door. A big four-blade ceiling fan was producing the only air movement. Like most long-time residents of Wheatland, Bill doesn't run the air conditioner on a mild day like this one.

Rick is sitting with me on the big couch. Neil and his friend, Jen, have just arrived. Neil has already made the introductions and the two of them are now lounging across from Rick and me on the small beige couch. We each have an open can of Budweiser beer. Bill is holding his in his hand; the other beers are on the coffee table between the two couches.

Neil is a fun guy. He is short like me, about five foot eight and thin, with light brown hair. His eyes always seem to be laughing, kind of crinkled in the corners. They go well with the smile that is always there on his round, tanned face. Neil works in Sacramento and lives alone. He spends a lot of weekends in Wheatland with his friends.

I remember the first time that I met Neil. It was at Red Hill, a local bar on the west side of town. My friends and I had been at the bar for a while, and it was probably around eight in the evening after a long day of duck hunting. Neil walked up to me out of the blue, and introduced himself as a game warden. He then started questioning me about the day's hunt, and maintained a serious poise as he walked me to a corner table. He then asked me to produce all of my licenses, duck stamps and everything else that he could think of. This took quite a while and to my embarrassment, we were beginning to draw a crowd. Neil kept it up; he had me just about convinced that I did something illegal when I saw that wisp of a smile creep across his face. I immediately realized that I'd been had. I love practical jokes. We were instant friends.

Earlier today, just prior to Neil and Jen's arrival, Rick brought me the contactor that I had asked him for. It was an electrical switch box mechanism that was enclosed in a black plastic box. I thanked Rick for the contactor, and left it sitting on the coffee table.

Oh, do you know what a contactor is? It is basically a switch used for starting electric motors. The switch is designed to connect three separate lines of electricity, usually three-phase. It contains three large brass electrical contacts that are fixed, and three opposing contacts that are spring-loaded. All of these components are housed in this rectangular black plastic case. It has external metal slots that are used to connect wires. Some people just call this switch a motor starter. I needed a three-phase contactor for one of my many garage shop projects.

Last month I had asked Rick if he had one. Rick is an electrician and these switches are pretty common in his line of work. He found this old model, which will do fine for my needs. This old contactor is much like any used equipment that typically finds itself sitting around in a workshop gathering dust. For some reason you simply don't throw it away. It will continue to sit-and-gather until the day comes when you need exactly *that thing*. My wife would see something like this in my shop and call it "man stuff." And yes, the black box was out of place on the coffee table.

"What is that?" asked Jen, pointing to the contactor.

All eyes fell on the black box. Rick looked to me for an answer, even though he knew perfectly well what it was, as did Bill. But Jen had asked and Neil seemed interested. This could be an opportunity for a story, and my friends were silently asking me to tell one.

"This?" I asked as I reached over and picked up the black box. I snapped the switch, which produced a sharp metallic **clack**. The contactor is spring-loaded and would make this loud sound each time the contacts were held down and then released. Snapping the switch manually wouldn't cause it any harm. I repeated snapping the contacts a couple of times as a distraction. I felt a story building in my mind. We had all afternoon.

I held the contactor in my hand but did not speak immediately; just sort of let the question hang in the air.

"You really don't want to know what this is. It—"

The screen door banged open as Steve filled the doorway, and then entered the room. Steve is one of Rick's cousins and Bill's nephew to be exact. Almost everyone calls him Stevie, and he doesn't seem to mind the nickname. Like most family members he was always welcome at Bill's house, and was probably just passing by. Stevie and his exact business interests were kind of a mystery to me. He always seemed to have plenty of spending money, though no one ever talked about where he got it. I try to be polite to my friend's family members, and if some bit of information isn't offered, I usually don't ask. Bill, Rick, Neil and I all looked up and said hi to Stevie. Bill went into the kitchen, returned with a Pepsi and handed it to Steve; then sat back down in his chair. Stevie took another step into the room and remained standing next to Bill by the front door. He thanked Bill for the Pepsi and was giving it his full attention.

Without any intentional prompting from me, the black box in my hand was beginning to take on its new identity.

"Jen, you seem to be a nice lady, but I don't really know you. I shouldn't be showing you this, or even talking to you about it for that matter," I said quietly as I leaned forward and placed the contactor back on the table. I retrieved my beer from the coffee table and sat back to drink it.

Rick reached over and nudged the contactor a couple of inches in my direction, picking up his beer before leaning back on the couch.

"Go on and tell her, Howard," Rick said without smiling. He was always ready for one of my stories and probably could sense one coming.

"Have you ever been to Reno, Jen?" I asked as I set down my beer and picked up the contactor again, turning it slowly in my hands.

"Yes, sure, I don't go there a lot, but usually get over once or twice a year. Why?"

"Oh, I just wondered if you knew anything about the town. Do you play cards, or the machines?"

"I like to play cards, but I'm not very good. Most of the time other people at the table will get mad at me because I'm too slow; so usually I just play the slots, or sometimes Keno."

"Quarter slots," I asked?

"Yeah, quarters, dimes or nickels. Sometimes even the dollar machines if I'm really feeling lucky."

I looked directly at her. Jen's eyes were a light blue, very sharp and clear. She had an easy way about her and didn't look away from my stare. I thought how some women would be uncomfortable sitting in this room full of strange men. Maybe she liked the attention. My next words were flat and serious.

"Jen, you're a friend of Neil's so I'm going to show you this. But what I'm going to say can't leave this room. It's illegal, and can get all of us into a lot of trouble. Do you understand?"

"I understand." Her voice was unsteady enough for me to know that she didn't understand anything, but then of course none of us did, *yet*.

"Jen, have you ever noticed when you drop your quarter into the slot machine and pull the handle, how the jackpot always manages to come up on a different line every other spin or so; and it really takes a lot of quarters to get the three of them to all be on the center line at the same time."

"Well sure, when they all come up that's a jackpot; that's how you win. Everyone knows that. You have to be lucky."

"Yeah, everyone knows that. But what they don't all know is that luck doesn't make the jackpot come up to the line. The machines are adjusted mechanically and set to pay off on an exact percentage. Some casinos set them down to a three percent payoff, some for a five or seven percent, and some might go as high as ten percent. But even at ten percent, that still means that someone has to put in one hundred dollars before the lucky guy can get ten dollars back. Do you understand that part?"

"No, I guess not; I don't really know how it works. I just know that it's fun to play and sometimes I win."

"I can win sometimes too. But this little gadget will win every time. Let me show you something." I leaned forward and turned the contactor so that she could get a better look. "This is called a Synchronizer. It's a custom magnetic device, designed specifically for cheating the slot machines. . . Neil, is she OK with this?"

"She's good, Howard, go ahead."

"OK," I said, taking a short sip of beer, then replacing my can on the table and leaning back. "Here's how it works. It takes two people to set up the slot machine. One should be a woman because she can carry a big purse and nobody will notice when she sets it alongside of her slot machine. Besides this box there's a battery pack that comes along to power it. The battery pack is not very big and will go into the purse with the black box. There is also a remote palm device, about the size of a matchbook. I have that built into a pair of slot machine gloves. Do you wear gloves when you play?"

"No, I just get dirty hands, but I've seen people use them. I know what you're talking about."

"Good, then let me explain. The best way to work this is to be next to the machine that your partner is synchronizing. The Synchronizer has a built-in electromagnet. It will stick to the machine through the thin leather of a purse. It needs to be physically attached to the machine you're working on. Your partner drops the quarters into his machine and you watch for a jackpot to come up. When the machine is showing a centerline jackpot on any line, the woman, while playing her own machine, just presses the correct button on her palm device and that jackpot line is locked.

It's that simple. All you need to do is drop another quarter and pull the handle. When a jackpot comes up on line one, two or three, you press the palm button again to select the next line on the Synchronizer like this: *clack*, as I spring the contacts closed. Drop in another coin, and spin again. Keep playing the machine just like normal until you've locked in each of the jackpot lines."

I continued snapping the Synchronizer as I explained this process. "The sound from the slot machine operation covers any noise that the synchronizer might make."

As I warm into my story, I can hear the stage whispers from Stevie talking to Bill. "He's lying isn't he? He's making this up, isn't he, Uncle Bill?"

Bill shrugs, "I don't know. You know how Howard is. He builds the damnedest stuff. Be quiet a second, I want to hear this."

"When you've locked in all three lines, you've synchronized the machine. This usually takes about twenty to forty quarters. At any time after that you drop in your final quarter and **clack**. All eyes go to the Synchronizer. I smile up at them. You push the engage button during the spin. The machine will lock up with all three jackpots on the center line and it will pay off in cash."

I look at Jen and then at my friends as I continue, but all eyes stay on the black box.

"The Synchronizer works every time, on any machine, because they're all designed and balanced the same way. The real challenge is to get a jackpot and leave the casino without causing any suspicion. There are a lot of casinos so I don't ever try to take more than one jackpot in the same place. This will work on any machine, even on the one, five, or twenty-five dollar slot machines. I don't ever play on them or play a progressive machine because they have to go get someone to pay your winnings, and you'll have to sign for the money. Quarter machines are perfect because the house doesn't make you sign your name or show ID for payoffs less than one thousand dollars. Just take the auto-pays two hundred, or three, or five hundred and be happy.

"You can easily stack up one or two thousand bucks in a couple of hours. So think of it as kind of like a job and don't get greedy. The greed will get you caught, and the casino boys aren't like cops. People who own casinos take cheating very seriously. I'm sure some of them would hurt you if they caught you stealing from their establishment."

Stevie edges closer to the coffee table. I'm still holding the Synchronizer and at this point have no intention of setting it down. This is getting good.

"Can I get a better look at that?" Stevie is moving now, attempting to reach past Jen.

I pull the box closer to me. "No, Stevie, this thing will just get you into trouble. You're better off forgetting that you ever saw this little box."

"Howard, how about letting me borrow it for fifteen minutes? My friend has a slot machine in his basement. It would be funny to try it on his machine. He would have a fit."

"Sorry, Steve, I told you this thing stays with me. I shouldn't even have told any of you about it. I really don't want to see you get into trouble."

My focus is on Stevie. Jen is completely cut out of the conversation now but from the corner of my eye I can see that she is relieved. She is starting to get that someone-take-me-home look, but so far Neil is still intent on the story. He isn't looking at Jen or responding to her body language.

Steve now settles on the arm of the couch.

"How do you know that thing will really work?"

"One of my old friends was a slot mechanic in Vegas. He helped me build the first one. This is the third. They work."

"How about selling it to me? Then you won't have to worry about what happens to it."

"Steve, this isn't for sale. I built it as a custom order for a man in Las Vegas and have already got the money for it in advance."

"Well, you can always make another one, can't you? I'll give you two hundred for this one." Money starts coming out of his shirt pocket.

I just sit there shaking my head. It's funny what your mind does. Here we are in this high stress situation, and I'm wondering why Stevie is wearing that long sleeve shirt on such a warm day. Six or eight seconds tick by. It seems like an hour. Everyone in the room is quiet as the drama plays out.

"Make it three hundred. . . five. . . seven hundred then," Stevie almost shouts, as more money lands on the coffee table. Stevie and I watch each other but neither of us says anything for a full minute. He shifts in his seat, completely ignoring Jen, and pulls an old warn wallet from his back pocket. He looks inside and probes the contents, then removes a small square folded piece of paper.

"I'll give you all of the money and this pink slip to my car; it's worth a thousand easy," he said placing his ownership paper on the coffee table.

"Steve, I—"

"This is all I have with me, but next week I can give you some more. How much do you want?" Beads of sweat are standing straight out on his forehead. Fingers are unconsciously patting his pockets, as if looking for some extra money he may have missed the first time.

Now, just like on any good fishing trip, comes the moment of decision— catch or release. I've done as much fishing today as I'm going to and have no intention of taking Stevie's money, but now the tricky part will be to make a clean release without anyone getting hurt. I am not about to underestimate Stevie. If I hurt him, he will hurt me. I went for neutral ground before answering. "How's the Pepsi holding up? Kind of warm today; I'm dry as a bone."

Rick was off the couch in a flash. "I'll get um."

We all looked toward the kitchen noises as Rick returned with a plastic banded six-pack tucked under one arm and a can of Pepsi in his other hand. He handed a beer to Bill and the soft drink to Stevie, and then set the six-pack between Neil and me on the coffee table. We each pulled off a can, kind of like breaking bread. Everyone took a beer except for Jen. She was starting to look a little pale. It must be the heat, or maybe the fact that Stevie had been all but sitting in her lap for the past five minutes. I guess I forgot to mention that Stevie was no small man. He weighed in at about two hundred and fifty. One massive leg was still on the arm of the small couch, but most of this ample frame was now pressing Jen into the upholstery. The remains of our six-pack rested on the coffee table, covering some of Stevie's money.

We sipped our drinks quietly for a while, each with our own thoughts. No one talked about the Synchronizer; like it never happened. Rick reached for another beer from the six-pack when I finally said, "Can't do it, Stevie. You're a good a friend. I would never be able to look myself in the mirror again if I let you get into trouble with one of my toys. Sorry, no."

Stevie took a long pull on his drink. He rubbed his sweaty cheek against his shirtsleeve, and then set the empty pop can quietly on the table. Slowly picking up his wallet, we all watched as he replaced the pink slip. He picked up his bills and tapped them on the table a couple of times as you would a deck of cards, then bent the money into a familiar crease. He gently replaced the folded bills into his shirt pocket. In one smooth motion his fingers returned from the pocket with a crumpled pack of Marlboros.

His eyes watched me as he lit the cigarette, inhaled slowly, then exhaled a dense white cloud of smoke across the coffee table.

"I knew you were bull-shitting her all the time." Stevie stood up and turned to leave; taking one last look at the Synchronizer that was still resting in my lap.

"See you guys."

Snapshot

Jack Harrison, Wheatland, California

*J*ack is the older brother my friend Ben Harrison. He is a lifetime resident of Wheatland, California. Jack and his wife Louise live in a small house next door to Ben's property. On most days you can find Jack in a mellow mood and mildly drunk, either in town or walking around his back lot with a beer in his hand. He is naturally funny and has a lot of local stories to tell. On occasion Jack will go on what he calls a "whisky-drunk" which can last from a couple of days to a couple of weeks depending on the money or mood. During these whisky-drunk times his personality will take change for the worst; I have found it best to give Jack a wide berth and wait for mellow Jack to return.

One Saturday morning Ben and I had just returned from duck hunting. I noticed Jack was changing tires on his old Dodge station wagon.

"Hi, Jack," I said as I stepped out of my side of the car. "You decide to put some new rubber on the old wagon?"

"No, I'm taking off the new tires," he answered, "putting on some old ones for the trip."

This answer really caught me off guard. "Why do you want old tires on your car, Jack?"

"Well, we're leaving for Ohio on Monday to visit with Lew's family," he said in answer to my question.

"But why are you changing tires, then?" I asked, still confused.

"There's a lot of highway between here and Ohio, and I sure don't want to wear out this new set of tires so I'm taking them off and putting on some old ones."

"Aren't you worried about flats or blow outs?"

"No, I'll be OK. I plan to carry a couple of extras when I make the trip."

Sure enough, later that morning I saw that Jack had removed all four of his new tires and replaced them with old warn ones. He had placed three more junkyard tires on the roof rack of the old station wagon and tied them in place.

Damn he is serious I thought, OHIO OR BUST?

January in North Idaho

My first year of living in North Idaho took a lot of getting used to. Winter rapidly changed from cold rain to sleet to snow. My little cocoon of a mobile home did a good job keeping me warm and dry, but some said that it was a mild winter.

In my second year, January arrived with temperatures that dipped near zero, and then fell colder still, finally registering numbers of around twenty degrees below zero. I woke up on one of these subzero mornings to find that my water system didn't work. When setting up the mobile the year before I had taken precautions against potential cold temperatures by burying all of my waterlines very deep; so I guessed that this current freezing problem was most likely within the mobile home itself.

God, where to start; the mobile home was skirted and insulated. I had visions of removing all the insulation and attacking the plastic water pipes with a hair dryer. This was terrible. Then a thought struck me. For the past year I had been heating my home with a wood stove that I installed; however the mobile also had a built-in electric forced-air system that I never used. There was a long heating air duct that ran full length under the mobile. This system had heat registers that were designed to supply warm air into each of the six rooms.

My plan was to open this heat duct to the underside of the mobile and hopefully warm up the crawl space. I removed one register then reached in with my hunting knife, and cut a hole in the duct. The cut was about six inches wide and one foot long. After removing the flap of aluminum to inspect the underside I found a black mesh cloth barrier. I cut the mesh as well, then shined a flashlight and was looking at bare ground below the mobile home. I cut another opening at the other end of the duct, and one more in a center room. Now I closed all of the registers, set the wall-mounted thermostat for about eighty, and turned on the forced-air heater.

My hope was that the pipes might thaw out in an hour or so. I opened a water faucet in the kitchen sink and waited.

Ten minutes later water was gushing into the sink. Who would have guessed how easily this could be done? I turned off the forced air heater, then went out to my shop and made up three twelve inch by eight inch pieces of plywood with 2 x 4's attached to the bottoms. I used these boards to close off the holes that I had cut in the heat duct. Once the boards were in place I replaced the floor registers and was ready for the next cold snap.

That same afternoon I was visiting my friend Al who lived about a half mile away. I couldn't wait to tell him the neat way that I had thawed out my house.

"Howard, sometimes you amaze me," he said. "I've lived here all of my life, and never heard of anyone thawing pipes with a forced-air heating system. Damn, I sure wish I could do something like that in this house, but I don't have forced air."

"You mean that this house freezes up?" I asked, swiveling my head to survey the nice cozy living room.

"Sure, my pipes freeze. When we hit these subzero temperatures the same pipes freeze every year. They're frozen right now. In fact I was just thinking about getting under the house with my cutting torch and thawing them out."

"Al, do you have an access to your crawl space from inside the house?"

He looked at me for a second before answering. "Yes, there is a crawl hole in the closet right there," he said, pointing. "Why?"

"You have that giant wood stove that can probably get this room up to ninety degrees. It seems to me all we would need to do is heat up the room and then direct some of the heat under your house. If it worked at my place it might work here as well."

"That sounds like a good idea, Howard, but how would you suggest we get that nice warm air to go under the house?"

I smiled as I explained the simple answer to his question. "I have an old squirrel cage blower from a forced-air heater in my shop. If we cut a piece of plywood to fit inside of your closet, we could cut a hole in the middle of it, and then we mount the blower to the plywood. It could blow warm air from your living room down under the house."

Al and I got busy. I went back home and retrieved my old squirrel cage blower while Al cut a piece of plywood to fit the floor of his closet. We mounted the blower to the plywood and cut a hole in the center, then plugged the blower into a nearby electrical outlet. The old blower started a flow of air into the crawl space.

"Now for the hard part," I said.

"What's the hard part?"

"Well, we have to heat this room up," I said.

"That won't be hard," Al smiled, opening the stove and throwing in several pieces of firewood.

"No, the hard part will be trying not to run out of beer while we wait," I laughed.

This actually proved to be the easy part because in less than thirty minutes water was running in Al's sink.

Dave remembers his apprentice years

Shortly after high school my friend Dave began his first job, working as a plumber's assistant. The company offered an apprentice program that Dave joined, eager to learn the trade. During his second year as an apprentice the company selected Dave to manage a twenty-unit apartment complex, as the *on-call*, maintenance-man. This new apartment development was built with county money. It was part of an experimental program which was designed to help poverty-level families. For many of the tenants this was their first real home.

Duties for this job included general maintenance of the complex and attending to tenant complaints. These complaints could be minor such as changing a light bulb or unplugging a kitchen drain. The more serious issues might include clearing a diaper-bound toilet, or opening a locked-from-the-inside bathroom door.

One day an older woman living on the second floor called to report a problem with her garbage disposal.

"Good morning," Dave said smiling, toolbox in hand. "I would like to have a look at your garage disposal unit."

The woman did not offer a greeting, but simply stepped away from the door to allow access, then followed Dave into the kitchen.

Dave being the professional he was first performed a preliminary inspection of the garbage disposal unit. He did this by running water into the sink, assuring a clean drain. Going under the sink, he disconnected the power supply to the garbage disposal, and then turned the grinding mechanism with a small Allen wrench that he carried in his toolbox. Once satisfied that the unit wasn't stuck in some way, he reconnected the power cord. Now Dave brought a bottle of liquid soap from his toolbox and poured a small amount into the sink. He turned on the water and then turned on the switch for the garbage disposal itself. Dave was pleased to see bubbles forming in the sink drain indicating that the unit was running properly.

He told the woman that she might have had some kind of stoppage, but the unit now seemed to be running just fine. "Please call me if you have another problem," he said, closing his toolbox and preparing to leave the apartment.

Three days later she did call, reporting the same problem.

Dave was once again met at the door. The woman stood aside while Dave proceeded to recheck her garbage disposal. Dave was careful not to miss any steps in his procedure and was again satisfied that the unit was working properly. Puzzled by this second complaint he assured the woman that the unit seemed to be functioning properly.

"That's what you said last time," she scoffed. Not waiting for an answer, she grabbed a large stained grocery bag that was sitting atop the kitchen counter and emptied its contents into the sink.

Dave looked first at the mess of garbage that she had just dumped into the sink, and then shifted his attention to the woman for an explanation.

"Just watch," she said, and turned on the switch. "See?"

Dave and the woman stood in front of the sink, both listening to the steady hum of the garbage disposal unit.

"See?" the woman repeated. "It doesn't work. That stuff will just sit in the sink all day, nothing happens."

High School

The three of us banded close together on the top row of hard bleacher seats. The football game was in progress but it did not mean very much to any of us. This was just a good excuse to be out late on a Friday night. A cheer went up and everyone around us stood up for the play. Dave remained seated, using the standing crowd as cover, and lit a cigarette. Cupping the cig carefully in his hand he took a drag, then passed it to Jerry, then it was passed to me. We all kept our eyes moving to make sure that none of the teachers spotted us smoking in the stands. In those years we could be expelled from school for this offense. The boy just below me turned around and asked for a drag. I passed the cigarette to him skillfully cupping it in my hand, and smiled with this shared secret. I noticed that a bottle was being passed between the three boys seated just below us. They were seniors; I knew them by sight but not by name. We didn't really associate with these older boys as the three of us were just in our sophomore year.

As I retrieved the cig I offered the boy some bold conversation telling him that we were going to get some beer after the game.

"Thought that maybe we would get drunk," I said. This wasn't true, but I was making conversation with a senior, and this kind of boasting sounded good at the time.

"Beer!" he snorted. "You can't get drunk on beer."

"You can't?" I asked, surprised.

"Nah," he said, "you drink some, and then you have to piss. It's impossible to hold enough inside at one time to be drunk."

Seniors are sure smart, I thought to myself. I left the football game with that wonderful piece of knowledge stored away. It took a few years before I would actually put his theory to the test. Man, was he ever wrong.

Bill Harrison and I duck hunting

The sun was well up and the few birds that were moving looked like tiny specks in the clear blue sky above us. Bill stood up, lit a cigarette and rested his arms on the top rim of the duck blind. He moved his head slowly as he surveyed the sky.

"There's a pretty good string of geese near the water tower," Bill said, indicating a thin dark line that I could just barely make out about three miles away. . . "Looks like two or three hundred ducks in that bunch heading towards the lake," he added, now looking at a dark cloud about four or more miles away, toward the east. . . "More geese way up high, back behind the old Bradshaw place," he pointed, turning slightly to his right.

I strained my eyes but couldn't for the life of me make out this last sighting.

"Bill, how can you tell which of those little spots are geese and which ones are ducks?"

Bill looked at me for a minute and seemed to be considering his answer.

"Well, it's pretty easy," he said. Bill extended his arm to point at a spot almost out of sight to the east. "Those are ducks," he said, then moving his arm to point toward a thin line on the horizon, he added, "and them are geese."

Reinhart

Reinhart has a personality and sense of humor that is hard to match. During his long and varied twenty-five year career as a job-shop tool maker he has found himself working for over twenty individual shops.

Reinhart specializes in composite plastics. This particular discipline is known as "soft tooling" in the aerospace industry. His accomplishments also include proficiency with conventional measuring equipment, and the more complex tooling optics. In addition to composites he had a solid well rounded background as conventional machinist. Reinhart has spent an untold amount of hours working with milling machines and engine lathes of all sizes.

This was Reinhardt's first day on the job in a small machine shop just east of Aberdeen Texas. Though it is only nine thirty in the morning it is already quite warm and Reinhart is well into his assigned project on the medium sized Logan Engine lathe. For Reinhart this was no big deal; just another day at the office.

As Reinhart finished his cut a tall man wearing a white shirt and striped tie appeared at his elbow. "Hello, my name is Gilbert," he said. "I'm the owner of this place. How you do 'in?"

"I don't know," Reinhart answered. "I've never got this far before."

Chief Barlow, Wheatland, California

Chief John Barlow was always an early riser. He would often leave his house around four thirty or five a.m., then drive around town for an hour or more before arriving at the station to begin his work day at six. He liked the town of Wheatland, having accepted the job as chief of police and moving here from San Jose with his wife Alice seven years ago.

John Barlow is a creature of habit. He likes things neat and in order. Every morning between six and six thirty he begins his shift with a large cup of coffee that usually becomes cold as he reads through the previous night's report. He then makes notes in the daily planner, and verifies the schedule of planned activities for himself and for his deputies. No one who worked at the station would even think to open Chief Barlow's office door between six and six thirty, knowing that their chief liked this half hour of quiet time.

One morning Chief Barlow had only just sat down with his cup of coffee when there was a commotion in the outer office followed by his office door banging open, revealing Jack Harrison, one of his constituents. The chief was not overly fond of Jack, and did not appreciate his morning routine being interrupted.

"What can I do for you, Mr. Harrison?"

"Well," Jack began, "Hank Swenson over in Sheridan has some old shacks that are left over from the days when migrant workers picked his peaches. Hank said that I can have one of the old shacks and I plan to move it to my place tomorrow morning. I need one of your deputies to meet me at the bridge by Camp Far West Lake on the Wheatland/Sheridan Road tomorrow at four a.m."

"I don't understand why you need a deputy, Jack," said Chief Barlow.

Jack gave the chief a puzzled look, and then explained his situation. "I'll put the shack on my trailer and move it on the back road between Sheridan and Wheatland. The road is plenty wide because the little house it's only twelve-foot square. My only problem is that I'll have to cross the bridge by the lake and it's kind of narrow there. I'd like to have one of your deputies to be there and stop any traffic that might be coming from the

Wheatland side of the bridge. It could be dangerous and I don't want to cause an accident."

"I see your point, Jack. Do you have a permit to move the house? It sounds like it's a wide load."

"Naw, I didn't mess with a permit. The shack is free and I couldn't see spending money on something that didn't cost me anything. Besides, at four in the morning the only place that I might have a problem is at the bridge."

"Jack, it's my duty to tell you that if you move that wide load without a permit we will have to give you a ticket. And that might cost you a whole lot more money than a permit."

"Look, Chief," Jack said, clearly peeved. "I did my duty as a citizen to warn you about what might happen at the bridge tomorrow morning. Now, if you don't have a deputy there and something does happen it sure won't be my fault because I did my best to get your help."

"Jack," said the chief sternly, "if you do show up at that bridge tomorrow morning my deputy will give you a ticket."

"Well," shouted Jack, "I sure-as-hell will be there!"

"So much for being a concerned citizen," Jack muttered almost to himself as he turned and left the office without bothering to close the door.

A few days later Chief Barlow was driving through town and saw Jack Harrison loading some bags into his car, which was parked in front of Big Al's Market. The chief stopped to have a word with Jack.

"Morning, Jack."

"Good morning Chief, how's the peace-keeping business going?"

"All is fine Jack; I'm glad that we didn't have to give you a ticket for trying to move that house across the bridge. My deputy had instructions to give you a ticket if you showed up with that house on a trailer."

"Yeah," said Jack. "I'm glad about that too."

"So did you decide to get a permit to move the house?"

"Nah, I don't need one anymore," said Jack.

"What do you mean? Aren't you going to move the house?"

"Well, the shack is parked in my back yard right now, so I don't have much need for a permit."

Chief Barlow's face reddened. "You never moved that house, Jack. My deputy was parked at that bridge for over an hour waiting for you to show up."

"Bridge?" questioned Jack. "Hell, I didn't cross the bridge. I pulled the shack straight down the main highway 65. There isn't any traffic at four in the morning, and it's sure a lot easier and shorter than messing with that windy old Wheatland/ Sheridan Road."

Fishing with Bill

Bill Harrison and I were bass fishing on Camp Far West Lake. I was standing on the bow running the electric trolling motor while Bill held down the back end of the boat. This morning Bill was currently out-fishing me about three fish to one.

"Looks like that one baby goose is sick," said Bill, pointing toward the bank near us.

I could see two large white adult geese on the bank about fifty yards away. I studied the birds that Bill had pointed out, and after a couple of minutes I spotted two baby geese that were much closer to the water.

"I can see the two babies by the water, Bill. What makes you think that one of them is sick?"

"No, the two chicks by the water are OK. It's the one lying down by the tree that's sick. See how that one adult keeps going back to the tree and making a fuss? He's trying to get the chick to stand up and come with the others. That chick isn't acting normal. My guess is that the baby goose is sick or hurt somehow and will probably die right there by the tree."

I let my rubber worm soak in the water and watched the goose activity for a few more minutes. I could see some movement at the base of the tree but I wouldn't have known that it was a baby goose without Bill pointing it out. Eventually the two adult geese lost interest in the straggler. They walked to the edge of the lake and joined the two healthy chicks. The four of them stepped into the water and slowly paddled away.

"Yep," Bill said, "that one is a goner."

"Bill, your eyesight has always amazed me. I wouldn't have seen that chick if you hadn't said something."

"Heck, my eyes are about shot," Bill complained. "I've already had a couple of surgeries on the right one, and my left eye isn't so hot either."

"Well, they still seem to be working pretty good," I said.

"Listen to this and then tell me if you still think my eyes are good." Bill smiled and began his story.

"A couple of weeks ago I was sitting around after dinner and my girl friend Debby wanted to go to Red Hill for a beer. I was kind of tired and didn't really want to go, so I told Debby to go on ahead, and that maybe I would be along later. She left and I took a short nap. After a couple of hours I woke up and decided that a beer sounded pretty good, so I went on over to Red Hill. When I got there I saw Debby's car parked in front.

"There was an old cowboy sitting straddle-legged on the porch in front of the screen door. I recognized the cowboy though I didn't actually know his name; he was usually with another scruffy old cowboy that looked a lot like him, maybe his brother. The two of them hung around Red Hill and were usually both drunk and already kicked out of the bar, or they were in the process of getting drunk and about to be kicked out of the bar. When I stepped onto the porch I could hear him mumbling unrecognizable words at the screen door. Once inside the bar I saw that Debby had a chair pulled up to the door and she was the one talking to the old cowboy.

'Hi, Debby,' I said. 'How are you doing?' Well, Debby didn't say anything to me. She just screwed up her face and gave me one of her dirty looks. I stood there for a minute or so, but she still wouldn't talk to me, just continued trying to talk with the drunken old cowboy. I shrugged my shoulders and walked over to the bar. Now I tried ordering a beer but Kathy the bartender was way too busy trying to kick the second cowboy out of the bar. I smiled remembering my first thought. The two old cowboys are still a set.

"I called to Debby, 'Come on over here and sit with me. Let Kathy throw those drunken cowboys out.' Debby wouldn't even look at me, so I walked over to her and tried to find out what was wrong. Kathy finally managed to kick out the second cowboy, and now Debby was acting like she was planning to leave with them.

'Come on, Debby,' I said, 'you don't need to be giving these cowboys a ride. They're big boys and can find their own way home. Come on over here and let me buy you a drink.' Well, she was still not talking and just gave me another nasty look.

"Now I was getting irritated.

'To hell with you,' I said. 'Do what you want.'

"I walked on back to the bar, called to Kathy, and finally managed to buy a beer. A couple of minutes later my nephew Rick wandered over and sat down next to me.

'How's it going, Bill?' he asked.

'Well, not so damned hot,' I answered. 'Debby is pretty steamed up about something.'

'What are you talking about?' asked Rick.

'She's about to take off with the old cowboys and she won't even talk to me. She's pretty mad about something,' I said, nodding toward Debby by the door.

'Hell, Bill, that's not Debby,' said Rick, smiling. 'Debby's sitting right over there,' he said, pointing to the *real Debby* who was sitting directly across from us on the other side of the bar."

"So," Bill said, "Debby and I have only been together for about eight years. What do you think of my eyesight now?"

The Long Drive

Several of my friends work for the local utility company named Pacific Gas and Electric. PG&E is a good company to work for with great benefits, but the company had a bad reputation for assigning jobs a long way from home. As an example of these long range job assignments, once four of my friends who were all living in Wheatland, California, had been assigned to jobs in Pittsburg, California. This particular job assignment was about one hundred and fifty miles from their homes. On many occasions when working on an assignment that was a long way from home my friends would rent a place near the job. When two of them worked on the same job site they often saved money by renting one room and bunking together. All of the men were married and didn't particularly like these remote assignments.

This time the four of them decided that if one of them would drive the others could cat nap in both directions and this way they could commute and come home to sleep in their own beds each evening. My friends worked out a simple plan that called for one man to do all of the driving for a whole week. Then they would rotate drivers and another would take his turn at the wheel, and so on until each had a week driving. The plan was working out pretty well and they were in their third week of commuting.

This week it was David's turn to drive. Al was slouching in the front shotgun seat and Ken was napping in the back seat directly behind David. Rick was awake; he leaned his head against the backrest and was watching the sky begin to get light over Al's right shoulder as fencepost after fencepost rushed by his passenger side window. The hayfields all looked pretty much the same with an occasional road sign or parked vehicle to break up the landscape. The car passed a large stack of hay bales. Rick noticed three or four hen pheasants and eight or ten almost full-grown chicks. The pheasants were doing their best to imitate domestic chickens, just hanging around the base of the haystack pecking and scratching in the morning sun. Then came more fence posts, more hay fields and an occasional parked farm implement, and then came Pittsburg.

The following day Rick once more watched the world from his widow seat. When the car reached the big haystack he saw that the pheasants were there again. On Thursday the pheasants were scratching in the morning sun once more. Friday morning Rick could just make out the now familiar haystack as a speck on the horizon.

"Hey, look at all those pheasants," he said.

My friends were all hunters so wildlife of any variety seldom passed unnoticed. Minutes ticked by.

"Where?" Al finally asked. "I don't see any pheasants."

"Right over there by the haystack," said Rick in a matter-of-fact voice, noticing that the haystack was still on the horizon but it now appeared to be about the size of a dime.

More fence posts ticked by.

"You mean that haystack?" asked Al. He was studying the haystack, now clearly visible and about the size of a grapefruit, still at least a quarter of a mile away.

"Yeah," said Rick, "must be twelve or fifteen pheasants pecking around at the base of it."

Eventually the car came even with the haystack, and the pheasants were there again doing their thing in the morning sun.

Al swiveled in his seat. "Good eyes, Rick."

Jack and Bob

The familiar sound made by tires crunching over gravel woke Jack Harrison from a restless Sunday morning sleep. Wondering who would be in his driveway this early in the day Jack glanced at the round dial of the old brass alarm clock as he rounded Lew's side of the bed. He noted that it was not that early—six a.m.—actually kind of late for most farm work in these parts, but Jack wasn't planning to be doing any work today. *What the hell?*

Jack opened the front door to see the unmistakable tall lanky backside of Bob Harris standing in his front yard using the toe of his boot to examine a rusty old hay-baler, "yard art." Jack shaded his eyes from the already hot morning sun. He could see the shiny hood of Bob's new Chrysler sedan parked in his driveway. This car was the envy of many folks in town. It was so new that it still wore paper plates from the car dealer in Sacramento.

"Come to take me for a ride, Bob?" Jack asked with an early morning attempt at humor.

Bob turned at the sound of Jack's voice.

"Well, I would always be happy to take you for a ride Jack, but actually I came over to ask you for a favor. Would you help me butcher a hog?" Bob asked in his normal, flat, matter-of-fact voice.

"I'm a fair hand at hog butcherin', Bob. When would you like to have me help you?"

"Well, I was kin'a thinking about right now today. See, I just got back from the Roseville Auction with this hog I bought. I'd like to take care of her as soon as we can. Kin'a like to get err' done before church this mornin'."

Jack looked across the yard but didn't see anything except Bob's car.

"Where's the hog, Bob?"

"Oh, she's in the car. Come look, she's a beauty," Bob said, already walking toward his shiny new Chrysler.

Jack slipped his bare feet into a pair of work boots that were handy just inside the door, then followed Bob across the lawn and was soon looking at a monster hog through the rear window of Bob's new car. This animal was big, dirty, and hairy, probably weighing in at over three hundred pounds.

Jack could see that the back seat had been removed to make standing room for the hog. Still the critter was not looking very happy. The large animal would have fit easy enough in the bed of a pickup truck but it was certainly out of place in this new Chrysler sedan.

"I was thinking that the big tree behind your house would be a good place to hang her. I know you've done a few of your own back there Jack, that's why I wanted to get you to help me," said Bob.

"OK," nodded Jack. "Let's get her out of the car and get to butcherin'."

With no further discussion, Bob opened the back door and reached in for the hog. She, however, had other ideas. The hog started squealing and began backing away. "Go around the other side," said Bob.

Jack went to the other side of the car and opened the door. Now surrounded, the hog attempted to escape by climbing the front seat, and managed to rip a great gash in the upholstery. For the next five or ten minutes Jack pushed and Bob pulled but the hog wasn't cooperating and the Chrysler was taking quite a beating.

"Hold up," said Bob. He pulled a red kerchief from his back pocket and mopped his brow. "This ain't working Jack, go ahead and close your door."

Jack closed the back door as Bob had asked, then looked up in time to see Bob open the front door of the Chrysler and bring out a rifle.

"What are you planning to do, Bob?" asked Jack, surprised to see the gun.

"Well, I might as well shoot her right where she stands and save on the rodeo," answered Bob. Then with no ceremony at all he aimed and fired. The hog dropped like a sack of wheat.

"This ain't exactly like I had planned," said Bob, "but we may as well dress her out here in the car."

Jack smiled over at Bob. "At least we got some shade, Bob. We sure as hell won't be able to move her now."

Decoy Roundup

It was Sunday morning near the end of January. I guess it must have been around eight o'clock as the sun was just up good. Duck and goose season has been closed for a couple of weeks but we still have some loose ends to clean up from this year's hunt, namely to make sure the two hunting blinds were sealed up for the season and that all of the decoys were picked up. My friends and I do most of our bird hunting on a twenty-acre pond that is actually part of a big rice field belonging to the Watts family. In the summer months this pond is planted along with the other five or six hundred acres of rice ground that is all part of the Watts Farm. After the rice harvest we have permission to flood this particular pond and set out our decoys so that we can hunt ducks and geese during the winter water fowl season. Our decoys stay in the pond for the entire three-month duration, but once the hunting season is over we need to remove the decoys and drain the pond so that the ground has a bit of dry-out time before spring planting.

This morning Brian, Rick and I had the chore of picking up the fifteen hundred or so decoys that we had set out for this past hunting season.

Now, if you would like to compare boring jobs I guess that decoy gathering would rank right up there. I would place decoy harvesting in a category somewhere between winding a ball from a hank of yarn and the task of raking fall leaves into five or six big burn piles. But that is not to say that you can't have a bit of fun with a boring job. As most of us know, the trick to this type of work is either finding a way to making it fun, or to make the conversation distracting enough so you don't think about the actual work you are doing. My specialty always ran toward the latter.

To help gather the decoys from the water, we had a small open boat that we pushed around the pond. Brian, Rick and I were walking in the pond lifting the decoys from the water, cutting away the anchor weight and placing the decoys into the boat. The weights went into a five-gallon bucket that was in the bow of the boat. When we had a boatload, which was about three or four hundred decoys, we went to the bank and unloaded. We sorted the decoys on the bank. Once all of them were collected, the three of us would load them into the trailer and drive them back to Bill's house to be stored away in the shed behind his garage until next season. With any luck at all we would have this job finished in a couple of hours.

It is a nice day, and we are all in T-shirts. We were also wearing hip boots. The duck pond was slippery, but not very deep.

"So Brian, what have you been doing for excitement down in Los Angeles.?" I asked, just making small talk.

"Not much, really, a couple of my friends and I have been doing some sailing," answered Brian.

"Oh really, I used to do a lot of sailing with my dad when I lived down there. Does your friend own a sailboat?"

"No, actually we rent a twenty-five foot sailboat from a place in San Pedro. It only costs us fifteen bucks an hour. We usually only stay out for two or three hours on a Saturday or Sunday; you can't even keep a boat in a slip for that kind of money."

"I didn't realize you knew how to sail, Brian. "Where did you learn?"

"Well," Brian answered smiling, "that's just it, we're all learning as we go. None of us actually know how to sail. That's another good reason to rent a boat instead of owning one."

"We sure did have a lot of fun waterskiing in the San Pedro harbor," I said. "Are you sailing inside of the harbor, or on the outside?"

"So far we've stayed on the inside of the breakwater. Last weekend we sailed way up to the north end but that turned out to be a bad idea."

"What do you mean?" I asked.

"Well, we didn't know it, but there are a lot of mud flats on the north end of the harbor. We sailed up there at low tide and ended up getting the boat keel stuck in the mud. It took us about three hours to get loose. The tide finally turned and the water came back in. It was actually kind of scary."

"Damn, Brian, you guys were lucky. If you had hit that mud flat as the tide was going out you could have spent the whole day stuck. You might have even wrecked the boat."

"Yeah, I know. We're going to get some charts of the area and take a look at the tide tables before we go out again."

"So after you were stuck last week did you call into the Coast Guard and let them know that you were alright?" I asked innocently.

Rick shot me a questioning look, but Brian didn't notice.

"No," Brian said. "The Coast Guard didn't know that we were stuck, so I didn't even think to call them about anything."

"It's no big deal," I said. "It's just that the Coast Guard likes to know about all boating accidents. They're on call twenty-four hours every day. Search and Rescue they call it. The Coast Guard logs all the boating accidents no matter how small."

"I still don't understand," said Brian. "I thought you just called the Coast Guard when you were in trouble."

"Well yes, that's true, if you're in trouble you call in a distress signal, then they send a ship out to help you. But any boating incident that lasts more than two hours can be classed as an accident. If the Coast Guard doesn't need to respond to these accidents they are pretty happy. When you qualify they might even pay survivors benefits."

Rick looked over at me again. The hint of a smile was just tugging at one corner of his mouth. He lifted a decoy from the pond and gave it all of his attention.

"Survivors benefits?" Brian asked. He looked at me, his face holding a puzzled expression.

Now let's just hold up a second. Rick knew that I was going to tell a story, and you know that I am about to tell a whopper, but Brian was a second-year college student at the time. He heard the word "money" and was prepared to listen. So who was I to disappoint him?

"Sure, just think about it, Brian. When I was in the Coast Guard I was on a three hundred foot cutter. We had about two hundred men. Each of us was making let's say five bucks an hour. That's what, one thousand dollars an hour? Now consider the cost of fuel. The four big engines burn about fifty gallons of diesel an hour. That's another couple of hundred dollars. Now, when our ship got a distress call they would go out and spend all of that money. A four-hour rescue could cost the Coast Guard about five thousand dollars. But if the accident victims rescued themselves the ship wouldn't need to leave the dock and the Coast Guard would save a lot of money. This money that they saved went into the Survivors Benefits Fund. It was paid out to the qualifying survivors of unassisted boating accidents. The Coast Guard would rather pay out a thousand or so as survivors benefits and avoid the trip."

Decoy gathering went almost unnoticed for the next hour as Brian and I discussed many possible scenarios where the

United States Coast Guard might find it economical to pay out cash money for would-be boating accident survivors.

"Well, it looks like you have the last one, Rick, let's head for home." I smiled at Brian as I turned and began walking toward the bank.

Bob and Stuart

Our first new home was quite an experience. We bought a tract house in a large development. It was a single story structure as were all of the homes in this particular subdivision. None of the homes had any landscaping whatsoever; just a house plopped in the middle of a dirt lot. I had no idea how much work it was to do something simple like planting a lawn for instance. Oh, first you had better put in a sprinkler system, and don't forget that the new place will need some landscaping, flower bed areas, cement walks, and how about that fence between you and your neighbor? All of these are very important items, and all need to be done before the grass seed is spread.

It turns out that most of the new homeowners have a very similar list of jobs in front of them, and in our little cul-de-sac many of my neighbors were perfectly willing to help with your job if you were willing to reciprocate when they needed your help. My neighbor Denny to the south and I teamed up to split the cost of a fence. To the north I had more fencing work to do. I joined forces with my immediate neighbor Bob, and with Stuart who lived on the other side of Bob. The three of us spent several weeks working together on this fencing project. We worked during the weekends and weekday evenings, which gave me plenty of time to form opinions about both of these men.

Bob is kind of a snob. He let everyone know right from the start that he is better than us average guys, and we are pretty lucky to have him around.

Stuart, on the other hand, is as good hearted as they come. Stuart is a big teddy-bear kind of guy, who is really very friendly. He will talk your arm off if given any chance at all.

Once this big fencing job was completed the three of us didn't get together very often. Bob and his wife Chris could be described as a "Ken & Barbie couple." Each of them would wave hellos in passing, but they always keep pretty much to themselves or with their own group of friends. They seldom mixed in with any of the neighbors or our cul-de-sac parties and activities.

Stuart and his wife Donna were just the opposite. They were always in the middle of things, and often invited the neighborhood group over for refreshments or an impromptu barbeque. Stuart came around my place all the time and was always talking to me about something. When I was in the garage or out in front of the house Stuart just had to come over and see what I was doing. I was usually nice to Stuart, as I was to all of my neighbors, figuring that he was good-natured enough and was just trying to be friendly.

It turns out that Stuart and his wife Donna were both teachers. They had all summer off from their jobs at the school district, so I wasn't surprised when Stuart got kind of ahead of me with the yard projects, as he and Donna could work on them every day of that first summer. Several of the other neighbors hosted house parties that first year, and as we were all pretty close to the same age, most of us got to be pretty good friends during this first year in the neighborhood.

The second summer I was still working on my first round of landscaping when Stuart and Donna decided to build an addition to their house. The addition that they designed was one big family room that was actually a second story. It was a single room about fifteen feet wide by forty feet long that jutted out from the roofline at the back of their house. The underside of this addition was designed as a cover for the patio in their back yard. The room had French doors that opened to a wide deck which gave them a great, unobstructed view of their back yard which now had a lush green lawn and ample landscaping.

Stuart and Donna had a big party to celebrate the completion of this room addition. They were very happy. I didn't immediately notice that our neighbor Bob and his wife Chris didn't attend this function, but as I stood on Stuart's new redwood deck with a beer in my hand, I found myself looking into Bob and Chris's back yard. I realized for the first time that I seldom saw the two of them anymore. They seemed to have their own group of friends and I couldn't remember the last time that I saw them at one of the neighborhood yard parties.

A couple of months later Bob and Chris put their house on the market. This was the first house that was offered for sale from the original group in our cul-de-sac. The SOLD sign appeared very fast. One Saturday afternoon I caught Bob out in front mowing his lawn.

"Hi, Bob, I see you've already sold your place. Where are you and Chris moving to?"

"We bought a home in Palos Verdes," Bob answered as he carefully guided the power mower around the real estate sign.

"Well, I'm sure it's a very nice place. I know that you and Chris will enjoy it."

"Hell, it doesn't have to be nice," said Bob, raising his voice. "I would move to the moon to get away from that jerk Stuart. I hate the bastard."

"Hate him?" I asked, surprised, wondering how anyone could actually hate Stuart.

"Yeah, I hate him; he's always running over to talk to me about something. Then he builds that monstrosity in his back yard. I can't go out into my yard to read a book without looking up and seeing him standing there smiling at me. Now I'm trying to grow trees on that side of the yard but it'll take a couple of years for them to grow tall enough to give me any privacy. I just can't wait that long. At least the new place is private and best of all, no Stuart.

I felt sorry that my neighbor Bob was harboring such resentment against a harmless teddy-bear of a man like Stuart. I hoped that this news would not reach Stuart, because he was a sweet sensitive guy and would be crushed if he ever heard how Bob felt about him.

Bob and Chris moved away and I didn't mention the conversation with Bob to anyone for a long time.

About two years later Stuart and Donna told me that they had purchased some property and were in the process of building a new house.

"Oh?" I asked. "Where are you going to build?"

"It's a great lot, Howard. It's in Palos Verdes; I can't wait to show it to you. You're really going to like it."

"Well, you'll have to invite us over when you get it built."

"Sure we will; we can go horseback riding," answered Stuart enthusiastically.

"Where do you get horses to ride?" I asked.

"Oh, Donna and I already have the horses. We have over an acre of pasture, and ride almost every day. The first thing that we built was the barn. There are equestrian trails everywhere in Palos Verdes. One of my favorite trails goes right past Bob and Chris's house; we see them all the time—I can practically spit into their pool when we ride by."

No Gathering

The vacation was going great so far. Tent camping this early in the year can get a bit chilly and we could even see some rain in April, but it is sure nice having the whole campground for just the two of us. Carol and I were not on any kind of schedule. We had a California state map, the bass boat, and our camping gear. If we had any plan at all it was just to have a good time, get in some fishing and then move when the mood struck us.

We spent two weeks in a beautiful campground at Lake Shasta, and as I said we—no kidding—had the place to ourselves. Just as soon as the tent was up Carol took off for a walk. She returned about a half hour later loaded down with twigs and pinecones.

"What's up with all that stuff?" I asked, laughing.

"Hey, it will burn. I love to gather firewood."

And she really did. We never went on even a short walk without Carol finding something to bring back for the fire. On several occasions she found a good stash of wood and asked me to help her with these treasures, but most of the time she simply considered this to be her job. There were plenty of gas stations and markets that sold firewood, and I did buy my share of the little bundles during this trip, but I cannot ignore the amount of wood that Carol brought into camp.

We drove on up to Lake Almanor, about one hundred miles east of Shasta, and set up camp. Once more we found a fairly empty campground with only a couple of motor-home rigs for company. Carol and I selected a very nice secluded campsite well away from the water and put up our tent. I began getting the boat in order and making myself at home. Carol went for a walk. About thirty minutes later she was back with her arms loaded with good-sized branches.

"Where did you find all of this firewood?" I asked her.

"Just the other side of the railroad tracks they've been trimming trees. There's a huge pile of wood over there."

And so for the next several days Carol made frequent visits to the slash pile on the other side of the tracks, and we enjoyed a big crackling fire every evening. We bought groceries in the town of Chester, but thanks to Carol's gathering I didn't find a reason to replenish my little firewood bundles. Fishing was pretty good and the weather was perfect.

After about a week we pulled up stakes and headed to a lake called Bullards Bar. This lake was pretty much due south of our current location. Camping here got a bit touch and go as the campgrounds were not exactly open yet. We checked in at the ranger station and they told us that we could stay in the campground as the scheduled opening was just a couple of days away. Water wasn't turned on yet so they said that we didn't need to pay.

As we drove into the campground Carol tapped me on the shoulder and smiled as she pointed to a big slash pile from some clearing that had obviously just been done. We had a nice fire that first evening but woke up around midnight to a downpour. I can't remember ever seeing so much rain in my life. It continued raining the following day and through the night as well. We managed to get a fire started but it took a lot of care to keep it going. We were running pretty low on dry wood.

Sometime during the second night the rain decided to quit. We awoke the following morning to a very soggy camp. Carol went off to do some gathering, and found enough dry twigs to get a smoky fire going that morning. We moved things around and attempted to dry out gear until about noon. When we finally got to fishing we found that the lake was still very cold and the bass were not particularly interested in our choice offerings. As we were still pretty wet and soggy from the toad-strangler the night before, we decided to break camp and head for Wheatland to visit friends and to dry out.

Carol and I spent two weeks enjoying modern conveniences such as a bed with a mattress and indoor plumbing, and then decided that it was time to resume our camping trip.

The spot we chose for our next stay was at Lake Oroville, also in northern California. Upon approaching this large campground we could see that our camping-alone experience was going to be a thing of the past. This campground was huge, offering at least one hundred sites. It was not nearly full, probably less than one third of the sites were occupied, but based on our previous campground stays this was a lot of people. This particular campground was the type that I call a No-No-Campground.

You may have camped in these places yourself. When you first enter the road leading into the campground the signs begin to appear. NO DOGS, NO WALKING ON GRASS, NO FIRES EXCEPT IN. . . , NO PARKING ON. . . , NO FISHING FROM. . . , etcetera. Plenty of signs—no, no, no.

The last sign that we saw just before reaching the pay station caught us by surprise. In big bold letters it simply said, NO GATHERING. This was followed by more writing in smaller text that went on to describe what kind of twigs, branches, pinecones, and other such cellulose items could not be gathered in this campground.

"But what do they mean by that?" Carol asked, obviously hurt, and taking this particular sign very personal.

We picked a nice site toward the back of the campground. It was a very big campsite with a semicircular drive in front that worked great for parking the boat. It also had a good, level spot to pitch the tent, which of course was the first thing on our agenda. There were lots of twigs and pinecones lying on the ground that Carol had to clear away before we could set up the tent. She placed these debris items near the fire pit, just to get them out of the way I suppose. I chose to ignore this activity that she called clearing as it obviously was not in the same category as gathering, so at this point we were still more or less legal.

Once the tent was up Carol busied herself with organizing the sleeping bags while I unpacked the remaining camping articles. This done, I removed a cold one from the ice chest and sat back in a camp chair. Carol walked up behind me. She had changed into shorts, hiking shoes, and a white hooded sweatshirt.

"I'm going to take a walk," she said. "Want to come?"

"No thanks. I still need to get the boat unpacked. Have a nice hike." My mind said *no gathering*, but I wasn't mean enough to say it out loud.

I watched Carol walk away from our campsite, her head slowly moving from left to right as she spotted choice firewood tidbits, which of course she wouldn't think of picking up.

About thirty minutes later I was back to unloading the boat. As I walked up to the boat I looked across the campground and could see someone with a white hooded sweatshirt heading in my direction. I thought the person must have been Carol, but she was too far away for me to be positive. She appeared to be carrying something, because the front of her white sweatshirt was brown, like she had things in her arms. *I wonder what that could be.*

As I watched the woman approach I was almost sure it was Carol. Then out of nowhere came a voice from a loud speaker. "IN THE CAMPGROUND. . . ." the bull horn began an announcement at full volume. Then it went on to say something about delivering firewood.

Yes, it was Carol; at the first sound of the speaker her arms dropped to her sides, she continued walking toward me, her pace quickened; she had been gathering. She rushed back to our campsite and without a word to me, went directly into the tent. She was certain that she had been caught in the act of gathering and would probably be prosecuted for this crime. About thirty minutes later one of the green ranger trucks pulled up in front of our campsite and the ranger called to me, "Do you need some firewood?"

I saw that the back end of his truck was full of small, neatly tied bundles of firewood.

"Sure, I'd like a couple of bundles. I'll get some cash and be right back," I added, turning toward the tent.

My wallet was in my Levi's pants pocket, which were lying folded in the corner of the tent. I fished the wallet from my pants, not wanting to disturb Carol, who seemed to be taking a nap.

About one hour later Carol emerged from the tent. She was acting kind of quiet. This was not at all normal and I thought she might not be feeling well.

"Are you OK?" I asked.

"I'm alright," she answered, not looking directly at me. "How much was my fine?"

"Fine?"

"Yeah, how much did the ranger fine me for gathering?"

Duck Hunt With Don Baker

Don Baker and I have been good friends for several years. We are about the same age and share many similar interests. Don and I both enjoy archery hunting and target shooting. Over the years he and I have joined with mutual friends and participated in several deer and elk hunts locally and out of state.

Don has one child, a son named Kevin who is one year younger than my daughter Felicia and a year or so older than my youngest, Aimee. When our families get together for an archery shoot us dads give a lot of attention to our kids. These events always seem more like family picnics than a competition.

In addition to archery, the two of us also have a passion for duck hunting with shotguns. During the previous archery seasons Don and I often talked about getting together to hunt ducks but when duck hunting season came around Don continued to hunt at his own duck club near Willows, about forty miles east of my home in Oroville, California, while I usually hunted with my longtime hunting partners in Wheatland, about forty miles south.

About the second week into duck season Don called me on a Monday evening and asked if I would like to hunt with him the following Wednesday morning. My bait route was now on an every-two-week schedule and it happened that I didn't have any work planned for that particular Wednesday so I gladly accepted Dons hunting invitation and we set the date.

I woke up early on Wednesday morning, hoisted my gear bag, hunting coat, shotgun and thermos that I had placed near the front door the night before, and loaded it all into the pickup. As I drove I sipped a first cup of hot morning coffee. Twenty minutes later I turned off of the main highway onto a familiar side road which led to Don's small house on Willow Street. He lived in the town of Chico which was known primarily as a college town, located about twenty miles northwest of Oroville. After the initial hellos were said I transferred my hunting gear and shotgun into the back canopy of Don's tan Datsun pickup truck, and then claimed the passenger seat. We were both kind of quiet this morning as Don drove the twenty some miles to his duck club.

Don and I sat on the lowered tailgate as we got ourselves ready to hunt. I pulled on my cold hip waders, remembering to snap them to my belt loops, and then traded my light Levi's jacket for the heavy camo hunting coat. After zipping the coat I removed my Remington shotgun from the protective cloth case, reached my right arm through the sling and shouldered the gun barrel up. I carried a small gear bag that had a mini-change of clothes, wool socks, warm gloves, and an extra hat. The bag also contained my thermos of coffee, a couple packs of Marlboros, matches, beef jerky, and two full boxes of ammunition. Don was ready about the same time that I was.

It was just a short walk from the parking area to the hunting blind itself. As we settled down into the blind it was very dark and still about thirty minutes before shooting time. Frost was visible on the ground but the pond itself was not frozen. I was enjoying a second cup of hot coffee while attempting to warm my fingers on the cup rim as I slowly acclimated myself to the unfamiliar terrain. At that precise moment a small flock of teal scared the crap out of me as they dive-bombed our position in a typical "out of nowhere" teal duck attack. I spilled my coffee as I attempted to hunker deeper into the blind but of course this was a little late for the hide-and-seek tactic between hunter and wildlife as the wily, sharp-eyed teal ducks had obviously pinpointed our position.

Darkness gave way to a hazy gray daybreak and the cattails on the far side of our pond could just be seen. The luminous dial on my Timex was reading seven a.m., legal shooting time. Right on schedule, two mallard ducks took an interest in our spread of decoys and Don began to call. I was never much good on a mallard call so I just sat quietly watching the birds as Don worked them with his call. The ducks made one pass quite high, then another slightly lower but again out of range. The birds reached the far west end of our pond and dipped their wings, intentionally losing altitude as they swung around for a third pass.

"This time," I whispered to Don as the birds dropped still lower and came toward us once again.

It is crucial for hunters to be in sync with each other when they rise up to shoot at these fast flying birds. Miscommunication at a decisive moment can cause the approaching flock to flare away from your blind at the last second. Unfortunately, the only way to work out this tactical precision is to spend a lot of time hunting with your partners.

If I was hunting in Wheatland my friend Bill would always take the lead and call the shot, but this was not Wheatland, and I was a guest this morning, so I was kind of figuring that Don would stand up to shoot. The birds were out in front of our blind with their legs down and their wings cupped for landing. The two mallard ducks were in classic position; this was storybook. Don and I had never duck hunted together before, and this was not the time to sort out who would be making the call. *Now!* I thought to myself. I waited another split second for Don to break cover, but finally just had to make the decision myself. "Take um," I said, standing as I raised the shotgun to a familiar position on my right shoulder, unconsciously locating the nearest bird, and simultaneously positioning it in my sights.

The trigger pull was smooth, controlled and deliberate, gained from years of hunting experience and countless hours of practice on the skeet range. My bird crumpled and I instinctively continued to swing the shotgun seeking the second bird. As my gun sight located the next duck I hesitated for a split second, giving my partner an opportunity, then watched the drake mallard fold at the sound of Don's shot. I was out of the blind in a second and retrieved the two birds that were both within ten or fifteen yards from our blind. I knew that I should have waited for Don to call the first shot in his own blind, but I was also kind of pleased with myself for not dropping that second bird.

"Nice shooting, Don," I said, returning to the blind. "Let's get us some more."

These first two birds proved to be the end of our duck hunting for the morning. The haze cleared to reveal a beautiful blue sky and the two of us sat quietly drinking lukewarm coffee, each hoping for another opportunity.

An hour had passed since we shot our two mallards when I heard a single honk from a goose. My fingers unconsciously located the wooden goose call hanging at my neck, bringing it to my lips as I slowly swiveled my head, trying to locate our visitor.

"There," whispered Don, indicating with his eyes only as he turned his head in the direction of the birds.

Two geese were about one quarter of a mile away, approaching our pond from the west. They were heading in our general direction. I gave one short blast on my goose call, and was pleased to hear one of the geese answer with a single deep honk of its own. I estimated about thirty seconds, and then gave another slow, deliberate single honk. Once more I was rewarded with an answering call. The geese were now near the edge of our pond heading directly for our position. They were low enough to shoot and if nothing changed their minds they would soon be in range. Without making any unnecessary body movement I called once again. The vocal goose of the pair answered me as the two medium sized birds continued winging their way in our direction. They were in a perfect position, about twenty-five yards high and directly in front of our blind.

These birds did not look big enough to be Canadian Honkers; *Brants*, I thought to myself as I watched their slow deliberate wing beat. My body began to coil up as I readied myself to stand when Don called the shot. *Now!* I thought, but waited one full second past the prime opportunity, then held another split second. I simply couldn't wait a moment longer.

"Take um!" I shouted. Rising to my feet and acquiring a target, now directly overhead, I pulled the trigger. My bird folded from the impact of lead shot and I rotated my body to the left, simultaneously swinging the gun toward the second bird that was now rapidly gaining altitude behind our blind. Finding the bird in my gun sight, I paused for a heartbeat waiting for the sound of Don's shot but this time it didn't come. I made sure of my target, adding a foot to the lead, and squeezed the trigger. The big bird folded up and fell to the ground.

Don was standing at my side.

"Sorry, Don, I didn't mean to shoot your bird; I couldn't wait any longer," I said. "What happened did your gun jam?"

"No, my gun didn't jam. I just didn't think you were actually going to shoot."

"What are you talking about? Why wouldn't I shoot?"

"Well, those were Brant geese."

"Yeah, I know what Brant geese look like. I killed three of them last weekend," I answered, still confused.

"You shot them at your club in Yuba County; they opened there one week ago. This is Glen County, and Brant goose season won't open here until next week."

Pheasant Hunt Private Property

Bernard and Ralph were just as happy as clams now that pheasant season would open the following morning. They spent a good share of Friday afternoon in preparation as they really had a lot of work to do making signs and such, but this was still their favorite day of the year.

Bernard had decided to accept Ralph's offer and spend the night at his house; they were both excited about opening day and stayed up way too late joking around, just like when they were kids.

The two men jumped out of bed at the sound of the alarm clock. Ralph slipped into coveralls and boots and ran outside to start the old Ford pickup, giving it a chance to warm up as Bernard prepared coffee in the small kitchen.

It was exactly four-thirty a.m. when they eased the pickup to a stop at the wide parking spot they had picked on Whitman Road just outside of Roseville. Ralph wasted no time in placing the large handwritten sign over their tailgate as Bernard set up the card table and single folding chair, then lit a Coleman lantern to get some light on the sign.

PRIVATE PROPERTY
PHEASANT HUNTING BY PERMIT ONLY
$20.00 PER HUNTER NO EXCEPTIONS

About five minutes later the first customer pulled to a stop behind their truck. The season had officially started.

"Sure, you can hunt all of this ground on the right side of the road," Bernard smiled, gesturing at the field with his hand as he answered the obvious questions.

"Just remember to keep this red sign pinned to the front of your jacket so we can identify you," Bernard said as he handed the man an eight by eleven-inch number sign made from heavy red construction paper. The sign had a single large number 1 painted in the center with white poster paint. Bernard pocketed the twenty-dollar bill, and then offered the man a safety pin from the collection in the coffee cup that sat near him on the table.

"Turn in at the first dirt road on your right up there about one quarter of a mile. Just park inside the fence and walk from there. Remember no shooting before seven, good luck."

About fifteen minutes later Bernard handed out sign number 10, gave his usual instructions and once more wished the hunter good luck.

"Well, Ralph, that was number ten, no sense getting greedy. What say we call it a season?"

Ralph started the Ford and made a U-turn. "Damn, I love opening day of pheasant season; I would almost give up my half of the $200 bucks to hear what Old Man Whitman has to say when he wakes up and finds all those city slickers stomping around in his corn field."

A Morning With Don

"So tell me something about this hunting spot you've rented," I asked Don as we passed through the small farming town of Gridley and I turned west on Colusa Bypass Road.

"Oh, well, it's a great spot," answered Don, pausing at the snap-sound of the hot cigarette lighter as it popped from the

dash, then bringing the glowing metal to the tip his cigar, "
. . . right on the river, lots of cover," he added through billows
of smoke.

It was around five-thirty in the morning and still plenty
dark. I was creeping along the unfamiliar road at about ten
miles an hour waiting for Don to locate the driveway that he
said was hard to find in the dark.

"Here, here," said Don, touching my arm and pointing to a
dirt road which suddenly appeared on the right.

As I began my turn I could see that the driveway led to a
big white house about fifty yards up on the left-hand side, and
I could make out a tall barn just past the house, also on the left.
There was a pickup parked in front of the barn. The truck was
pointed away from us with the lights on.

"Wait, stop," said Don, reaching over and grabbing my arm.
"I just remembered there's a better place to park. Back up."

"What is this crap, Don? I thought you had permission to
hunt here."

"Yeah, I have permission. I just don't like to talk to that guy
early in the morning. He's always crabby in the morning. We
can park down the road a-ways."

I backed out of the driveway and began driving up the
road.

"Don, if we end up in jail. . . ."

"No, no, we're OK, park here. We can walk in along the
river."

I came to a stop and parked in the wide pull-out that Don
had indicated, thinking very seriously about simply turning
my truck around and finding breakfast somewhere in Gridley.
"Don, we should—"

"Come on, my blind is just about one hundred yards up
the river."

I followed Don on the narrow foot path that ran along the
edge of a plowed field to our right. The river was on our left.

Don's one hundred yards took the better part of one quarter mile to reach. Once there I could see several large pieces of cardboard and big Styrofoam blocks that had been scattered about.

"Damn," said Don. "Some kids must have wrecked my blind. Wait a sec, I'll get it back together," he said, as he retrieved two pieces of broken Styrofoam block and added them to a third, making a kind of U-shaped enclosure on the river bank.

I sat on the side of the bank getting the lay of the land. We were overlooking a small tree-lined river. This was probably good wood duck habitat, and some mallards or pintails might actually fly by; however, due to all of the trees, the ducks would be forced to fly near the middle of the river and might pass our spot on the bank. Unfortunately if the birds flew low along the river the way that I thought they would, there was no way that we could see them approach. I could imagine that if a duck did come by, we would only get one chance, a snap-shot. This would be kind of like trying to swat flies out of the air. Then to top it off, if one of us did manage to hit a bird it would simply fall directly into the river and float away. Without a dog we didn't have a chance in hell of retrieving a duck.

"Great spot you found here, Don." I leaned back against the Styrofoam block. "Hand me one of those little cigars."

It was good and light now. I had altered my position some and poured a cup of coffee, while Don kept an eye on the river. Apparently he was hunting. I didn't bother to load my shotgun and had absolutely no intention of doing so. I turned at the sound of a car engine and saw that a white pickup was driving on a road that ran along the back of the plowed field. The truck looked to be heading in our direction.

"Looks like we have company, Don," I said, pointing toward the approaching vehicle.

"Well," said Don standing and stretching his neck. "It doesn't look like the ducks will be flying today. We may as well go."

"Wait a minute, Don. I don't think I'm quite ready to go. I'd like to see just how crabby your farmer friend is when you talk to him in the morning."

The pickup stopped at the end of the dirt road, about twenty yards from us. Two big men wearing cowboy hats stepped from the truck and began walking in our direction.

Before the men could reach us Don called to them.

"Morning, the hunting is pretty slow today."

"Morning yourself. This is private property. Pack up and get out," was the only answer Don got in reply.

"But I was told that the river is public access," said Don meekly.

"You was told wrong, but if you're asking to get tossed in that public access river, that's just fine with me. Right now your ass and your truck is parked on my ground. Get movin' and don't come back."

There was not much room for further discussion. Don and I started walking back down the narrow path. Don turned to look over his shoulder. I swiveled my head in time to see that the two men were now picking up the Styrofoam and carrying it to their truck.

"Kids," I said to Don.

As Don and I were almost at my truck I reached down and picked up a sign that was lying face down on the ground. We had walked over this sign in the dark on our way into Don's blind. The sign read, POSTED NO HUNTING NO TRESPASSING.

"Darn," said Don, "I sure wish we had seen that sign this morning. They must have just posted this property."

We made a U-turn and started for home. As I passed the

farm driveway I glanced to my left and could see the white truck returning.

"You were sure right about that guy, Don. He is really crabby when you talk to him in the morning."

The Ranchero

David and his cousin Peewee were born and raised in the town of Wheatland, California. Besides the fact that they were related, the boys had always been best friends. Now that high school is behind them they both work for Don Perkins at his garage near Four Corners. The two boys have experienced plenty on the job training and they are willing to tackle almost any kind of farm or over the road equipment. A typical day at Perkins shop would usually include a good share of heavy mechanical work. Most of the time the boys were paid in cash for their labors, but on occasion the pay for work would be in the form of barter. The item offered in trade for their services could be an old engine, a new pump, or even a vehicle of some description. Their pay for overhauling the Dodge truck transmission that belonged to Jeff Styles of Sheridan last week was a maroon 1967-Ford Ranchero.

I looked at the little truck parked in front of Bill's house and asked David if he would like to sell it. I needed a small truck for weekend fishing bait deliveries, and thought that the small Ranchero would probably be a good vehicle for my wife or for my helpers to drive.

"Well, I'll talk to Peewee; it's half his," David answered. "We were thinking about cutting the top off of it and making a rabbit-hunting mobile."

On further inspection I noticed that the little truck was missing a radio, but aside from that minor flaw, it seemed to be intact without one dent that I could see. All of the glass was good and the six-cylinder engine purred quietly.

"OK, David, let me know. I'll give you a good price if you decide to sell it."

The following weekend I returned to Wheatland and went in search of David and Peewee to ask them what they had decided to do with the little pickup. I found the two of them swimming at the Young Farmers Pool.

"So guys are you still planning to make a rabbit-hunting mobile, or would you like to sell the little Ranchero to me?"

David grinned at Peewee. "Well, it's kind of too late for that little truck," he answered.

"Oh, did you sell it already," I asked?

"No, not exactly, we just kind of killed it," said Peewee, now grinning as well.

"Killed it?"

"Last Wednesday we took it out to the field by Dry Creek and were taking turns doing some laps when Peewee lost control on a curve and rolled it," answered David.

"Damn, it's a good thing that you weren't hurt," I said, concerned.

"Nah, Peewee wasn't hurt, but I figured if he could get it to roll over once, I could do a lot better. So I got her up to about sixty, and when I hit the curve just right, it rolled four and a half times. I pretty much rolled that little truck into a ball."

Cheese Room

One winter day late in January, a man by the name of Richard Morris called to ask if he could rent some space at my locker plant. I told him that I did have space available, the old ice-room, but it wasn't refrigerated. Mr. Morris assured me that the space would be just fine with him because what he had to store was two pallets of cheese, and it would not require refrigeration this time of year. He said that he would only need the space for one month. I accepted fifty dollars cash for the month of February, and gave Mr. Morris a key to the room. The cheese arrived a few days later but I never saw or heard from Richard Morris again.

This was my third April in the bait business, and as usual business began to heat up, as did the weather this time of year. I had plenty of things on my mind but could not completely ignore the smell outside of my rental storage room that seemed to be getting stronger every day. I decided to investigate one evening toward the end of April and was surprised to discover that the two pallets of cheese that once measured about eight feet wide, and four feet tall, was now measuring something like twelve feet wide and three feet tall. This melting pile of cheese was definitely the cause of a bad smell and also seemed to be spreading wider as I watched. This was not a good thing but I did manage to set the problem aside and out of mind for the time being.

Business continued to improve until I found myself working sixteen to eighteen hour days toward the middle of June. Wednesday was a short route day and I returned to the locker plant around three thirty. That was when I received an unexpected phone call from the Butte County Health Department.

"Howard, this is Bill Riggs from County Health. What the hell have you got locked up in that back room of yours?"

"Uh, bait. Catfish bait, Bill," I lied in my most sincere voice. *I'm going to be hung.*

"Oh yeah, bait? Is it any good," Bill asked, now sounding interested?

"Good? It's going to be great. It's my secret recipe. Would you like to test some out for me when it's ready?" I answered. *A fisherman; please God, let him be a fisherman.*

"Sure, thanks, Howard, but just exactly how long do you plan on keeping that stink locked up in there?" Bill responded in his no-nonsense, *I'm-no-stupid-fisherman voice.*

". . .Two weeks," I told him meekly, now hoping for a stay of execution.

"The first of July then; I'll be in touch," says Bill, and hangs up.

Early Saturday morning, June twenty-ninth, the temperature not yet ninety-five degrees, the Steer Killer's son Bobby and I cautiously opened the heavy wooden door to the old ice-room. We were greeted with an odor that could be described by no man. I backed my old '57 Ford pickup truck to the dock, and the two of us began shoveling. The stuff was mixed with paper packaging and wax of some kind. It didn't want to be shoveled, so we resorted to scooping up most of the rank, slippery material by hand.

God, don't puke, I told myself, *it can't help.* After three dump runs and about five hour's work, the cheese was gone. All that was left to do was the wash down. I gave Bobby the little bit of soap we had, and left to finish the last dump run by myself. Afterward I drove the '57 straight to the grocery store for more soap and a six-pack of Coors. Once inside the store I remembered how ripe I must be, but it was too late. People didn't stop and stare; they grabbed their kids and ran.

I picked up the first extra big box of Tide laundry soap that I saw, passed on the beer, and looked for the shortest check-out line. Great! I spotted a line with only one person, and she only had a few packages. I nonchalantly took my place in line behind the lady shopper. As we waited I tried not to notice how nervous she was getting. The woman certainly knew that something bad was standing very close behind her, but to her credit, she never turned around.

Unfortunately for both of us the checker was becoming nervous also. Heck, by now the terrible smell had probably spread through the entire store. Our checker knew that it was one of us but didn't look up. He just kept on ringing up groceries with his head down. The frazzled checker fumbled with the last couple of packages and started making mistakes. It took a full five minutes to check the six or eight items. When he finally handed the lady her bill, the poor woman realized that she needed to write a check. She produced a pen and began frantically stabbing at her checkbook. On the third attempt she successfully completed writing the check, tore it from the book, grabbed her stuff and bolted for the door.

My friendly smile met a cold stare. Now the checker knew with certainty who the culprit was, and the huge box of Tide soap really colored in the picture. Once in the parking lot I still wasn't completely in the clear. About five or six local citizens were cautiously zeroing in on my truck. The men were walking around the parking lot with noses in the air, sniffing like dogs on the hunt; all of them heading toward the '57 Ford. Somewhat rattled, I slid behind the wheel and prayed for a fast getaway.

We scrubbed on that room into the night. Finally I made the beer run, then we scrubbed some more. The Killer's son went home after we drank all the beer. I drooped against the fender of my '57 still inside the gate of the locker plant, wishing I were someone else, anyone else. A friend, Don's brother Ray, drove up to the gate and got out of his car. When he saw me he yelled, "What is that terrible smell? Is that coming from you, man? Damn, your old lady will never let you back in the house, let alone back in bed."

He was pretty close to right. After dropping my clothes—boots, belt and all—into the trash barrel, I washed in the backyard using bar soap and a garden hose. Then I climbed into the bathtub, washing and scrubbing my body with every cleaning product that wouldn't remove skin. When that painful procedure was over I showered a couple of times and finally got permission to sleep on the couch. It was a full two weeks later when I passed the daily sniff test and was cleared to sleep in my own bed.

The old ice-room was always called the Cheese Room after that weekend, and years later I was positive that I would still get an occasional whiff of dead cheese on a warm evening.

I was kind of disappointed that Bill from the Health Department never did call back or come around to check up on me. I sure would have liked to shovel a scoop or two of that fresh catfish bait into the back end of his nice gray county pickup.

Wood Run

he old brown Cadillac pulled into a convenient space in front of my shop, ignoring the custom-made **NO PARKING** sign. As the car eased to a stop Don shot me a smile through the dirty front windshield, then leaned sideways and seemed to be wrestling with something next to him on his front seat. A moment later he walked in carrying a white paper bag.

Eyeing the familiar package in his hand, I said, "Beware of Greek's bearing gifts."

"Glad I caught you," said Don, ignoring my comment as he lifted two cups from the bag and handing one to me.

I stood and watched Don, smiling, as he began his typical coffee ritual; first setting his coffee cup on the workbench, then filling it to the brim with cream. He slowly began stirring in eight or ten cubes of sugar as the excess tan colored liquid ran over the edge of the white Styrofoam cup and onto the otherwise clean surface of my workbench.

Now leaving the coffee to get cold, Don moved to the wood stove and pulled out a cigar.

"Hope you got a minute; I been wanting to talk to you."

"OK, one minute," I chuckled, knowing full well that Don would beat around the bush for at least ten minutes before actually talking about anything. I was also fully aware that whatever this was, somehow it would end up costing me. I sipped my coffee and tried to look disinterested as Don warmed up.

Don is not a man to do anything in a conventional way. His style is to dream up some goofy scheme and then spend hours trying to convince people that it will work. He will often talk so long that the idea kind of starts making sense. Once the talking stops, however, Don will start the project and then fall down on the follow-through. The man is always dressed a bit on the grubby side, but this dress-down look is just another part of his style. Don is a born salesman and knows it.

I am often amused by the short cuts that Don comes up with. I know that in most cases his schemes will take a bad turn and end up in disaster; but for some reason Don loved to talk to me about his new ideas. He knows that I will usually end up giving him a hard time, and will seldom actually participate.

This past year Don had spent most of his time assembling a disjointed array of clunky old vehicles, saws, and wood cutting equipment. He was now looking for ways to make a faster buck in the firewood business.

I casually glanced at the clock. Don had been talking for about thirty minutes, and had yet to come to the point. This was going to be expensive. I gave him my hurry-up look.

His words started coming a little faster, and then Don paused and took a long pull on his cigar. *Here it comes.*

". . . So around here I've been getting eighty bucks a cord, and in Sacramento I can toss it off the truck for a hundred. But think about Reno?" He paused, giving me time to think about Reno I guess. "They don't have any trees around Reno; it's desert. The wood they do burn is mostly pine. *Pine* for Christ sake; like burning cardboard. Can you imagine how much money we can get for a load of Black Oak in Reno?"

Did he say we?

"Don't be thinking *we* Don. I don't do firewood."

"Well, err, I was thinking about, kind of a sample run—just to test the water. . . ."

Gathering momentum, he said, "I. . . been thinking about your little Datsun flatbed pickup, and how cute it would look with a load of oak, and how cheap we could make a run on Reno. Bet we could pull one-fifty, maybe two hundred a cord. The stuff would go like hot bread. Just park in the middle of a residential area and take orders. End of the day we spin the load. Then I come back two, three weeks later with Big White and fill all the orders."

I held up my hand to stop Don for a second. "Let's see if I got this straight. We use my truck. I help cut a load of oak. I drive two hundred miles one way to Reno, then spend the rest of the day door knocking, taking orders for *you*, after that we split the *maybe* one hundred fifty bucks. Don, this is beyond stupid! Once we take off the price of gas and a couple of sandwiches, then possibly a night over, it sounds like I work my ass off, beat the crap out of my truck and probably end up spending my own money to make this all happen. At best we break even!"

"Sure, this is an order taking trip. The real money comes when I run in with my Big White truck and kick off six cords."

"So take your big truck and leave me the hell out of this swell deal!"

"No, no, listen; you're missing the best part. See, we do our door knocking, cop to it—you know that will be some fun."

He gets a cold stare from me.

"Get a few orders, then we spin the load to the highest bidder, take the money to the green table. We drop it down, one flop that doubles it. Now we each have about a hundred. We don't hesitate, double-down again and run with the winnings. Not bad, had a good time, got a couple of free drinks, some laughs, and two hundred in your jeans for the trouble. What are you messing around with right now, anyway? It looks like you could use a free trip to Reno."

Somewhere along the line I must have smiled. This was so far out I liked it. Why not make his day?

"OK, tell you what. Give me the two hundred, I'll drive and maybe knock on a few doors. You can do your own gambling."

Don had stopped listening after the "OK." He knew he had me.

The following morning we hit the woods early. Don started his normal procrastinating and lit a cigar. I started my saw. We were in a good slash pile of dry black oak. Even with his messing around, the little truck loaded fast. Don was right about one thing. We had stacked the load tight to the top of my three-foot racks and once loaded, it did look kind of impressive.

Cutting wood combined with fresh air always makes you hungry. We sat down to enjoy our lunch and discussed the four-hour drive to Reno. I suggested we call it a day and leave early the following morning. Don lit another cigar, nodding agreement through thick curls of grey smoke.

No matter how much grief I lay off on Don, we are really good friends. The drive was going fast, as it will when the conversation is steady. I just sat back and enjoyed the game. It had been a long time since I had let Don set the hook on one of these Tom Sawyer deals. We talked about some of the selling that we had done individually or together and by the time we got near Reno, we were both pumped and declaring, Reno really needs good firewood! Maybe we can pull three, four hundred out of this little load!

It was cold in Oroville yesterday, and it was cold again this morning when we left town, but like the man said, Reno was a desert, and the day was starting to get pretty warm.

"Turn left your next chance. I see a lot of chimneys over there. . . . Good, this looks like the place. . . Stop somewhere. . . Where is that other pack of cigars?"

Canvassing door-to-door, or "door knocking" as Don calls it, can be a real drag for some folks, but I have always enjoyed talking to new people and kind of make it a game. When I was a kid I almost got myself thrown out of the Boy Scout troop because I sold too many boxes of candy for a fund-raiser. Our allotment was two cases per boy. I sold my initial two cases so fast that I wanted to sell more. I walked to the local drug store and bought a receipt book, then went back to selling, taking money and handing out receipts. By our next scout meeting I had sold twenty cases, not realizing that the candy order had already been placed based on the two cases per boy projections. My scoutmaster was furious. It worked out though, as most of the other kids didn't sell any candy.

Don had picked a good place to start. The street he chose was wide and the houses were big, with nice yards, and large front windows. The homes were well set back on their individual properties. This provided most of them a good view of my little orange wood truck that was parked on the street, mid block.

Let's play. I knocked on the first door, then a second, and actually started settling into my sales pitch by the third door. "Hi, my name is Howard. I know that it is a little early, but have you thought about firewood for this year?". . . And on to the next door. . . Sure, no smoke coming out of any of these chimneys today; it must have been ninety degrees but I continued on.

A live one!

"A hundred and fifty isn't bad for oak. It's really been a long time since we had a nice oak fire. This will be a great surprise for my husband." She picked up her checkbook from a nearby counter, opened it, and ponders for a moment. "You know, I believe that I may have surprised him enough this week."

"I know the feeling; thank you anyway," I said, trying not to laugh as I backed from the porch and started towards the next house.

Don and I met at the corner to compare notes. I had one definite, maybe at one-fifty ". . . when my husband gets home" and one positive. . . "I'll give you a hundred, if you can't do any better; come back."

Don had several names, addresses and phone numbers written down on his small lined note pad. The comments read, "Come back this evening," "I know my husband will be interested," "Come back next month," and "Please call tonight."

Grinning, Don told me that he also had one invitation for a nooner.

"Let's move the truck and do it again," said Don, reaching out for the keys.

My knuckles barely hit the door when it opened. *Wow!*

"Hello, my—"

"Come in," she turned, leaving the door open as her red-sandaled feet walked down a polished hardwood hallway that angled toward the rear of the house. I followed with visions of sugarplums dancing in my head, down the dimly lit hall and into what must have been a den. Scanning the room, my eyes settled on the biggest cop I had ever seen. He was sitting on a barstool, still huge, talking on the phone. His monster hand went over the mouthpiece.

"You the guy selling wood?" Not waiting for my answer, he said, "Sit!"

My eyes went slightly out of focus as I sat on the edge of a beige couch quietly staring at a large set of deer antlers mounted over the fireplace mantel. My mind began playing head games with me as it flashed color pictures of a little orange wood trucks with a big blue **CALIFORNIA** license plate. I felt beads of sweat forming on my forehead as I pondered the possible fine for peddling out of state without a license. Impound? Morning court? Would my small stash, a single one hundred dollar bill, be enough to make bail? It seems very warm in here. *Stop it; think fun; look pitiful.*

He cradled the phone and turned to me.

"Is that oak on your truck?"

"Uh, yeah, sure, it's black oak—the best."

"How much a cord?"

"We're asking one fifty for this load."

"Well, I'll need more than that little load. Can you handle three or four cords?"

"No problem; we're taking orders today. Let me write down your number and I'll call before our next run. We can work out a good price depending on how much you need," I said casually as my fingers reached for my open shirt pocket and retrieved a pencil and note pad.

Standing now, the officer took my pad and wrote down his information. "Don't you forget me," he said, handing back my pad and pencil.

"Oh, don't worry, I won't."

I spotted the truck backed into a driveway down the block. Don was beginning to remove the nylon tie-down straps as I walked up to him.

"You aren't going to believe what just happened to me!"

We unloaded the truck in front of the garage, making sure the door wasn't getting blocked by any of the wood. Our new customer stood by looking very pleased with his purchase as the pile continued to grow in his driveway.

Sitting at the bar enjoying a first well-deserved cold beer, Don spread the crisp bills out in front of us. We did the easy math, deciding that after expenses we each had forty-five dollars, an actual profit.

I was kind of tired, a good tired; almost watching in third person as Don's dumb plan became a reality. Our ninety dollars rested on the green felt, centered on the Come line. The new shooter threw a five... then came a seven. . . .

"You lose!"

The Green Chicken

*F*riday got here quickly, *Just a few more boxes to unload from today's route,* I thought to myself as I finished cleaning up my bait truck for the week. I loaded the small aluminum hand-truck once again and stretched my back. The sun was setting as I stacked the last of the unsold merchandise back into the freezer, and then I got a little sloppy and decided to leave a dozen or so empty boxes in the front refrigeration compartment of my truck. No big, I'll get them tomorrow I said to myself, anxious to be finished.

Damn, it got hot today! The news said one hundred eight degrees and I am sure it reached it. This temperature is not unusual for a mid July day here in Oroville, California. It is still pretty warm now at eight p.m. It's kind of funny how you gradually get acclimated to the heat. You can sort of plan your day around it. As the weather warms up, I find myself shifting more and more work into the evening or early morning hours. My delivery routes typically take ten to twelve hours to complete. That kind of steady schedule makes for long days. I really enjoy this business but it sure feels good to be finished for the weekend. I stretched my back again, locked up the bait truck, and leave the locker plant behind, looking forward to a shower and a cold beer as soon as I get home. Water skiing may be on the agenda tomorrow.

My schedule consists of a different route each weekday, all of them being in a circle. Some routes are slightly longer than others but all of the routes start and end here in Oroville. If I were to draw the route-week out on a note pad it would look like a sketch of a five-leaf clover. The product that I distribute is fishing bait. I am a wholesaler. My customers are local stores, markets, sporting goods shops, gas stations, trailer parks, and some rather unlikely locations that also sell fishing bait. They all retail the bait to fishermen who then enjoy the warm summer days and evenings sitting at their favorite lake or river, or cruising the shore in boats, "trying for the big one." I sell all kinds of bait, some of it is favored by the many different species of fish but the determining factor for bait sales is really established by the many different species of fisherman. My job is to stock the shops with products that their respective customers will be asking for. Worms are usually the bait of choice for trout, perch, bluegill, crappie and other pan fish, but when it comes to catfish the selection gets pretty extensive. For example, many fishermen prefer clams, while others swear by anchovies, and still others will not consider fishing with anything but fresh chicken livers. I sell all of these products, and have learned from experience how much bait a given store will require for the week. I also have a pretty good notion which unique species of fisherman they cater to. The object is to maintain a good supply of bait. Overstocking a store now and then is permissible but allowing one of my customers to completely run out of bait is simply not an option.

Monday morning came around and I remembered I had left a bunch of empty boxes in the truck. I got started cleaning them out before restocking for the day. *What the hell?* Under the pile of empty boxes I found two flats of chicken livers, forty eight eight-ounce containers. Well the chicken livers are spoiled for sure I thought. My truck refrigeration wasn't turned on to keep the compartment frozen so this bait has been sitting in the heat all weekend long. No real big deal I will have to throw this bait away with the next dump run.

The best thing for me to do right now is to put the spoiled bait into the freezer and deal with it later. I loaded up my truck and head out for the day. I make a mental note to tell Alice, my chief bait packer, about the spoiled livers. We sure don't want to get them mixed up with the fresh ones.

Thursday morning rolls around and there is no loading for me today. It sure is nice to have the boys help me pack up the truck. It gains me a full hour jump on the day's work. They are Alice's older boys, real nice kids. I left Alice a list last night, and this morning my truck was almost completely loaded when I got to the locker plant. There is nothing more for me to do but to head down the road. All of the customers are friendly and most of them know me by my first name. I adjust my radio and settle into the familiar route.

It is my practice to restack the flats of bait in my truck as I sell products throughout the day. If I don't keep them stacked low they will fall over when I turn corners. On my fourth or fifth stop I was restacking when I found the green chicken livers. I knew immediately that the spoiled livers from Monday had somehow found their way back into my truck. Now, when I say "green," I don't mean that they had a slight green tinge; nor did they simply have some light green spots like mold on cheese. These livers had somehow turned from their normal dark red to a brilliant bright green color, very similar to something found in your garden. I moved the spoiled livers to the bottom of the pile, fairly sure that I would have enough good bait to get me through the day. Wrong! I had almost twenty stops on this route today and nearly everyone seemed to be out of chicken liver. I couldn't believe it.

By the time I got to May's Corner, I still have one flat of livers left, twenty-four containers, not counting the bad ones of course. That might be enough, I thought to myself optimistically. May's Corner is a small Mom & Pop quick stop, convenience store near Black Butte Lake. May is busy at the register with a customer, so I wave a cheerful hello as I head toward the back room to check the freezer stock as usual. This store does an active business and I am really not overly surprised to see that the four dozen containers of liver I had left the week before are almost sold out. Damn, now I only have two dozen in my truck.

May caught me as I started out the door. "Oh, Howard, make sure that you leave me plenty of chicken livers; the guys are catching catfish and I'm going through it pretty fast."

"Yeah, May, everyone has been buying livers today. I still have some left but am running pretty low."

"Gee, I don't want to run out this weekend. See what you have left and give it all to me."

I ran out to the truck to re-check my stock, and then came back into the store.

"Sorry, May, I only have two dozen left, except for the specials."

"What specials?"

"Oh, I have four dozen special cups of chicken liver. I'm working on something new, but haven't really got any fishing reports back yet." Technically this was not a lie. *They were certainly special and no reports to date.* I knew from my personal fishing experiences that catfish liked stinky bait and this would fill that bill. My only real concern was that this liver might be too rotten and soft to hold onto the hook.

"Well, bring in everything, the special stuff too. I don't want to run out."

Five minutes later I returned with a fresh stock of bait.

May took a quick look at the new bait. "Green livers, yuck!"

"I told you they were special."

"Yeah, but green, will it catch fish?"

"Green should be a good color for catfish. I really can't say just how good it will work yet. Tell you what May. This special stuff should sell for more money, but go ahead and sell it for the same price as the regular liver, and if it doesn't catch fish as good as I hope, I'll restock with the red chicken liver next week."

The following Thursday I packed the truck, keeping in mind that we are having a big run on chicken liver. With Murphy's Law firmly in place, most of the chicken liver that I sold the previous week was still on the shelves. I had plenty with me when I got to May's little store near Black Butte Lake.

May wasn't really into fishing herself, but she was an excellent storekeeper. She had good instincts and paid attention to her customers, which included listening to all of the fishing stories. I figured that I would have some exchanging to do, and might even get scolded, but wasn't prepared for what actually happened.

"Hi, Howard. Want a cold drink? Help yourself."

"Hi, May, how's everything with you? I'll take you up on an ice tea. How are your boys doing, catching anything?"

"Yeah, they've been doing great. Getting lots of crappie, and catfish. They're really doing good with the special chicken liver. You were right about that stuff. Make sure to leave me three or four flats of it. I've completely sold out."

This I wasn't ready for.

"You know, May, the special bait was an experiment; I didn't want to make very much of it until I got some feedback."

"OK, bring me what you have."

"That's the thing, May; I don't have any more with me."

I could see the hurt expression in her eyes. She was already feeling sad just thinking about letting her fishermen down, and I was almost at a loss for words now that the conversation had taken this unexpected turn.

"Tell you what, I'll make up some more, and bring it in next week."

During the drive home I pondered on this new product. How hard could it be to duplicate the process? *Freeze, thaw, heat and refreeze. Presto, green chicken livers.*

Weeks went by. No more nice July weather. This was August, with temperatures reaching over one hundred fifteen degrees. I sweated over the chicken liver project like a mad scientist. Alice and the boys helped almost every evening. I even got into setting cooking timers and making notes, like I knew what the hell I was doing, but all of my attempts failed. The best that I could come up with was to turn the red livers into a muddy brown color. During the second week I found that by adding a little bit of water I could replicate a kind of a ghastly gray color. I also ruined several T-shirts and did manage to produce lots of evil smelling stuff that we had to throw away. I tried everything short of green dye, but never could duplicate that first brilliant green. The project came to an end when after about a month, May quit asking me for the special livers. She was still disappointed, but did seem to sympathize with me when I told her sincerely that I was still trying to perfect my process but simply wasn't quite satisfied with the results.

As years passed my best friends would laugh and point to the Green-necked Pheasants they saw on the side of the road, always claiming that these were green chickens. One of my buddies suggested that I should try to trap them and see if they were green inside. We all enjoyed the joke, but I never did actually get around to telling May the details about my special catfish bait formula.

Dad's First Hunt

My folks came to visit midweek. Mom had plans to spend most of her time with my kids, her grandchildren, and I wanted to give Dad a close-up look at my business, the bait route. My plan was to drive Dad around on one of my daily routes and show him what I actually did for a living.

It was the third week of August. The hot spell broke last week and our daytime temperature dropped from one hundred-ten degrees to the current mid to low nineties. This was a welcome change as it also treated us with cool evenings. Eighty-five-degree nights are not exactly jacket weather, but it is a promise that the hot summer is over and fall is around the corner. My seasonal bait business can provide a pretty good living in the summer but it just barely breaks even during the fall and winter months. As the weather gets chilly, fishing ends for all but the most serious fishermen. Bait sales typically decline to almost nothing by mid winter. I always meet this time of the year with mixed emotions, knowing that the busy bait season is almost over and our money will start getting tight. But on the bright side, hunting season is just around the corner.

As a rule I can cut the bait route back from once-a-week deliveries to once-every-other-week on the first of September. This gives me a lot of time for hunting. First will be archery deer season which starts at the end of August and runs through the first two weeks of September; then I will break out the shotgun for duck hunting in mid October.

Today is Thursday; this is typically a very busy route day. I call this the Marysville route. I have twenty-five customers to call on and my driving distance will be about two hundred and fifty miles. Dad has been a good sport; he got up early with me this morning and we had a quick cup of coffee, then we both went down to the locker plant to load the refrigerated truck for today's route.

My dad was very interested in my loading process and asked a lot of questions as I stocked the five individual compartments of the truck. Frozen bait was loaded in the front two compartments and containers of live worms were loaded in the back. Working the route consisted of restocking customer locations and driving between stops. About fifty percent of our time was devoted to the customers and the remainder of the day was spent driving between these stops. Dad did his best to help with the work and eventually he and I fell into a routine where Dad could move some of the bait around as I made out the bills and collected money. Our day went quickly as bait was transferred from the truck to the many customer locations.

Dad was happy to be taking part in this new experience and our conversation went nonstop. I'm not sure how it came up but at some point during the day Dad and I got on the subject of deer hunting. My dad had lived his whole life in the city and knew very little about this subject. I was not exactly an expert myself, having only taken up archery deer hunting about five years previously, but I was more than happy to share some of my archery hunting experiences with him.

At around eight o'clock in the evening we said good-bye to our last customer and headed for home. By the time we arrived at my house, Dad and I had decided to go on a short hunting excursion the following day.

Deer hunting season wouldn't actually open for about one more week, but I didn't feel that there was any particular reason to bother my dad with this technicality. I was always pumped up about bow hunting and I guess my enthusiasm was rubbing off on my father. Preseason scouting was a big part of hunting and it was very important to me. I had a new bow this year and was really anxious to get into the woods. My friend, Don Weaver, owns a large parcel of ground east of town, and had offered me an open invitation to hunt on his property with my bow. This would be a kind of scouting trip for me as I would not shoot a deer out of season, but it couldn't hurt anything to let my dad believe that he was on an actual hunting trip.

I met Dad the following morning and gave him my spare pair of hunting boots. "As I recall we have the same shoe size," I said. "Go ahead and put the boots on. You might as well get used to the feel." The weather was still pretty warm so I explained to him that we would get our gear together this morning, then drive to Don's place and try our luck in the late afternoon. I told him that the deer bed down in the heat of the day but would probably begin walking around as they head for water later in the day. I wanted us to be there when the deer would most likely be moving around. I went through all of the pre-hunting motions, talking to Dad about archery gear while getting my equipment ready at the same time. We spent some time in the back yard as I first sighted in the bow with target arrows, then made a few practice shots with the razor-sharp broadhead arrows before placing the bow back into the hard travel case then loading the case itself into my truck bed.

I fitted Dad with some of my camo clothing and then added it to the gear bag. We filled our two canteens with water, packed a couple of candy bars and some basic survival food into two fanny packs, which I added to the gear bag as well. I rounded up two flashlights and asked him to remind me to stop for fresh batteries before leaving town.

"Hungry?" I asked, glancing at my watch and noting it was almost one o'clock.

"Sure," Dad said, "thought you'd never ask."

Once we left the main highway, the county road leading up to Don's property was little more than a dirt track through the trees. This was a county road but not well maintained. It was rutted, rocky, narrow and steep, with trees and bushes growing right up to the road edge. Many of the larger trees had branches that stretched out and hung completely over the road to join with trees and branches on the other side. This tree-covered canopy tended to darken the roadway and made the time of day seem much later than it actually was. I was driving pretty fast attempting to beat the falling sun.

I knew this road very well but my dad didn't. He made up for this lack of knowledge by bracing his left hand firmly against the dashboard and grasping the padded door handle with his right hand in a death grip.

"Do you have to drive so damn fast?" he finally asked.

"We'll be there pretty soon," I answered, not looking at him, as we fish-tailed around a sharp hairpin turn to the right.

"I'd like to get in an hour or two of hunting before it gets too dark."

"I'd like to live to see another day," Dad said, clearly unhappy.

I did ease off of the gas pedal a bit, but I doubt that Dad noticed this subtle effort to reduce my speed. His knuckles were white against the dashboard. A mile later I took a right turn that led onto Don's property and followed this crude driveway another one hundred yards.

Suddenly a cable appeared in front of us. It was stretched across the road about two feet off the ground. I sure wasn't expecting this cable to be draped across Don's driveway and quickly jumped on the brakes to avoid running into it. The brake pedal went to the floorboard without slowing my truck at all. I was shocked by this sudden malfunction, but recovered quickly and stomped the emergency brake with my left foot, causing the rear tires to lock up and skid. The truck slowed, and then stopped just an inch or two short of wiping out my grill on the heavy wire cable.

"What was that all about?" Dad asked.

"I don't know," I said; already out of the truck and looking underneath. "The brakes just went out."

It only took a second to locate the problem. I could see brake fluid was dripping from a line that hung down on the front driver side of the truck. The brake line was clearly broken. "I must have clipped a rock or a tree root. The front brake line is busted."

Dad looked over at me. "What are we going to do?" He asked, clearly concerned.

"Go hunting," I shrugged.

I walked around to the back of the truck and opened the gear bag. I pulled out two camo shirts, flashlights, fanny packs and binoculars.

"But what about the truck?" Dad asked, not moving.

"Dad, the truck is broken and we can't fix it right now. We might as well go hunting."

I offered him one of the camo shirts, then removed my T-shirt and slipped on the other long-sleeved camouflage hunting shirt. I thought about changing into the camo pants but decided to stay with my Levi's. Once my fanny pack was strapped in place I began replacing batteries in our flashlights. Dad slowly removed his blue polo shirt leaving it folded on the front seat of the truck. He changed into the camo hunting shirt, adjusted the fanny pack belt and snapped it in place around his waist. I handed him one of the flashlights.

"Here, Dad, put this into your pack." I lifted my bow from the back of the truck; then I gave him the binoculars. "Let's go," I said.

The terrain was flat and heavily wooded with a mix of buck-brush, pine, live oak, and black oak trees. We walked side by side for about one quarter of a mile and I let Dad get accustomed to his new boots as I explained the lay of the land ahead. We were approaching a long draw. I pointed Dad toward the left-hand side of the divide and told him that I would walk on the right. The idea was that I might spook a deer and it would run toward him, or he might spook a deer and it could run into my arrow. We would meet at the dirt road that crossed at the end of the draw about two miles from where were now standing. I told Dad that it might be getting a little dark by the time we reached the next road but he should just stop at the road and wait for me, not walk down the road in either direction.

We separated and started our sweep of the long draw. I was watching for deer but angled in a way that I could keep an eye on Dad at the same time. A small doe broke cover about fifty yards out in front of my dad but Dads pace didn't change and I don't think that he saw the deer. Then a little three-point buck appeared out of nowhere and walked slowly up my side of the draw, going out of sight once more behind some brush. I stopped walking and watched for movement, but never see that little buck again. Dad continued walking and I lost sight of him as well.

It took me another half hour or forty-five minutes to reach the narrow road at the end of this draw. Once there I begin walking up the road and am happy to see Dad sitting on a stump about one hundred yards up the road. He had managed to walk a straight line on the hillside and hit the road perfectly as planned. I was glad he had done as I asked him to and not decided to walk any farther down the road because it was beginning to get dark and walking around at this time of day could be an easy way to get lost in the woods. He was facing away from me and didn't move as I approached.

"Hi, Dad," I said, almost within touching distance.

He jumped, nearly falling off the stump as he turned to face me.

"Jesus, you could give a guy a heart attack."

"Sorry, Dad, I thought you must have heard me stomping up the road. I really didn't mean to startle you. See any deer?"

"No, I did hear something running but I didn't actually see anything. How about you?"

"One doe and a little buck."

"Really?"

"Yeah, you scared them both out of the brush and they ran towards me, just like we planned. Turn on your flashlight and follow me; it's not too far to my truck."

The small dirt road angled slightly uphill and intersected into the main road. Once there, we turned left and walked side by side until we got to the driveway which leads into Don's property.

About that time Dad remembered that the truck was broken.

"How are we going to get the truck fixed?" He asked.

"Sorry, Dad, but I don't think that the Auto Club will be an option."

"Then how do you plan to drive down that road without any brakes?"

"Carefully," I said, opening the driver's side door. "That is unless you would like to drive?"

He opened the door on his side and got in. "Your mom is going to be pretty mad if you manage to kill us both."

I offered a tired smile at his dry humor, but my mind was already adjusting to the driving task ahead. Backing slowly out of the driveway, I considered the fact that this was the last level ground we would see for a while. Our next twelve miles would be downhill in the dark without brakes. I started our descent down the county road driving very slowly. Once we got going I pushed down the emergency brake just to get some feel for how quickly it would stop us. The truck did slow down, and then came to a stop in the middle of the road. I realized that even at this reduced speed the emergency brake was not very effective.

I decided to put the truck transfer case into four-wheel-drive low range. That would be a very low gear, but the compression of the engine would keep us from going very fast, and at this point driving slowly would be a good thing. We started down the hill once again. Shadows loomed out of the dark and the truck headlights allowed me to see more of the winding road than I really wanted to. I wished that we were driving in my old Ford instead of this new Dodge because the Ford had a hand emergency brake located just under the dash. This truck had a newer foot actuated design which was really much more difficult to control in this type of situation. Damn, a curve was coming up way too fast. I let off of the gas pedal with my right foot and immediately pressed down on the emergency brake with my left foot. The transmission and engine did a good job slowing us down, allowing me to creep around the curve at finger-tensing seven or eight miles an hour. I reached down with my left hand and pulled the brake release lever, allowing the truck to roll free again.

My confidence was building and I decided that my slowing down technique would work just fine as long as the truck speed didn't get much above ten miles an hour. I got pretty good at reading the road and didn't need to use the emergency brake again for three or four miles. My neck was beginning to get stiff and tense. I was sweating more from the concentration than from the warm evening. Once we were safely at the bottom of the hill, I looked over at my dad. He was nestled peacefully against the passenger side door, his left arm holding onto the padded door handle tethering him in place, sound asleep. Our nerve racking twelve-mile descent on this little back country road took us the better part of an hour to complete.

I put the truck transmission back into standard drive and moved the transfer case lever into high gear. Feeling comfortable now that we were back on flat ground I adjusted the radio to a country station and pulled out onto the main highway to begin a slow ride home. Around eleven thirty I set the emergency brake for the last time in my own driveway.

"Dad, wake up. We're home, wake up."

He opened his eyes and looked around. "We got here pretty fast."

"Yeah a record, fifty miles in just under two hours. Let's see if we can find us something to eat."

I knew this wouldn't be a problem, especially with my mom around. We found almost a whole ham in the refrigerator. I cut several thin slices of ham. Dad made the sandwiches, adding mayo, cheese, lettuce, and tomatoes. I opened two beers, handing one to Dad.

"I don't understand how you could have been so nervous on the drive up to Don's and then actually manage to sleep on the way back when we didn't have any brakes."

"Well, on the way up you were driving like a wild man. Coming down I could see that you intended to drive in a more civilized manner. Oh, and thanks for the hunting trip. It was truly an experience." Dad hoisted his beer in a toast.

Tractor For Sale

*B*eing a city boy, I was really fond of cars. My first was a '52 Mercury that my buddies and I pushed by hand into my parents back yard when I was only sixteen. A couple of weeks later my folks were somewhat amazed when my friends and I actually drove that car out of the back yard under its own power.

This Mercury and the multitude of cars that followed did not do anything to prepare me for my first tractor.

My purchasing methods were basic, sound, and strictly scientific. I needed a tractor, had two thousand dollars to spend, and the local paper to shop in.

The second ad that I read in the classified section met all of the conditions and qualifications. Two hours later I was the proud owner of a John Deere Model 50. The fact that this tractor was practically an antique did not faze me for a second. It was love at first sight.

"I'll be back for my truck," I told the farmer as I climbed aboard my new tractor, preparing for the ride home. "Oh, what about the guarantee?" I joked.

"Well, I can't guarantee it for you, but it always seemed to run good," replied the farmer, absolutely playing it straight.

"Just kidding," I said. "You will guarantee that it will get me home won't you?"

"Oh, sure, no problem, have a nice ride."

And off I went. I lived six miles away. That tractor ran great, bumping along the road in sixth gear. I made a left turn from the county road into my driveway. The tractor engine coughed, bucked once, and then died just inside of my front fence. I worked on the engine for the next two weeks before bringing it back to life.

That farmer really knew his tractors.

Plumbing, Cows, & Baby Chicks

*N*orth Idaho is one of the most beautiful places that Mother Nature has pulled together. The rolling landscape is mostly farm country bounded by evergreen forests, high-peaked mountains, lakes, rivers and small streams.

Two main highways pass through this region of Bonner County, but any turn off of these interstates will land you on a hard packed dirt-and-gravel county road. These rural roads are lined with wire-fenced fields or pastures holding cows, horses or other less typical livestock. You will see barns of every description, houses that range from mere shacks or small mobile homes to palatial estates. There is also a fantastic array of multicolored farm equipment in various states of readiness or disrepair.

The sight of a tractor towing incredibly wide implements or passing people riding horses on one of these county roads is just about as common as seeing a kid on a bicycle in any metropolitan area.

I live in this rural community. My twenty-acre parcel is bounded on the south side by a county road called Samuels. On the north side my neighbor owns a full section, six hundred and sixty acres, and just to the north of him is the beginning of Kootnie National Forest. To say that my home is way-out-there would be kind of an understatement. I plan to build a house on the property in the next couple of years but for now the instant housing mobile home suits me just fine.

Moving in last fall was chock full of surprises—some that required quick changes of plan. I found out that when you choose a piece of undeveloped ground for your home, a person needs to be flexible.

My property terrain is on two elevations. It has an upper bench containing about ten acres, and flat lower pasture ground that is also about nine or ten acres. On the division of these two benches is a sandy hill that rises about forty feet high running north and south. The upper bench is more wooded, and offers wonderful views, but the access to this upper acreage would present a big obstacle in the winter. I chose a spot below this sandy hill for my mobile home. The location was just about in the center of the property and I felt that the hill would offer some protection from the more severe winter storms.

Having landed the trailer in this desirable location, my next step was to arrange for water and power. The power part was fairly straightforward. I met with the Northern Lights Company engineer and conveyed my thoughts, which he transcribed to his clipboard bound paper form. We then exchanged handshakes followed by my personal check for twelve hundred dollars. Power was on its way.

Now, to find water. In this part of the country finding water can be taken quite literally. Local wells had reported depths ranging from shallow wells at thirty feet to deep wells that can reach three hundred fifty feet. Some areas claimed that there was no water at all, just wet, blue clay that is known to plug any pump but will not produce a steady flow of drinking water.

"So how do you go about finding water," I would ask.

At first I thought people were putting me on when they began talking about walking around with coat hangers and witching a well, but eventually I realized that they were stone serious, so I began making some phone calls on the subject. These calls lead me to the witch.

On a cold, foggy fall morning the "witch" arrived at my doorstep clad in dark brown rain gear. A wide brimmed hat covered most of his weather-wrinkled face. I guessed that the man was old but he had one of those faces that did not reveal secrets of age.

The witch greeted me then turned from my trailer and walked slowly away. I began to follow him. I was carrying several freshly cut wooden stakes and a hammer. It was not my intention to kill this witch but to assist him by marking the spot when he found water.

He carried a small plywood box in one hand with a wire running from it to a long metal rod that was held firmly in his other hand. The rod was aimed straight away from his body and was swaying gently from side to side with the movement of his walking. Occasionally the man would modify his direction and venture slightly to the right or left and then return to his original course. Eventually he came to a stop. The metal rod was bouncing up and down violently as if determined to leap from his hand.

"Put a stake here," he said, pointing at the ground beneath his feet.

I pounded a stake into the ground as instructed and then stood up and looked around to get an assessment of the location. My mobile home was a long way off. The witch must have read my facial expression and sensed my concern.

"You can choose any spot on the property for the trailer, but the water is here," he said, emphatically pointing toward the freshly placed stake. "There is a good flow of water about forty feet down."

After living in cities most of my life, it was a bit unsettling to find myself standing in the middle of an old hay field discussing the best place to drill for water, the conversation being held with a grown man calling himself a water witch.

The well driller moved his huge rig into position. He backed up a long trailer that held the equipment, and then set up the drilling tower that would be used to drill my well at the spot I had previously marked with the wooden stake. It was mutually understood that once the drilling began he would charge me by the drilled foot. The well driller did not offer any opinions as to how I had determined this particular location for my water well and seemed only mildly surprised when he struck water at exactly forty feet.

My new well casing, spray painted red, protruded about one foot above ground level. When looking from the front window of my mobile home, the open panorama was unspoiled by the introduction of this new piece of plumbing. The short projection of pipe was almost hidden in the pasture grass. If the pipe been painted any color but red it would have been nearly impossible to see.

Papers and sketches littered my kitchen table. I had spent the entire morning wrestling with the basic concept of pumping water. The pumping system consisted of three main components. The first thing that will be needed is a pump of some kind. The pump could be either above ground, such as that used on shallow wells, or the more preferred style a submersible pump which would be installed inside of the well casing.

Then a pressure tank is needed. It could be installed almost anywhere in the system. This thirty or forty-gallon metal tank is used to provide constant pressure in the system. It is also designed to absorb the sudden shock of water pressure that is produced each time the pump is started.

The third key piece of this mechanical puzzle was a pressure switch. The switch could be mounted almost anywhere in the system but usually found itself attached to or very near the pressure tank. The switch will activate the pump when the system pressure was low, then it would break an electrical circuit and stop the pump when a desired pressure was reached. All of these main pieces of hardware are usually placed near the opening of the well and are then protected from the elements by the construction of a pump house.

I did not have any difficulty comprehending the technical concept of this water pumping system. My issue was focused on the necessity for an ugly conventional pump house. I looked again at my beautiful open field clad only in soft brown grass, and tried to imagine what it would look like with an outhouse-style wooden structure parked smack dab in the center.

North Idaho can get pretty cold. Reported low temperatures have been in the minus twenty to thirty-degree range. These extreme conditions will freeze the earth, driving frost levels down well below the surface of the ground. Water pipes that were previously buried below this frost zone will be safe, however pipes that are not buried "pretty damn deep" will freeze and could possibly break. Local horror stories attested to this fact of nature. I wanted to bury the water pipes deep enough to be safe. The question is, just how deep should this be? Local lore places this pretty damn deep safe-zone at anywhere from three to seven feet. Not being a man of half measures, I chose to go with the deepest estimate.

The backhoe driver had finished for the day. Today's digging produced a major hole behind the house that would eventually be used for a septic tank with two long shallow runs that were intended for use as a leach field. I was standing at the bottom of my newly dug eight-foot deep ditch that ran in a straight line from the new well to within a couple of feet from the mobile home. This ditch would be used to run the main water piping from the well to my house. It would also carry the electrical cable that would power the pump.

Surveying the ditch at this below ground level, I had a fantastic idea. If this ditch is deep enough to insulate the water pipe, couldn't it also be used to insulate the pressure tank? *Why do I need an above ground pump house?*

I climbed from the ditch, walked home and went straight to my kitchen table. Once there I opened my eight-by-eleven ruled tablet and began to design an underground pump house.

When I bought the septic tank from Gill Brothers on Highway 95, I noticed that the outfit also made big sections of concrete pipe. I had already purchased my septic tank but returned to Gill Brothers the following day and ordered two sections of concrete piping. Each section was four-foot in diameter by four-foot long.

The system that I designed worked something like this: A submersible pump would be placed in the steel well casing. This pump would be connected to three hundred feet of pipe that would run underground until it reached inside of the two sections of four-foot diameter concrete pipe that had been placed on top of each other at the mobile home end of the ditch. The concrete pipe sections would become a wall for my underground pump house. This concrete casing would be home for the pressure tank and pressure switch. From that intersection of plumbing it would be relatively easy to make the short run of piping which would connect my mobile home to the water supply.

Once this system was connected and tested I could backfill the long ditch, leaving only the four-foot concrete pipe open. I would then build a front porch for the mobile home. The closed-in porch would act as a cover and also an access for the underground pump house. Neat idea, don't you think? I built the system and it worked perfectly.

An early cold snap caught me by surprise with freezing temperatures around the first of October, followed by six inches of snow in early November. I had completed every part of my water pumping project except for actually building the front porch. I placed a sheet of plywood over the open four foot wide hole as a temporary measure that could prevent a bad accident, and winter really came in earnest. Snow fell for the following months, producing a beautiful white landscape.

Water flows hot or cold at the kitchen sink with a twist of the handle. The bathtub shower produces a strong spray of hot water and the toilet always flushes without hesitation. My newly installed potbellied wood burning stove will hold a fire almost all night long and I never use the electric forced air heater. My little home is warm, comfortable and dry. Life couldn't be better.

March brought cold showers of rain that worked like magic, melting months of winter formed ice and snow. I awoke one morning to find that the water system wasn't working. My first thought was that a pipe must be frozen, but how could that be? It was thawing outside—melting, not freezing.

After a few minutes of investigation I found that the melting snow was my problem. Water from rain and melted snow had found a way into my below ground pump house. In fact, over two feet of water had accumulated in the hole. The rising water had floated my pressure tank off the ground, causing it to break free from the attached piping. This was an unforeseen development, for sure. Working in hip boots, I managed to plug the pipe section where the pressure tank had been attached. It was obvious that the tank could not be returned to the hole until the front porch was built, but where would it go in the meantime?

The local hardware store provided everything I needed. The project was really pretty easy. Once the Y-valve was installed on the faucet that supplied water for the washing machine, I ran a short length of garden hose from the new Y-valve connection into the bathroom where it was then attached to the forty-gallon pressure tank now residing in my bathtub. As I said before, the pressure tank could be almost anywhere in the system, and it should work just fine in the bathtub. Problem solved.

There was just this one small drawback, almost not worth mentioning, but when I took a shower and was in the process of rinsing the soap from my face, my warm bottom would very often come in contact with the surface of this ice-cold metal tank. This did not happen every day because I was very careful. The icy fingers only grabbed my butt about every other day. God, I hated that water tank.

On my way home from town one day I stopped at the store to pick up some groceries. Somehow I managed to leave the shopping center with a small black dog along with my weekly food supplies. Don't ask; I named him Max.

April brought more rain but it was much warmer. It also brought some sunshine that began drying the ground. One morning it brought a beat-up, blue farm truck bouncing up my driveway.

The tall thin man stepped from the truck and introduced himself simply as Vern, a local cattle rancher. He was looking for a farm hand that would be willing to drive a tractor during the planting season. Up to this moment I had not been actively looking for work, but this was a small town and word gets around. We struck an agreement and I began working for him the following morning.

I woke around four a.m., packed a sack lunch while the coffee was making then laced my boots and walked outside to check the weather. The dog met me at the front door. "Well Max, want to go to work today?"

The day was chilly and a light rain was falling. I took another walk around this old piece of farm equipment. During our question and answer exchange the previous day, Vern had asked me if I could drive a tractor. I had answered flippantly that I could drive "anything with wheels." That particular exchange was replaying in my mind as I took a closer look at the old yellow D-2 Caterpillar. It definitely *did not* have wheels, not even a steering wheel, but my immediate concern was that it also seemed to be missing a starter motor.

I must have passed some kind of test that morning. Vern was not in sight and did not come to my aid in any way. He had simply pointed his arm and asked me to go get the Cat, and then walked off in another direction. After finding a rusty old crank-handle under the seat, I tentatively inserted it into a beckoning hole through the radiator. Then with one mighty turn of the crank, I managed to get this beast started without breaking an arm. I cautiously maneuvered between the combination of floor pedals, side levers and a stationary throttle until the machine was turned around. Once this little operation was under my belt, confidence was building quickly. I managed to keep the Cat going in a straight line down the short dirt road and then maneuvered it onto the bed of the farm truck which was parked at a cement-loading ramp. I spent the next couple of days improving my Cat driving skills by clearing small trees from one corner of a big odd shaped field.

The little Caterpillar was soon replaced with a big John Deere 4020 tractor that I used for disking, harrowing and fertilizing this sixty-acre field. Once my dirt preparation work was completed, Vern moved in with a smaller tractor that he used for the actual seed planting.

My farm-hand chores would vary slightly from day to day. Vern leased several fields from land owners in the area and I would often move equipment over the road from one field to another, then plow, disk, harrow, or work on fences as directed.

The farming day would begin way-to-early and end oh-so-late. My dog Max was becoming quite fond of riding on the tractor.

Max and I were just finishing up a small ten acre field one evening when I saw the now familiar blue Chevy pickup pull in and park by my yellow Ford. Vern said that he would like me to come over to his place the following morning. It was time to sort the cattle. He asked if I could ride a horse. "Sure," I said, "as long as it has wheels."

Knocking the alarm clock to the floor was not a wonderful start. I tossed off the warm blankets and swung my feet to the cold floor without giving a thought to the possibility of glass. After retrieving the still ringing broken faced alarm clock from under the bed, I had managed to cut my right foot and left hand; all of this by 4:02 a.m. The blood could be cleaned up later as I was not about to be late for my first real live rodeo.

I let the warm water churn at the back of my neck, glad to see that the bleeding from my foot had almost stopped. Backing away from the showerhead to inspect my hand proved to be a mistake as the Jack-Frost-cold pressure tank took this opportunity to grab both cheeks of my ass. "Damn!"

The weather was warming some but it was always chilly in the mornings. I continued wearing long johns under my work clothes. I was also still wearing my trusty heavy-lined Carhartt jacket. Outside I started the Ford, and then prepared breakfast for Max that consisted of puppy chow mixed with milk and warm water. I ate my breakfast standing at the kitchen counter as I slammed together a quick lunch and refilled my military style canteen with water.

It was just short of five a.m. and still pretty dark when I pulled to a stop in Vern's dooryard. Several men were standing on the long wooden back porch, smoking and drinking coffee from large white mugs, so I knew that I wasn't late. I entered the house through the back door. Vern was sitting at his big kitchen table, still eating breakfast. We nodded our hellos as I fixed myself a cup of coffee, wondering, not for the first time, how in the world this thin man ate such a huge breakfast each morning without gaining weight. We often started the workday in this kitchen. Vern would sometimes give me instructions for the day's work around fork-loads of food. He never once asked me if I had eaten or if I would like to sit down. *Strange man,* I thought.

This morning I took my coffee outside and joined the other men on the porch. I recognized a couple faces but no introductions were offered so I kept quiet as well. Heads turned at the bang of the screen door as Vern crossed the porch with his typical long strides and headed toward the barn. Coffee cups rattled against the Formica top of the porch table and the men hurried to catch up with Vern. I took a quick detour to my pickup, grabbing gloves, canteen and lunch. No telling what this day will bring.

I wonder where Max is off to. My missing dog didn't actually worry me as he was no stranger to this farm and often plays with Vern's dogs.

Being accustomed to working early mornings, it always strikes me as funny how I never seem to notice daylight coming. One second it's dark, then the next I can see almost every detail. Seven horses are saddled and tied at the corral gate. They are creating their own fog bank as they rattle tack, stomped feet, and exhale jets of warm air into the cool Idaho morning.

There is very little conversation as each of the men picks out a horse, leads it from the group and mounts up. I waited for the others, and then untied the last horse at the gate. Her name is Smoky, an Appaloosa with a gray coat spotted with big brown freckles. Her rump is brown with small gray freckles. We would get to know each other soon enough, but for now

I was simply hoping that she will let me get aboard without making too much fuss.

I had been taught to ride as a kid, but my last time on a horse was many years ago. Fortunately Smoky is very gentle. The success I enjoyed landing my bottom in the saddle on the first attempt had everything to do with her disposition and very little to do with my expertise as a horseman.

Once mounted, I got my first good look at the lay of the land. Cows are scattered as far as I can see. Most of the cattle are full-grown, but there are a lot of baby calves mixed into the herd as well. I have no idea how many animals are in the herd or just how big this field actually is, as the fence line goes out of sight over the horizon. The horsemen broke into two groups; we separated and began riding along the fence line in opposite directions. The idea was for us to ride to the back of this big field so that we were behind the cattle. Then we planned to drive the entire herd into a large corral that was standing open near the point where we started riding.

I rode along side of a man named Don. He was Vern's son-in-law, married to Vern's only daughter Debby. Don was currently separated from his wife. They had one son who was twelve years old. I told him that I had a daughter the same age and that she was living in California with her mom. It took us about thirty minutes to encircle the cattle. During the ride Don and I enjoyed a pleasant conversation, only to conclude that aside from our kids being the same age, our similar marital status, and a mutual relationship with Vern, we didn't actually have much in common.

One of the cows I was herding did not want to go the way I wanted her to. She and her calf kept trying to swing back around Smoky and me. I was working pretty hard to prevent that from happening. Smoky finally had enough. She lunged forward and bit the cow on her butt. The pecking order was now firmly established we did not have any more trouble with that particular cow.

As we worked the cattle out of the two far corners of the field, the cattle began to group up. Or I should say the cattle began to form into a herd. Once in this herd, they were much easier to push, I mean, easier to drive. Within about three hours, my first cattle drive had come to an end. All of the cattle, nearly two hundred of them, are now penned in one medium size corral.

Upon closing the gate on the last of the cows, Vern went to an inside gate that led into another smaller corral. Don was manning a gate that opened into yet another small corral. Now the sorting started. The idea was to separate the steers from the heifers and calves. Vern wanted only heifers and calves, while all of the steers were intended for Don.

The four other men and I are tasked to drive individual steers or heifers and calves through the gates that Vern and Don are controlling. We single out an individual animal and attempt to haze it through a gate, this done by much hat waving, arm spinning, shouting and a good share of running around. Some animals are chased successfully through the intended gate, but very often a wily critter will veer at the last split second, leaving us would-be cowboys winded and dusty hanging against the wood rail fence. Thirty minutes of this activity has the sorting crew red faced and crap splattered. Most of my new comrades are leaning forward, hands on knees, gasping for breath, and hoping for a second wind. The cattle, however, are not even breathing hard.

I walked over to Vern and asked him if I could give the sorting a try with Smoky. He took a quick look at the remaining number of cattle in the corral and then at the battered sorting crew, and gave me the OK.

Smoky and I were pals now that we had some history. I mounted and rode confidently into the corral. I didn't realize that something was about to change. The gentle horse that had carried me across the pasture was a mere memory. I found myself seated on a cat-like creature that responded to rein or body commands with split second agility. Once pointed at the cow of choice, Smoky would run, turn, stop, lunge or veer. She might snap her teeth at the cow or actually bite. Her front legs shot from right to left in her relentless pursuit.

The steer or heifer that Smoky had singled out would dart through the opened gate, rolling its eyes, seemingly happy for the chance to escape this monster. It only took about ten minutes for me to realize that Smoky knew this game much better than I did. Once she had me trained, the sorting got real easy. I would kind of point her at a cow or steer, then lean forward in the saddle, not touching the reins at all. Smoky would take it from there. All I had to do was hang-on, which was not exactly a walk in the park.

The last calf cleared the gate and I walked Smoky from the corral back to the large field. The other men and I unsaddled all of the horses and gave them a good brushing before setting them free to run on their own.

Lunch is burgers and chips with homemade baked beans and potato salad. I ate four helpings of everything, never giving a thought to my peanut butter sandwich which I would find the next day pounded flat, still wrapped in foil, in the inside pocket of my jacket.

An afternoon siesta is not on the agenda. Once more at the corrals, we have the job of separating the calves from the heifers. The actual sorting is fairly easy because we were working in a much smaller corral. Once the heifers are gone the calves are herded into a long narrow loading chute. At the end of this board chute is a metal clamp contraption that will firmly hold the calves and allow us to rotate them onto their sides while Vern and Don de-horned, vaccinated and converted bull calves into steers. The babies are then set free to rejoin their moms. Most of the caves now have bloody heads from the horn removal and a new yellow number-tag dangling from a right ear.

My job is to keep the calves headed in the right direction. This loading chute was built for full size animals, the problem being that the small calves can actually turn around in the chute and cause a major traffic jam. When this happens I have to jump inside of the chute and manhandle the culprit back into the right direction. The frightened little calves charge into me, banging their small heads against my legs as they attempt to escape. This activity is amusing for the first half-hour or so, but as most of these little guys are about the same size, their hard heads and newly formed nub-horns are beginning to take a toll on my legs. As time goes on it seems as if each baby calf is intent on pounding the same painfully bruised area, and my Levi's are offering very little in the way of padding or protection.

I found Max sleeping peacefully in a shady spot near Vern's back porch. There is a black and white Collie looking dog sound asleep in the same general area. Obviously Max and his new friend have had a very hard day.

Easing my yellow Ford into second gear I leaned back against the padded seat and pointed the truck toward home. As rodeos go, this one was pretty tame. There were no bucking horses, calf roping contests or bull rides. The only spectator event had been my impromptu cutting horse exhibition. All else was just plain work. I am bone tired, and wishing that Max would offer to drive.

Once home I removed my outer layer of clothing and tossed all of it out the back door. The dirty clothes could be dealt with tomorrow, maybe. I took one step toward my bedroom when I noticed what looked like a blood trail in my hallway. Following the tracks into the bathroom I leaned against the doorjamb and studied the two red footprints contrasting against the white, gold-flecked linoleum bathroom floor. It took a full minute or more for me to figure it out. *I cut my foot; was that today?*

My eyes moved from the floor, coming to rest on the green painted steel pressure tank. "You have grabbed my ass for the last time!" I said out loud, suddenly mad.

It should only take a half hour at the most to put the tank back into the underground pump house. I had been checking the hole every day or two, even removing the cover on sunny days. It had been completely dry for the past week. I closed the red handle of the water valve leading to the pressure tank, then loosened the garden hose coupling at the bottom of the tank one full turn. Water began trickling from the forty-gallon tank and ran down the bathtub drain.

I went into my bedroom to select a clean work shirt and pair of Levi's for this last little job. After pulling on my tall work boots without bothering to lace them, I walked to the kitchen in search of a cold beer. Two Budweiser's were looking back at me from the second shelf. I removed both of them and drank the first while still standing in front of the closed refrigerator door. Walking back toward the bathroom, I opened the second can of beer. I leaned against the bathroom doorjamb, holding the cold beer can against my cheek as I watched water slowly trickling from the tank. *This is taking too long; there can't be much water left. Maybe I should unscrew the hose a bit more.*

I gave the hose connection a half turn. *Bad plan*; gushing water erupted against my hand, blowing the garden hose aside it hit the front wall of my bathtub. Not stopping there, the water angled upward to the ceiling and then rained down, soaking me from head to open boots.

Unbelievable!

My head started ringing. *Ring...ring...ring!*

No, it isn't my head; it must be the phone I realized. I didn't get many phone calls and kind of forgot that I had one.

"Hello," I answered into the handset.

"Your chickens are ready."

"What?" I asked, not sure that I had just heard correctly.

"This is Cornie's Feed Store," said the woman at the other end. "Your hundred baby chicks are here."

Water was beginning to puddle at my feet. Mud was running from my boots onto the otherwise clean kitchen floor. I had a vague recollection of ordering chickens in another more peaceful life, before starting back to work.

"OK, I'll be there in the morning."

"No, tomorrow is Sunday, we're closed. You have to come now!"

Back to the bedroom for yet another change of clothes. The wet ones were unceremoniously thrown at the bathroom floor, to help sop up some of the water.

"Come, Max, we're going after chickens."

At Cornie's Feed Store one hundred white, chirping baby chickens were waiting for me in three open cardboard boxes. I positioned the three boxes of chattering chicks and one bag of feed on the front seat of the Ford. This made a snug fit against my side as I started the return trip home. Taking the long way around, we made a quick stop at the small convenience store on Highway 200.

Once re-provisioned with two six-packs of Budweiser, I was on my way back to tackle the soggy mess that had started so innocently just two hours earlier.

It only took a couple of minutes to remove the now empty pressure tank from the tub. After carrying it out to the edge of my underground pump house I returned to scatter several dry towels on the bathroom, hall, and kitchen floors. One hour later the pressure tank was installed and back to functioning.

Now I had to do something with the baby chickens. It was still a bit too cold for them to survive outside during the night, and due to my long work hours, the chicken coop was not quite ready for occupancy. Without another thought I brought the three boxes of noisy, bouncing puffballs into my kitchen and arranged the boxes on the floor. Then as an afterthought I found some heavy bowls that the chicks wouldn't capsize, and gave them all a ration of food and water; *Now, for that long overdue shower.*

Sunday was just another workday during planting season. The alarm rang at four a.m. as usual, and I woke up sore in places that I didn't even know existed. Even my hair hurt. I kicked the damp towels into a pile as I made preparations to go to work. Before leaving I fed the baby chicks again. Their food and water was almost gone. I placed a clamp-on-light bulb inside of each box, and then partially covered the boxes with cardboard to help keep the chicks warm during the day. Max got to eat in the pickup on our way to work.

I have an easy, square, flat, forty-acre field to work today. The sky is clear and by about eight in the morning the day has started to warm up. The disking was going real well so I worked on through the entire field without stopping for lunch. At around one o'clock it was actually getting hot. I stripped down to my long johns top for the first time this year and the warm sun is feeling pretty good.

After switching the disk blades for the harrow-set I got in one round before calling it a day. My legs are still kind of sore from the beating they took yesterday, and sitting on the tractor seat all day hasn't done much to limber them up. I hung onto the side of the tractor for a minute, listening to the hot engine gurgle as it cooled. Max was at my feet expecting me to move. Finally my legs un-cramped a bit and decided they could make it to the truck.

The dust-free breeze blowing in through my pickup window feels just fine. I have actually taken off my long johns top and am down to a V-necked T-shirt. Max has his head poked out of the passenger side window and seems to be thinking the same thing I am. He does that a lot.

When I opened the door to my mobile home the hot blast of stagnant air almost pushed me back out. Damn, it must be over a hundred in here. Leaving the front door open, I walked on in a couple of steps. What the hell is that smell? Oh, damn, I had completely forgotten about the baby chicks. When I got to the kitchen, there they were, all dead. Every one of them was lying on its side, not a sound or movement from any of them. *Crap.* I went over and opened both of the kitchen windows, then went down the hall and opened the back door as well. Who could have expected this kind of hot day?

I looked at the baby chicks again. Probably couldn't make one chicken sandwich out of the bunch, I thought to myself sarcastically. Then I thought I saw one of them move. I hurried to the sink and filled a glass with water. Dabbing water on my fingers, I flicked some of it on the chick that I saw move. It moved again, and I flicked more water. Another chick blinked an eye, and I continued flicking water. Then the first one was trying to stand, so I reached over and set the chick on her feet. More were moving, so I kept flicking water, and standing them up like toy soldiers. Pretty soon the chicks were not only standing, but actually walking. More and more of them were coming around! A miracle.

I worked as fast as I could, flicking water, getting more water, and standing them up. There were only about fifteen or twenty chicks left on their backs in the cardboard boxes and I had high hopes for them as well, when I suddenly realized that eighty or more of the little buggers were now running around the kitchen and who knew where else. I made a mad dash and closed the front door just as one of them was wobbling for freedom. Then I closed the back door as well and started the big chicken round up.

The good news was that once the chicks were back in the cardboard boxes they were trapped. The bad news was that they were pretty damn fast and my legs were still going pretty damn slow. It took me almost an hour to catch all of the amazingly recovered dead chickens. A couple of times I thought of calling for reinforcements, but Max might not play this game as well as Smoky had. God I was tired; the white sea of noise and feathers was finally contained.

Back outside, I surveyed the almost finished chicken coop. It took about fifteen minutes and all the energy I could muster to patch a few holes, make a minor adjustment to the heat lamp and then move the newest members of my little farm into their new home.

As I watched the baby chicks patter and peck around the coop, I made a silent oath never to allow chickens into my house again.

A Time For Planting

It is still dark and cold. Some frost is on the ground, but the calendar says that it is spring, and by God I am going to plant my first crop. During the long winter I had done my homework on this subject and asked a lot of questions at the feed store. I was very new to farming of any kind and hungry to know what kind of pasture grass would do well in my area. Everyone around here has been helpful and this question asking has given me a lot of good information from some of my new friends and neighbors.

When planting a pasture, it turns out that you don't simply scatter grass seed like you intended to plant a front lawn in the city. In this part of the country the proven method is to plant first year pasture grass with a cover crop of some kind. Oats or barley seems to be the best choices. The idea is that the cover crop will grow fast and protect the young grass shoots from the elements. Then the cover crop can be harvested. This harvest can pay for the initial farming investment, and possibly even show a profit. The following year there is no need for a cover crop as the pasture grass will have a good root system in the soil and can do just fine on its own.

I did some basic measurements and had figured out how many acres to plant. The guys at the farm store took it from there and did the math, sending me home with six large bags of pasture grass seed and ten much larger bags of oat seed. These seed bags have been stored in my shop for the past two weeks, and I was straining at the bit wanting to get going on this project.

Dressed in warm clothing including thermal underwear, two sweatshirts, heavy work gloves, and my trusty insulated Carhartt jacket, I climbed aboard my John Deere 50 tractor, cranked up the engine and pointed her toward the front field. Three months ago I got a great deal on a practically new two-bottom plow. I was pretty sure that the John Deere would pull this new plow but I was yet to put it to the test. Needless to say, I was a little apprehensive as I pushed forward on the hydraulic lever controlling the three-point hitch, and dropped the new plow into my front field for the first time.

Looking back over my right shoulder, I was delighted to see two straight, smooth, dark brown furrows emerge to the surface as they were cut from the straw-colored grass. The tractor easily pulled my new two-bottom plow around and around the oblong ten-acre field. It took the better part of a day for me to plow that field the first time. The next couple of days found me disking, harrowing, fertilizing, and finally seeding pasture grass with a cover crop of oats.

Spring rains and then summer sun worked nature's miracles on my new pasture. Around the middle of June, I stood on the hill at the north side of my property, proudly looking over my field of golden oats waving gently in the light afternoon breeze.

Then like a hammer blow, a horrible thought struck me. How was all of that brown waving stuff going to get into my barn? I had visions of walking through the field carrying a heavy bag. No, that wouldn't work; there was way too much work for one person. How about several farm workers walking through the field dragging heavy bags?

Not to despair, my first phone call put me in contact with a local farmer who would be pleased to combine my field. We set a date for the following week.

The farmer arrived on the scheduled day, and introduced himself as Ned. He told me confidently that we were looking at about two hours work. Smoke belched from the huge green combine as it eased into the task, cutting a twelve-foot swath in my virgin oats. I began to climb my hill so that I could get a good view of this operation. About the time I reached the top of the hill, the noise from the combine stopped.

Before completing his first round the combine had quit running and was now resting quietly at the far end of my field. I walked back down the hill and across the field to see what was wrong. In a brief conversation Ned explained the problem, which could easily be fixed with my help. The farmer borrowed my truck and went to town for parts. I went to my shop for tools and then began unbolting pieces of the combine that Ned had indicated earlier. When Ned returned a couple of hours later he and I worked together until dark, repairing, replacing and adjusting various pieces of hardware on this antique behemoth.

The following morning my farmer friend arrived shortly after eight. He had a cup of coffee with me and then cranked up once again and went to work. The green monster completed almost two full rounds, and then pulled into the pit with new troubles.

"Major problems," Ned told me, sadly shaking his head. "I've busted the shaker box. Do you have a welder?"

Fortunately I did have a welder and also had enough metal lying around to make the necessary repairs. After watching me work for an hour or so Ned decided that I had the job under control, and that he had pressing issues in town. He promised to return the next day and wished me good luck.

I welded and fabricated in the hot sun for the balance of the day. Sometime after dark the machine was back together. I took a long shower, had a cold sandwich, and went to bed, dreaming fondly of farm workers dragging bags through my field.

Waking early on the morning of day three, I rolled out of bed at the sound of vehicle tires crunching up my driveway. Damn, I hurt everywhere. As I dressed in clean work clothes, I could hear the sound of Ned's combine running in the field. I reheated some of yesterday's coffee and made a quick offering of puppy treats for my dog Max. He and I climbed the hill and found a comfortable spot to watch the day's work. I could only hope that my weld job would hold up and that I would see the last of the green monster.

As predicted, two hours and the job was completed. I almost sang for joy when the combine made its last round.

Ned was standing near the fence. He was looking over my newly cut field fidgeting with his hat and looking sort of perplexed, so I asked him what was wrong. He said that he was trying to figure out whether he should charge by the acre or by the hour.

"Oh, charge by the hour," I said. "It will sure make it a lot easier for me to figure out my welding and mechanic rate."

Ned nodded and left. No bills were exchanged.

Spring came again the following year and the pasture grass in my front ten-acre field was just beautiful. I have other fields that should probably be re-seeded but for some reason the planting bug has never bitten me again.

The Great Goat Hunt

*T*hursday was the day for a weekly auction held in our neighboring town, Bonners Ferry. I had never been to a livestock auction before and some of my new friends told me that it was a lot of fun. I was beginning to get into the swing of North Idaho events and decided to go see what this auction was all about. The friends that told me about the auction had warned that parking could be difficult for late risers, so I made a point to get there early and selected a good spot in the large parking area. I had arrived at the auction yard around eight a.m., and after asking around I found that the bidding would not actually get underway until about ten. There was a restaurant across the street so I went there to have breakfast while waiting for things to get started.

Walking back across the street after a great breakfast, I could see that a good-sized crowd had arrived. I was glad that I had come early as the parking lot was indeed brimming over. Not expecting to know a soul here, I was surprised to hear my name being called from someone in the group. A neighbor by the name of Art rushed up to me and asked if I had brought my pickup truck.

"Sure, I have my truck. Why?"

"Well, I just bought a Billy goat that they decided not to run through the auction," said the neighbor. "I drove my car this morning and don't have a way to get it home. Would you mind bringing it to my place?"

"Don't mind at all. Load it up," I said, already walking away. "My truck is at the far south end of the parking lot."

I found out that the livestock auction would not actually begin until around noon, however I was told that there was a flea-market auction that always began promptly at ten. I mixed into a crowd of milling, slow moving people and eventually ended up inside of a large metal building. Once inside I could see that the walls were lined with tables which held an endless assortment of boxes upon boxes of clothes, small appliances, tools, gadgets and farmyard equipment, some which was impossible to for me to identify. The auctioneer was already in the process of auctioning these items. He sang out in a loud clear voice rapidly acknowledging new bids and then immediately calling for the next higher bid amount. His quick cadence prompted a lively bidding session, with much good-natured commentary from the crowd. I soon learned that a minimum bid was fifty cents, which seemed to assure at least one bid for every offering. The auctioneer knew his audience very well. Most of the items were sold individually, however at times he would skillfully group two or more boxes of dissimilar articles together and sell them as one lot to make sure that even seemingly worthless objects would be sold along with the more worthy offerings. People scooped up these treasures as they won the bid and proceeded toward a far door to pay for their new possessions. As the auction moved along the benches that lined the walls were swept clean in its wake.

I was gradually becoming familiar with my new surroundings and eventually realized that the metal structure we were in was actually three individual buildings which are all connected. I looked behind me and noticed that the first room was now completely clear of both people and boxes. The crowd behaved like one body as we hovered around the auctioneer. With him in the lead we slowly moved from one item to another, and eventually from room to room, while he picked his way through the vast array of unusual offerings. All of these indoor treasures were auctioned off before noon and the crowd slowly moved outside to the rear of the metal buildings so that we could view yet more items. These additional auction items were bigger than the ones that were inside of the building, and I noticed that the crowd had begun to disperse. I was now looking at several farm implements, a garden tractor, an old pickup truck and two beat-up cars. Once these last articles were sold the remainder of the people began walking toward the big white building adjacent to this first auction site. Following the slow easy flow of foot traffic, I now found myself inside of the large white arena-looking building. I noticed that the beer concession stand just a few feet to my left was getting a lot of action. Now fortified with my own pitcher-size Styrofoam cup of amber liquid, I once more merged into the flow of moving people and eventually found a place to sit.

As I looked around I realized that this building was designed specifically for the livestock auction. The room that I was in was like a barn, with a very high ceiling. It had a fenced-in dirt arena in the center. The arena was made from open rail fences, and was surrounded with coliseum style seating. Board benches provided seats and a good view for the large group of spectators. Some folks brought padded cushions or draped their jackets over the boards, but most simply sat on the well-worn wooden benches and didn't seem to mind the discomfort.

When the auction started animals were paraded into the main arena through a gate on the right side of the open rail fence. Once the animal or group of animals was in view the auctioneer began his quick descriptive narration. Bidding went very fast, and it took me a while to understand exactly what was going on. Once the winning bid was made, the single animal or group of critters was promptly escorted out of a gate on the left side of the arena, and new stock was brought in from the right again. This whole process was done very smoothly and extremely fast.

Suddenly the auction was over. When I glanced at my watch I was surprised to find that it was already three p.m... I would have guessed that it was closer to one-thirty or possibly two at the latest.

I stood for a long moment looking at the creature that now occupied the bed of my pickup truck. This thing-from-hell wasn't exactly what I was expecting. The Billy-goat was an evil looking monster with dirty, shaggy, black and brown hair. It had a large set of menacing looking black curling horns which began just above its eyes and protruded eight or ten inches above its head. Standing erect, his back was five or six inches taller than my three-foot truck racks. The goat had large oblong vacant looking multicolored eyes that seemed to be looking in several directions at the same time. Eventually these disturbing eyes stopped wondering and the animal tensed up as he noticed me for the first time. The goat fixed me with a cold, blue-gray eye I knew immediately that we were not going to be friends. The air around my truck had taken on a very pungent unpleasant odor that proved to be coming from this gross looking beast.

Even though the day was cold, I drove with both windows open. It took several miles of driving before the smell in my cab dissipated enough to actually chance closing one window on my driver side.

My neighbor Art lived about one quarter of a mile from me, on the same road as I did so it really wasn't much of an inconvenience making his delivery. When I arrived at the farm however, Art wasn't home. The family had several children and the oldest boy, about twelve, met me as I parked in the yard behind the house. I explained the reason for my visit, and asked him if he could handle the goat. The boy said that his dad had gone to town and would be home soon. He introduced himself as Timmy and assured me that he had a vast amount experience with goats of every description.

Timmy promptly climbed onto the bed of my pickup. I joined the boy and began to untie the short piece of restraint rope, actually bail twine that attached the goat's neck to the front rack of my pickup. I intended to hand the rope to the boy, but at this precise moment all hell broke loose. As the rope was undone, the goat leaped upright on its hind legs, towering above us his front legs with sharp looking hooves were waving menacingly. Timmy and I each jumped in opposite directions, and the goat took this opportunity to leap from the back of the truck, running for parts unknown. The goat did not seem to be having any trouble sorting out this new terrain as he crossed the open field at an impossible speed, then disappeared into the trees on the north end of the pasture.

The boy Timmy and I spent the remainder of that afternoon searching in vain for our escapee. I eventually got home around six in the evening, soon after to be called by my neighbor. He didn't seem to be particularly upset that the animal had run off and told me that the goat was purchased for meat. He then suggested that I take my bow and go on a goat-hunting expedition the following day. His last words were; "Shoot on sight."

The following morning my kids left for school, but soon came running back into the house wild eyed, reporting that an evil looking, foul smelling creature was lurking in our pasture. I went outside knowing exactly what it was that they were describing. We all looked around, but the goat had vanished yet again.

Early the following day, I answered the knock at my front door and found Timmy standing on the porch. He said that he had located the goat, however, his dad was once again in town, and did I have a gun?

Loading Felicia and Aimee my two children, our dog Max, the neighbor boy Timmy, and my twenty-two bolt action rifle into the front seat of the pickup, we drove the short distance to the neighbor's house. Timmy went inside; he returned moments later with two additional children and a small rifle of his own. It took a bit of shuffling around to get the optimum seating arrangements. We ended up with my two girls and Timmy's younger siblings in the back of the truck with the dog. Timmy and I remained in the front with the guns.

Following the boy's directions, I drove for a couple of winding miles of dusty county road. I was initially kind of amused as I thought of this strange safari led by a twelve-year-old child that I didn't really know, until the unwelcome thought of my neighbor coming home and finding his children missing entered my mind. I could easily imagine how uncomfortable it might be attempting to explain to the county sheriff how I was simply taking all of the neighborhood children on an early morning goat hunt.

Fortunately this gloomy thought process did not stay with me for long as my guide prompted me to take a left turn off of the main road. We were now traveling on a small narrow track that soon passed through an open wooden gate. We drove another half mile or so along this rutted path that actually turned out to be a long driveway which ended in a farmyard.

On one side of this yard there were several corrals made from white board fencing. The small corrals were holding goats of various sizes and colors. Timmy tapped me on the shoulder and pointed at our wayward Billy goat, lying down in a back pasture near the far end of this series of fences. I never did find out how Timmy had previously tracked the goat to this remote location. As the crow flies, we were at least three miles from his house.

The goat seemed content, and didn't even look up as we all verified his location. A farmer met us in the yard and we explained our reason for being there. I then casually asked the farmer if we could simply shoot the animal where it was and avoid another long chase.

To this day I don't know why the goat farmer agreed to this idea, but he said OK. We didn't waste any time. Taking careful aim, Timmy and I both opened fire. The goat never moved. We drove to the back of the field and loaded the dead animal into the bed of my pickup, then gathered all of our junior hunting crew and with a shy wave of thank you, left the goat farmer's yard.

When we returned to my neighbor's house I was now slightly irritated to find that he had not yet returned home. It was starting to get warm and this goat still needed to be cleaned, so without hesitation I dropped off all of the neighbor children and went back to my house. I quickly located my hunting knife and a wide bladed skinning knife. I also found an old deer bag in my hunting gear and once again returned to the neighbor's farm.

It took about thirty minutes to clean and skin the goat. I left it neatly wrapped in the white linen deer bag, hanging from the bucket on his large Ford tractor.

Later that morning neighbor Art called.

"You messed up."

Visions of killing the wrong animal popped into my head. *Pedigree, State Fair quality, no doubt; probably a priceless animal—oh, God.*

"What's wrong?" I asked quietly.

"Well, you left the whole thing. Should have just been half if it hanging there when I got home. You sure earned your share."

Two weeks later I ventured back to the auction. I parked early in the near empty lot as I had done on my first visit, and then casually strolled across the street for breakfast. I returned to the auction area early and was on time for the first bid at the flea-market auction. Within a half hour I was just getting into the swing of things and beginning to have a good time. I had offered two bids on an item that I didn't particularly need and was prepared to bid once again when my neighbor Art, now my new best friend, tapped me on the arm.

"Hi, Howard, are you driving your pickup today?"

"Well, yes, Art, I have the pickup. Why?"

"Well, it's the damnedest thing. I just bought a ram, and I'm driving my car again today. Think you could bring him home for me?"

Old Green

*Y*ears of leaves, pine needles and tree bark covered most of the old green truck. I could see that it had one flat tire on the front but the back tire on the passenger side and the two driver side tries seemed to be holding air. I couldn't imagine what kind of a mess I would find if I looked under the hood. My friends had bought this property and simply asked me if I could remove the old truck. It really shouldn't be much of a job. I would just take off the flat tire and get it fixed, then I'd ask one of my buddies help me tow the truck to my place.

Once I get her home I will call the junkyard guy to come and get it. The whole job shouldn't take more than two or three hours at the most. Easy money, I thought, considering the fifty bucks they gave me to make the truck go away.

It only took a couple of minutes to remove the flat tire. I placed it in the back of my pickup and started for home, planning to take the tire into town the following day. When I got to my place I decided to air the tire up just on the off chance that it might hold air. The following morning I was pleased to see that the tire was still firm. I put a tow chain in the pickup bed and drove over to get my friend, Larry, who said that he would help me with the tow.

Back at my friends' property, Larry and I mounted the tire and then hooked up the tow chain. Larry drove my truck and I climbed into the old green International. One hour later the old truck was unhooked and resting peacefully in my yard. Now that the truck was out of the bushes and some of the leaves and bark had blown away, it didn't look quite as bad as I had remembered. I couldn't see any dents or any really bad rust spots. I began to get interested and tentatively raised the hood to get a look at the engine. The straight-six cylinder engine actually looked clean. I was really surprised to see that everything appeared to be in place. Getting very interested now, I checked the oil and found it was full and clean, so I decided to add some water to the radiator and see if she had any leaks. Once satisfied that the radiator was holding water, I got the battery charger hooked up. *Might as well go all the way,* I thought to myself.

One hour later my battery charger was reading in the green "trickle charge" zone so I got into the driver's seat and turned the key. The engine came to life without any hesitation. All of the gauges were reading normal and the old six-cylinder engine remained running at a smooth idle, actually sounding better than my own pickup.

Maybe this rig wasn't quite ready for the junkyard after all. I unhooked the battery charger and got in to take her for a little drive. Everything worked fine except for the brakes. No unusual sounds were coming from the gears or from the engine. The four-wheel drive transfer-case worked perfectly in both low and high range, as did the locking hubs. Into it now, I went to work on the brakes. Four hours later after one short run to the auto parts store, the brakes were working just fine. At the auto parts store Gilbert, the store owner, and I had placed the year model of this truck to be a 1955 vintage. I was beginning to like this old truck. Maybe I had a new wood-hauling rig.

The old green International proved to be a great wood truck. It could climb any hill and ran off road as well as it did on solid footing. The suspension was very heavy and it was almost impossible for me to overload the narrow eight-foot bed. My neighbor and wood cutting buddy Ken was really impressed with the loads of firewood that I managed to bring home during that fall wood cutting season.

Winter came and the old truck found a home parked between the small dump truck and the big twenty-foot, long-bed hay truck. Things around my farm usually get a name of some kind and this truck was no exception. We began referring to the International as Old Green.

My two girls spend most of the year in California but would come to visit us in the summer. They are getting so big. My oldest, Felicia, was fourteen this year and Aimee will be twelve in July. Our other two kids, Jimmy, eight, and Crissy, twelve, live with us all year long. All four kids get along just fine with only a minor amount of turmoil as you might expect with that many children living under the same roof.

As the summer days got longer and hotter, our kids began hanging around the farm a bit more than usual. Their favorite swimming hole was only about one-half mile away, but a hot summer day in North Idaho can often make distances seem much longer. Horseback riding was out of the question, the archery equipment remained hanging on the rack near the back door, and nobody seemed very interested in going for a hike. As the group activity director, I woke up one morning with a great idea.

"Felicia, how would you like to learn how to drive?"

"Drive?"

"Sure, Honey, I'd like to teach you how to drive a car."

All of the kids were suddenly interested in this exciting possibility. The five of us walked outside and the kids followed me as I headed toward Old Green.

"This isn't a car, Dad, it's a truck," said Felicia.

"True enough, but trucks and cars all work the same. When you learn how to drive one you can drive the other. Do you want to learn how?"

I loaded all of the kids into the old truck and began driving toward my shop. My glance fell on Felicia and I noticed how her eyes were spending a lot of time looking at the various pedals, gauges, and levers. She may have even noticed the steering wheel for the first time. At the shop I tossed four old tires into the back of the truck and headed into the big front field.

I stopped four times in the field, dropping off a tire at each stop. On my last stop, it was time to start the lesson. "All of you kids will have to go to the fence and watch; I'll be there in a minute."

I turned off the engine, placed the four-wheel-drive transfer case into low range, and then shifted the transmission into second. I stepped out of the truck.

"OK, Felicia, slide over here under the wheel." I pointed through the window. "That pedal on the left is the clutch; you have to hold it down with your foot when you turn the key and start the truck. Once the truck is started you push your other foot down on that small pedal; that's the gas. Now you let the clutch pedal up slowly and the truck will begin to move. If you let it up too fast, the truck will die, and you'll have to start over again. Now, what I would like you to do is start the truck, and drive around the tires. See you later."

"Dad, wait, what about the other pedal and the other levers?"

"Felicia, you can drive with the two pedals that I just showed you. I'll be by the fence."

"Dad, are you sure that I don't need to know anything else?"

"Oh yeah, try to turn the steering wheel before you drive through any of the fences. Have fun." I walked away and joined the kids at the fence.

We all waited. Soon the engine started. Then the engine revved. . . the truck made one tentative jump forward. . . the engine revved again. The truck made a leap forward and continued moving. . . the front wheels turned slightly to the right. . . then turned back straight. The wheels turned again and the truck began advancing toward one of the old tires. It rounded the first tire and began to seek out another.

I figured that second gear should hold her speed down to about five or six miles per hour. I smiled—my baby girl could drive.

"OK, kids, back to the house, we can watch from there."

Old Green bounced and weaved around the field, sometimes rounding a tire and sometimes not. Dust rolled from the wheel wells, and the engine revved with glee. A small head with light brown hair could sometimes be seen looking through the top spokes of the steering wheel. The siblings continued to watch with me for fifteen or twenty minutes, then found other interests. Old Green happily kicked up dust in circles that my eye noticed had started to become more uniform. I left my post thinking about her next lesson. After about an hour Felicia walked from the field and found me.

"Dad, I think I broke the truck."

"Why, Sweetie, what happened?"

"Well, it just stopped running, Dad."

"Did it make a noise or anything?"

"No, Dad, it just stopped going."

"Come on, Felicia, I'll fix it," I said cheerfully, already walking toward my shop. She followed.

"But Dad, how do you know what's wrong with it?"

"I think that I know," I said. "We'll see." At the shop I picked up a five gallon Jerry Can of gasoline normally used for the tractor. "This will probably solve your problem."

Gasoline now in the tank, the old green truck was back in action and continued making circles and raising dust for the remainder of the afternoon.

The next morning I walked with her into the field. "I think you're ready for another gear, Felicia." I got into the truck on the passenger side. "Go ahead and start her going." She did as I asked.

"Now push the clutch pedal to the floor." When she did that I shifted into third gear. "Give it gas, and let up on the clutch."

The truck leaped forward and my daughter was delighted.

"Let me try that, Dad."

"OK, slow down then push in the clutch and put it back into second gear, give it a try." She did it, "Now clutch back in, and back into third gear." She did.

"OK, now stop and let me out." I walked from the field laughing to myself. She now had a top speed of about ten or twelve miles per hour. I better show her how the brake pedal works before she finds forth gear on her own.

My daughter and Old Green raced around the field all morning. I listened to the tone of the engine as it revved and slowed between gears. Eventually both the girl and the truck ran out of gas just before noon. I filled up the gas tank while Felicia came in for lunch. She and I both returned to the field that afternoon, and I spent all of five minutes explaining the boring operation of the brake pedal. Once this was understood I felt that my usefulness as driving instructor had just about come to an end. Felicia continued driving around the field and I took the other kids to town for ice cream.

That evening we all sat on the front porch eating ice cream

cones. Felicia was dirt from head to toe, the wide smile never leaving her dirty face. I noticed that the old green truck was parked in the field within inches of the wire fence, just a short walk from the house, and a long way from the nearest tire. I believe she has it.

After breakfast the following day, I asked Felicia if she would drive the truck out of the field and bring it to the shop.

"You want me to drive it there by myself, Dad?"

"Sure, Honey, it's just like driving in the field. All you'll need to do is steer it through the gate. I want to fill the truck up with gas, and I'm getting tired of carrying the cans all the way out to the field."

I hid out in the shop doing my very best not to peek around the corner of the building, as I listened to the careful progress that the truck was making as it approached my shop. When I heard the engine shut off I emerged from the shop carrying a can of gasoline. Felicia was still sitting behind the wheel smiling at me.

I put the five gallons of gas into the truck and then called to Felicia who had wandered off.

"Come on over here, I'll show you where the reverse gear is so that you can back away from the shop." Felicia backed up smoothly, stopped, then found a forward gear and returned to the field.

Circles in the field were now often stopped, and the truck would go backward for ten or twenty feet, then it would stop, pause, and then resume the dusty forward circles around the tires in the field. Once I had to laugh as I watched Felicia back the truck around all four of the tires. The truck engine would always rev as it raced from tire to tire, not unlike our 4-H barrel racing.

We had lunch and the whole gang was sitting in the front yard.

"Why don't you guys go down to the creek for a swim?" I asked.

"Na, it's too hot to go swimming, Dad," said Jimmy.

"Well, maybe Felicia will drive you to the creek," I responded, trying my best not to smile.

"Will ya, Felicia," begged Jimmy.

Crissy and Aimee were already up and running for their swim suits and towels.

"Dad, I don't know how to drive on the road," said Felicia.

"Listen, Honey, it's just as easy as driving in the field. If you see a car coming from the front or behind you, just stop. Don't pull over to the side of the road or anything, just stop, and they will go around you. The people that drive on these roads are all our friends, and they'll recognize Old Green."

"OK, I'll try it."

"If you have a problem, Honey, just leave the truck and walk back, you know it's not far."

The kids loaded up into Old Green with Felicia firmly planted behind the steering wheel.

My wife looked at me in disbelief. "You aren't really going to let her do it, are you? Surely you're going to go after them!"

"No, I'm not going after them. Felicia has been driving in the field for two days and hasn't even hit a fence. I think she can make the one-half mile trip to Grouse Creek and back without a problem. This will probably be the safest trip to the swimming hole that those kids ever have," I laughed.

Old Green started and cautiously drove down the center of my driveway, then stopped at the end and turned left on the county road. I watched Felicia make the next left turn on Grouse Creek Road, then continued watching her progress until she was out of sight. The creek was only about one-quarter of a mile farther but I knew it would take at least five more minutes for them to reach it at her current rate of speed.

About two hours later, the old green truck came into view on Grouse Creek Road. It stopped at the corner, then made a right turn onto the county road and then slowed for a gradual right turn into our driveway. Four smiling, wet children emerged from the old green truck. Jimmy was clamoring for an ice cream cone and asking if Felicia could drive them to town.

John

You just had to understand John; the man who invented night motorcycle polo on the golf course. Yes, this was the same John who set fire to the wooden stool in the machine shop as his friend Admiral, while seated on that stool, dialed in his finish cut on the lathe. To say that John enjoyed a practical joke was like noticing that rain water is wet.

One day John found a huge dildo and brought it home. After spending some time looking for a good way to spring this wonderful treasure on his wife, John decided to hang the object from a string that turned on the light in their master bedroom closet. It took several hours before his wife, Mickey, found a reason to turn on the closet light. She produced a satisfactory scream to John's delight.

Mickey should have known better than to try for retribution, but she did her best. Several days later Mickey sent John off to work with the dildo resting quietly in his lunch box. It was hidden just below the two foil-wrapped tuna sandwiches. John came home from work that day and said nonchalantly that he had lost his lunch box. He went into great detail, explaining how he left the lunch container on top of his car when he first arrived at work. It was first break when he got hungry and realized where he had misplaced it, but some *bastard* had stolen his lunch box from the parking lot. He was forced to eat from the catering truck that day. John went on to ask Mickey to buy him a new lunch box and thermos. He carried a brown-bag lunch for several days and went without coffee until a new lunch box and thermos were purchased.

It was almost six months later when Mickey discovered how devious her husband could be. At the beginning of her weekly art class she opened her art-supply box. Yes, the dildo reappeared to yet another red-faced scream as Mickey slammed down the lid of her supply box. She attempted to regain her composure as she looked around at the surprised faces of her classmates. It was very embarrassing for Mickey as she tried to convey the reason for her sudden alarm. When she explained herself the classmates did comprehend the mean joke, but it was impossible for Mickey to explain John.

I sat at my cluttered office desk and looked once again at the short note written in John's familiar scrawl.

> Please pick-up an extra case of Coors.
> I don't plan to drink any of your
> North Idaho home-brew crap.
>
> J

No telling when he would get here—today, tomorrow, next week? I knew that this note was all the warning I would get. Actually I was kind of surprised that he gave me any advance notice at all. As young men, John and I had been roommates for more than a year, and have been best friends for another fifteen years since that time. I wouldn't say that I understood John, but I was sure looking forward to seeing him.

I looked away from John's note, now paper-clipped to the desk calendar, and once more focused my attention on the legal documents piled in front of me. I re-read the real estate contract yet one more time and still couldn't fully understand what this hodgepodge of words was attempting to convey. Lawyer talk, damn, why couldn't they simply write in English?

This is a nice little real estate office. My coworkers are all friends and we enjoy the business. I glanced across the aisle at Darlene, a top sales agent. Maybe she would help interpret this gibberish. The ringing desk phone changed my direction.

"Hello, this is Howard."

"Howard," said Karen, the office secretary, "there is a man from the IRS in the front lobby. He has asked to see you."

"Thank you, Karen. I'll be right up." I was already reaching for my jacket that hung from the clothes tree near my desk. It had to be John.

The real estate office reception lobby was nicely decorated with one small couch and two comfortable armchairs. Our secretary was seated at her desk, which occupied one corner of the same room. Karen appeared to be very busy with paperwork, but glanced up and gave me what's-up look as I entered the room.

John was sitting comely in one of the armchairs. He was wearing a conservative brown sports coat, brown slacks and a matching tie. A leather briefcase rested across his knees and his face maintained a serious IRS-type composure.

He stood as I extended my hand, and ignoring the handshake, pulled me into a bone crushing bear-hug embrace.

"Hi, Brother."

"Hi yourself John; damn, it's been a long time! Let's get out of here," I said, starting for the door. "Karen, please take messages for me. I won't be back today."

Karen looked at the two of us and nodded without speaking. Obviously she had never seen one of her coworkers hugged by an IRS man before.

It had been raining earlier, but now the street was semi-dry as I angled John across the two lanes of Second Avenue, heading toward the nearest bar.

Sandpoint, Idaho, is a great place to live. The downtown section has evolved into a pleasant mix of businesses that cater to the local residents and an ever-growing tourist trade. Storefront windows are always decked out with eye-catching displays and colorful signs offering encouragement for shoppers. Restaurants and bars are numerous. Most of them sell good food at reasonable prices. The bar I was headed for at the moment was called Wheelers. It is technically a restaurant, combination deli and beer-wine bar. Some of my friends claim it's kind of "yuppie," but I could never see that and it is definitely one of my lunch time favorites.

"Hi, Bob, two Coors," I said to the proprietor as John and I adjusted the tall bar stools into preferred positions. Two frosty bottles appeared immediately and Bob retreated out of sight without asking for payment. John lifted his beer and tapped it to mine, then took a long swallow as his eyes explored the local adornments. I hoisted my own beer and said, "Great to see you, John. What's up with the tie?"

"Oh, my company is doing some work for an outfit in Spokane. I had a meeting with them this morning and managed to turn the business trip into a visit."

"How long can you stay?" I asked.

"Got a flight out Saturday afternoon. Do you think this little town has enough beer to hold me for three days?" John asked, smiling at me over his now empty bottle.

"We'll see," I answered, laughing. "Bob, another round," I called toward the back room.

"So," John said. "When I was on that long plane ride I thought up a great gag."

I gave John my attention, not speaking.

"Picture this. You and your wife go into a grocery store. You get a shopping cart and load it up with a couple of cases of beer, a bottle or two of bourbon, a couple bottles of gin, maybe some vodka and three or four bottles of wine. Now as you head for the register you toss in a big box of Pampers."

I sat smiling as I envisioned this purchase.

"OK," continued John, "once the checker has totaled up your bill, you pull out your wallet and look inside. Then you say to the checker, damn, that's more money than I have with me. You look perplexed at your wife for a second; then tell the checker to take back the Pampers. Try not to smile when you get the dirty look.... "What do you think?"

"Perfect, John, but I can't do it in this town. They know I don't drink gin."

We both laughed, and then fell into pleasant conversation as friends will do when catching up. After a couple more beers, I called Bob over to settle up and also asked him to give me two six-packs to go. I paid up and hefted my purchase from the bar-top. John and I walked from the bar into the bright mid-afternoon sun.

"Where's your car, John?"

"It's the red one over there," said John, pointing toward a Ford sedan parked on the far side of the street.

"I'll drive," I said, walking to the driver's side of the car.

John got into the passenger seat, pushed a key into the ignition and reached for a beer from my package. He opened one beer and handed it to me, then got one for himself and nestled back into the leather upholstery.

"Let's go!"

I took a quick sip from the open beer, then placed the can between my legs and pulled away from the curb. My home is exactly fourteen miles from town. The route consists of one mile on Highway 200, a left turn onto Highway 95 for nine miles, then a right on the south end of Farm to Market Road for three and one half miles, then a left on Samuel's Road for the last half mile. The highways are both interstates, Farm to Market Road is a good paved secondary road, and the last one, Samuel's Road, is a well kept county gravel road.

I began the drive in my usual way along Highway 200 and then intentionally failed to make the left turn on Highway 95, taking a sip from my beer as we drove through the junction. I had decided not to take my normal route home and was pondering a slightly longer, more interesting route. John was looking at the passing scenery, which was all new to him, and I made a gentle left turn onto a rural, unnamed, unpaved road that continued for about five miles.

Pop. . . another cold beer touched my arm.

"Isn't it beautiful out here, John?"

"Yeah, like a lot of nothin'. How far out do you live?"

"Oh, it's not real far," I said, noting that the sun was setting and rain was beginning to fall as I made a right turn onto Upper Grouse Creek Road. By now we are way the heck out of our way and going farther out of the way by the minute.

Pop. . . the road was getting rougher and the water-filled potholes were getting deeper. Water and mud splashed up on the windshield as we continued upward for another ten or twelve miles. The road climbed steadily, with a lot of switchbacks thrown in. Snow was beginning to appear at the roadside.

"Nice drive," from John. "Damn, is that snow on the side of the road?"

"Yeah, it'll be gone in a week or so if the rain keeps up."

We were now driving in what could be described as a muddy slush. The car was slipping and sliding through every turn and the front window was completely brown except for the two clean arcs left by the wipers. At the summit the road leveled out for about one half mile, and then we began to drive downhill on what was locally called Lower Grouse Creek Road. We were currently about fifteen miles from my house, but I didn't share this bit of information with John. The woods made the road look like a tunnel. It was now very dark.

"How's your beer?" asked John. . . *Pop*.

"I'm ready, thanks."

The rain stopped when we got about half way down the hill, but all the potholes were full of water that continued splashing over the hood. I did not turn off the wipers, and was constantly pushing the spray button to keep our windshield semi-clean. John had been pretty quiet for the past fifteen minutes, and I glanced over to make sure that he hadn't fallen asleep.

"Almost there," I said, "just another mile or two."

At the end of the road was a T-intersection. I made a right turn, then a quick left, then another right turn. We traveled one more short block and then made a right turn passing through an opening in the fence which was my driveway. I pulled to a stop in front of the house and turned off the ignition.

"We're here!"

John opened his door to step out; then pulled his leg back quickly as my dog Max growled his greeting.

"Max, it's OK!" I yelled from my side of the car. "Don't worry, John, he just growls but won't bite." I chuckled as Max came to my side of the car and stuck his head in as the door opened.

"It's black as hell out here; I can't see anything," said John.

"Hold on a second," I said, walking past him and opening the front door for some light. "OK you can see now, come on in and meet the family. I'll show you around in the morning," I had been married for over a year but John had not met my wife Susie or her kids, Jimmy now seven and Crissy who would soon be twelve.

We settled down for a great evening meal and John got a chance to entertain a new audience. He was a big hit with the kids and managed to keep Susie red faced with laughter. The following morning I handed John a cup of coffee and we wandered outside for a brief tour of the property as the smells of breakfast were beginning to drift from Susie's kitchen.

"You picked a good day to come, John."

"Yeah, why is that?"

"Well, today is auction day at Bonners Ferry. We never miss the auction it's a blast." By the time we got back from our walk Susie had breakfast ready. We sat down to a full-blown country spread with fresh eggs, fresh home grown sausage, homemade biscuits, garden supplied preserves, fresh squeezed orange juice, and more strong hot coffee. The kids jumped up from the table to help with the dishes in order to get ready for the auction.

I cannot begin to tell you how much fun the flea-market auction is. They sell everything a person could possibly imagine. The minimum bid is fifty cents, and the bidding goes fast. The long-time auctioneer makes sure that everything sells. He will auction off a complete box rather than individual items if he thinks that some of the things in the box may not warrant a bid. At times the auctioneer will group two or three boxes for bid, knowing that there is really only one item that is worthwhile. You can be sure that at the end of the auction everything will be sold and the shelves will be clear.

As the bidding started, John got right into the swing of things and was soon the proud owner of an old single-stitch Singer sewing machine. Don't ask! Shortly after that, John bid again, winning a worn, brown, leather doctor's bag, which he said would be perfect for holding his new sewing machine.

At the end of the flea-market auction our group took a seat in the livestock auction and watched several lots of horses pass through the bidding process. All of us were getting pretty hungry by now so we stopped for lunch at a small sandwich shop on the outskirts of Bonners Ferry and then returned to my house in the mid-afternoon.

John and I kicked around my little work shop and had a few beers as we caught up on old times. I started a fire in my shop-stove and even though it was summer time the heat it produced felt pretty good. As the sun went down we both found ourselves standing closer to the hot stove. Susie was soon calling us for dinner so we headed to the house for yet another round of good home cooking. After dinner we moved into the living room and I think that John was very surprised when we found both of the children engaged in preparing a fire in the wood stove.

"That's one of their chores," I said, following his gaze. "The kids make a fire every morning and each evening. My job is to make sure there's plenty of wood in the shed. They take it from there."

This evening it was all about John. I played straight man as John delighted my family with his stories. Susie and the kids were hearing most of these stories for the first time, though many of them were very familiar to me. The evening passed quickly and soon both Jimmy and Crissy were fading. Susie, John, and I stayed up for another hour and then called it a day.

We all woke early the following day and I suggested a drive to Hope, Idaho, which was about fifteen miles east of us. We spent a nice day sightseeing and feeding the deer that were not exactly pets, but would practically eat out of your hand. By the time we got home it was almost dark again. This evening was a bit more normal with the kids sprawled in front of the TV and the adults talking quietly at the kitchen table.

Saturday morning I showered and came into the kitchen to find John helping Susie with something at the stove. I poured myself a cup of coffee and sat down between the two children on the couch. John's travel bag and new/old brown doctor's bag were by the front door.

"You packed already, John?" I called into the kitchen.

"Well, yeah. I have to get going pretty soon."

"What time is your plane?" I asked.

"It leaves at one thirty."

"Well, you have plenty of time. It's only eight o'clock."

"Are you sure? I was thinking it would take about four hours to get from here to Spokane."

"It'll be OK," I said. "I know a shortcut. You have plenty of time for breakfast."

We sat down to another one of Susie's trucker-special breakfasts. I was amused to catch John checking his watch a couple of times, but to his credit he didn't say anything.

After breakfast John said his goodbyes to Susie and the children as he got down to business, packing the muddy Ford. I stood close by and watched the kids begin a familiar game of keep-away from Max with the Frisbee. I had seen this game played many times before. Max would usually let the kids throw the Frisbee for about two minutes before snatching it away from one of them and ending the game for the day. I laughed as Max made an unbelievable leap and grabbed the Frisbee out of the air.

"Game over!" I yelled. Then I turned to my friend John. "Damn, it was sure good to see you." I watched John as he smiled back, but he didn't start the car. Then as an afterthought I said, "John, it was kind of tricky getting here. Do you think you can find your way back to town?"

"I can find my way back," he answered quietly.

I had him.

"Would you like me to go with you? My car is still in town, anyway."

"Well, sure, I can put up with you for a couple more hours."

"Susie, I'm going to run into town with John," I said as I moved around to the passenger side.

"Have fun," she answered back, smiling.

John eased the Ford down my driveway and made a left onto Samuel's Road. At the first corner he looked over at me and said, "Left here?"

"No, you can go straight, John," I said smiling to myself.

As he approached the next corner he asked, "Left?"

"No, take a right. I thought you knew how to get back to town."

Fifteen minutes later we were parked in front of my office in downtown Sandpoint.

"You bastard," John said, looking across the seat at me.

"What do you mean? I asked innocently. "I told you I knew a shortcut,"

"Hey John It's only nine thirty; and about a one hour drive to Spokane.

Wheelers is open, want a beer?"

Dead Rabbit

Kids are just naturally inquisitive and the questions they come up with can often amuse or completely take you by surprise. My youngest, Jimmy, is usually quiet in school but once he gets home he is absolutely full of questions; especially when it comes to his favorite subject, hunting. Jimmy loves the very thought of hunting and simply has to know everything to do with tracking, scouting, or the use of hunting equipment. I can't remember the last time that he wore anything but his favorite camo hunting pants while playing and I am beginning to worry that they may begin walking on their own.

When my friends come to visit, Jimmy will often sit quietly and listen as the men talk about deer, elk, or bird hunting. The conversation sometimes involves decoys, calls, guns, bow preferences or new equipment.

I enjoy a bit of exercise every day, but resist jogging, pushups or weight lifting. I prefer to keep in shape by shooting a few arrows every morning. I began my morning routine as usual today by quietly getting into my clothes, lifting the compound bow and belt-quiver of arrows off of the wooden peg in the hall and gently opening the back door. I was very quiet but, Jimmy still heard me. "Dad," he called from his bed, "can I come?"

"Sure, come on," I answered, stepping onto the porch. I started a slow walk across the yard.

Jimmy busted through the back door, shirt halfway on, and pants halfway up, with boots in one hand and his small tan-colored recurve bow in the other. Looking back I couldn't help smiling as he sat on the porch step and proceeded to pull on his tall boots, not bothering with the laces. He stuffed the corners of his shirt into the still open pants as he ran to my side.

"Morning, Son," I said ruffling his short blond hair. "Did I wake you up?"

"Nah, I just wanted to shoot with you this morning," he answered.

I had set aside this upper section of my property for a walking archery range. It is about seven acres of hilly ground that could be farmed, but I always felt that it was just too pretty. There is a big grove of birch trees that runs the full length on one side of this acreage and several large pines are scattered randomly across the hill. The views of our valley from this high spot are wonderful. During the winter we can walk up here in the evenings and on occasion will see the Northern Lights. Most of the ground is covered with a heavy, thick leafy bush that some of the neighbors call Salal Brush, but I have never confirmed that local name.

Jimmy and I are walking on a narrow path that will meander through the brush connecting six covered hay-bale target-butts. As we walk this path he and I will shoot at the individual targets. Some of the targets come into view at a range well over one hundred yards but we never shoot that far. Each target can provide a shot that is long and difficult or can be made quite easy by simply walking closer and selecting a better spot to shoot from.

In the early morning we often find deer on the target range. Jimmy will reach over and touch my leg to let me know that he has spotted them. The deer always run off as we approach, but we know that these local deer aren't really afraid of us target-plunkers. Target shooting on a walking range is very good hunting practice, and as I said, Jimmy likes everything that relates to hunting.

Jimmy and I walk side by side up the hill until I stop to knock an arrow for my first target. I take carful aim and shoot. Now we walk closer to the target. Jimmy is choosing a spot that he feels is in his shooting range. It is my turn to watch and wait quietly. I stand slightly behind Jimmy as he makes his first shot. Now we move to the hay bale and retrieve our arrows. This will be our normal routine as we continue around the seven acres for our morning shoot.

Jimmy knows that I will let him shoot at the targets from any distance that he chooses, but he also knows that he is only carrying one arrow. If he lost that single arrow by completely missing a hay bale, he is probably finished shooting for this morning. I taught first my girls and then Jimmy to shoot this way. When they first began shooting, I handed each of the kid's one arrow, then placed them directly in front of a target bale. I ask them to shoot from there knowing that they wouldn't completely miss the bale. Once they were confident that they could hit the hay bale every time, they would move back on their own, making the shot more difficult. Occasionally the kids shot from too far back and did miss the target completely. They would usually move closer for their next shot. I never pressed the kids to hit the bull's eye, but hitting the hay bale almost every time helped them build confidence, and they also spent a lot more time shooting and a lot less time searching for lost arrows. The kids each learned that one arrow was enough if you didn't miss.

At the last target I stood to one side and watched as Jimmy came to a full draw. I noticed his concentration as he held on the target for a long second, and then smoothly released the string. The small silver arrow arced into the bale hitting the red plastic coffee can lid that we used for the bulls eye. His arrow landed just inches from my own. The boy was getting pretty good. Jimmy was six years old.

That evening at the dinner table we were almost finished eating when Jimmy asked, "Dad, how do you make a *dead rabbit call*?" Jimmy had been hanging around my shop, listening as a friend and I talked about coyote hunting the week before. I knew that he really meant "wounded rabbit call" which was a common call used by predator hunters, but I just couldn't pass up this opportunity to mess with him.

"Well," I said, shifting slightly back in my chair and looking at him seriously, "put your right hand across your mouth and press the palm down hard on your lips." I motioned with my own hand, and watched as Jimmy carefully positioned his right hand over his mouth.

"OK, now place your left hand over your right hand and press it down real hard." He followed my instructions and covered the right hand with his left.

"Now talk," I said. Jimmy struggled with this predicament for a minute, his face getting red from the effort.

"**I can't**," he finally said, in a rush, as he removed both hands.

"That's right," I smiled. "Dead rabbits can't make any noise either."

For years afterward when Jimmy was getting a bit too chirpy, I would look at him and simply say, "Dead rabbit." Both of his hands would come across his mouth and his eyes would smile back at me. The boy really got that Dead Rabbit call down.

Hauling Old Junk Around Town

*A*fter two continuous weeks of rain, I was happy as I looked out of my bedroom window to see stars shining down from a clear morning sky.

I had promised to help my friend, Jay, with the task of moving an old Chrysler station wagon from its current storage location. This old car had come into his possession over five years ago. Jay had plans to restore the car into a thing of beauty, but this restoration project was not quite at the top of his priority list. The wagon has been peacefully parked all this time at the home of Jay's friends Larry and Margaret. Jay had once rented a room from them in Renton, Washington. The small garage behind their house was never used and became a handy storage spot for the car, but now the house was up for sale and the old station wagon simply had to go.

This was not my first attempt at towing a car. I knew that these jobs seldom went one hundred percent smoothly. The key was to bring plenty of tools, just in case. Another good idea would be to plan on getting dirty, as the need for crawling under the vehicle was always a possibility. The tools were already neatly arranged in the bed of my Jeep Wagoneer. This tool assortment included special items like extra chains, bale twine, come-along, high-lift and a bottle jack, and a long crow bar. There was also a large box of mechanic tools.

I began to get dressed with the second part of this scenario in mind. My Levi's are stored in descending order from the best, near new pants stacked near the top of the pile, to the worst, paint splattered, torn pairs that tend to migrate towards the bottom of the stack in my closet. Grabbing a pair from the bottom of the heap, I pulled them on and then found a patched, paint spotted work shirt that would be just fine for this dirty job. Sitting on the side of the bed, I laced up my tall work boots, and then shoved a red bandanna into my back pocket. I was dressed and ready to go. Coffee was already made, thanks to the auto timer. I poured a cup, and then emptied the remainder of the pot into a big stainless steel thermos. Glowing green numbers on the stove clock flipped from 4:59 to 5:00 as I turned off the kitchen light and walked out of the back door leading into the garage.

Once in the garage, I made a quick survey of the semi-cluttered workbench and open toolboxes, looking for anything else that we might need for our job today. *Nope, I think we have enough.* Opening the side garage door, a cold morning breeze found its way under the collar of my Levi's jacket. I shrugged deeper into my coat. This was a reminder that winter was getting pretty close; today was November second.

As I went into autopilot on the five-mile drive to Renton, I thought about my friend Jay. My parents and his were friends. Our families joined in a lot of outdoor activities; so we had been thrown together as kids. I was the oldest of the children with one brother and a younger sister. Jay is about five years younger than I am. He also had a younger brother and sister. All six kids were expected to "play nice" and enjoy whatever plans or activities the adults set in motion. Jay and I somehow managed to stay friends and shared experiences like first cars, first motorcycles, first beers, and several other firsts. We were comfortable with each other and had many years to know how well we worked together.

Wells Street in Renton is an old neighborhood. Streetlights are far apart, casting a faint orange glow on the houses, which are mostly dark. I spotted Jay's El Camino parked in front of the small white house that belonged to Larry and Margaret. Driving slowly past the house, I can make out a figure standing near the garage door at the back end of a long driveway. I began backing down the driveway with practiced ease, and stopped about ten feet short of the now open garage door.

"Coffee?" I asked as I stepped from my Jeep.

"Sure," said Jay, accepting the thermos. He removed the stainless steel cup and poured.

I peered into the dark garage and tried to sort out objects that seemed to blend together.

"We got any light in here? I can't see a damn thing."

Jay reached into his jacket and produced a small penlight. "This is it," he said, handing the light to me.

I pointed the light at the station wagon, and then bent down, shining the beam under the car looking for foreign objects or debris. Jay sipped at his coffee as I slowly walked around the car doing a quick inspection of all four tires.

"At least the tires are up. Let's pull her out and have a look."

Not waiting for a reply, I walked to the back of my rig and opened the rear tailgate. I removed a light tow chain and brought it over to the front of Jay's wagon. Jay found one end of the chain and began crawling under his station wagon. I picked up the remainder of the chain and began walking backward toward my car uncoiling the chain as I moved. Once at the back of my Jeep, I made up a loop in the chain and placed it over the trailer ball. Jay had already hooked his end of the chain to the wagon.

"You ready?" I asked.

"Ready," said Jay. "I'll shine the flashlight at you when I want you to start up, then again if I need you to stop."

"OK."

We headed in opposite directions for the two vehicles. I eased the Jeep forward until I felt a firm tug, then held down the foot brake and waited. A couple of seconds later Jay flipped on his flashlight. I began to drive slowly forward. The light went off and didn't come on again so I continued my progress up the driveway for several yards. The light blinked again so I stopped and cautiously eyed the wagon in my rearview mirror. It continued to roll for a couple of feet and then came to rest.

Jay was shining his flashlight around the back of the garage. He returned with two short pieces of two-by-four that he placed in front and behind the driver's side rear wheels of the wagon. I went to the front and unhooked the chain, first from the wagon, then from my Jeep. I opened the tailgate and dropped the chain into the back-end of my Jeep, and then began wrestling with the rented U-Haul tow-bar. Jay came to my side and lifted one end of the bar. We both sidestepped toward the wagon, and then laid the tow-bar on the ground directly under the front bumper. Jay began untangling the cinch chain on his end of the bar, while I did the same at my end.

"Ready?" I asked.

"OK," said Jay.

As he lifted his end of the bar I clipped on the top cinch chain. We then moved over and attached the other end as well. Jay and I worked together adjusting the bar and cinching it in place.

"Looks good to me," I said. "I'll get the Jeep." Swiveling in the driver's seat, I began backing up. I kept my eyes on Jay, watching for hand signals. He stopped me by closing his fist, then motioned back a couple of inches, and then stopped me again. I heard a familiar clank as Jay dropped the heavy hitch onto my trailer ball.

I opened the Jeep side door and removed the portable lights and electrical cable. I then grabbed a rag and wiped four circles of dust from the top of the wagon so that the suction cups would stick. Jay got busy hooking up the safety chains as I brought the wiring over the top of the wagon and plugged it into my trailer receptacle at the back of the Jeep.

"Want to help me check the lights?" I asked.

"All right," said Jay, already walking toward the back of the wagon.

I reached into the Jeep and pulled on the running lights.

"Taillights," said Jay.

I turned off the running lights, turned on the ignition switch, and dropped the turn indicator lever down.

"Left turn."

I raised the indicator all the way up.

"Right turn."

I walked back to the wagon carrying a ball of hay-bale twine. We both went to work tying the taillight wire to the wagon. Once finished, the ball of twine was returned to my Jeep.

"Where did you put the coffee?" I asked as I walked toward Jay with my empty cup.

I topped off my coffee cup. "Ready to roll, big guy?" I asked, smiling at Jay.

"Yeah, I'll walk along side for a while listening for rattles or rub noises."

"Good plan." I got into the Jeep and started slowly up the driveway, then made a wide right turn into the street. I drove slowly as Jay walked on one side of the wagon and then the other for about fifty yards. Once satisfied he came up on the passenger side of the Jeep and tapped the window. I stopped to let him in and then headed for the highway. Keeping a close eye on the rearview mirror I drove carefully for a couple of miles. The traffic was still very light which was always good just in case the unforeseen happened.

"Did you get a Trip Permit?" I asked.

"Yeah, I picked it up yesterday. Didn't you see it taped in the rear window?"

"Sorry, I should have known that we were legal," I said, smiling.

Jay laughed, "Aren't we always?"

After five or six miles I could see that this tow was going pretty good. I relaxed a little and glanced back at the old car.

"Damn, Jay, I sure hope we never get tired of hauling old junk like this around the countryside."

Jay swiveled and looked back at the wagon. "No, you just can't buy this kind of recreation."

"Are you still up for the trip to Idaho?" I asked.

"Sure, when do you want to go?"

"Well, the auto parts store called yesterday and told me that the starter motor has arrived. I should be able to get it back in the truck today and maybe do a little tune up tomorrow. How about next weekend? I'm thinking we should plan on three days to be on the safe side."

"We're pretty slow at work right now," Jay answered. "I can take off a day or so. Sure, next weekend will be fine. You know if we wait too long we could catch some bad weather."

"You're right, I would be happy to do this trip without any snow. I better bring along some tire chains though, just in case. Damn, speaking of cold, I hope I get a chance to fix the heater."

About seven years ago I had moved my family from Oroville, California, to Sandpoint, Idaho. To facilitate this move, I had purchased an old Chevrolet two and a half ton moving van. Once in Idaho, I removed the van box and converted the truck into a twenty-foot flatbed. This truck then served as a farm truck, hauling hay, wood, and farm equipment. When I moved our family from Idaho to Washington last month, I used the same truck for this second household move. Now the plan was to return to Sandpoint with the big truck and pick up the last miscellaneous items that were left behind. The main thing that we were after was an old 1950 Chevy dump truck that actually belonged to Jay.

My old farm truck was basically sound. It had a big block 400-inch engine and two 50-gallon side fuel tanks. The main problem with the truck was that it had a fickle starter motor, which I was planning to replace. The heater core was shot, and I wanted to get it repaired or replaced, but when messing with these older vehicles, parts are almost nonexistent, so I was hoping that the weather wouldn't get too cold on our trip.

Once the station wagon was deposited at its new home, I brought Jay back to Renton, then swung by the U-haul rental store and returned the tow-bar. My next stop was at the auto parts store to pick up my new starter motor. I decided to buy a set of plugs and points as well because I couldn't remember when the truck had its last tune up.

I installed the new starter later that afternoon and was satisfied that it was working properly. It took about one hour to finish the job and I crawled out from under the big truck just in time to wash up for dinner.

Sunday morning found me back to work on the old truck, installing plugs and new points. Then kid projects and honey-do's took care of Sunday afternoon so the heater core remained on my maybe-later list.

The following Saturday morning Jay arrived at my house early. He has a small overnight bag, a warm looking red plaid hunting coat, and a big coffee thermos.

My gear is already packed behind the truck seat, including a well-stocked toolbox. I have a big wooden packing crate lashed down on the forward end of the flatbed which is holding chains, chain binders, miscellaneous tie downs, a come-along, wheel chalks, and a couple of crow bars. The truck is gassed up and I figure that even if we get poor mileage it should make the three-hundred-mile trip to Idaho without needing a fill up. I had never driven the truck very far without a load, and do not have any idea of what kind of gas mileage we can expect, but I guess we will find out.

I smiled as Jay took possession of the passenger side. It really didn't matter which one of us started the drive because both of us would get ample opportunity for wheel time. Pulling away from the curb, the big block engine snapped through the gears, easily pulling the empty truck.

About fifteen miles into our trip I was climbing a steep grade on the south side of Tiger Mountain when the engine began missing badly. Within a couple of hundred yards our speed dropped from around sixty-five to forty and I was wishing for a turnout.

"There!" shouted Jay.

Pulling into the turnout, I eased to a stop without killing the engine. Jay was already out and opening the hood as I rounded my side of the truck. It only took about one minute for us to assess the cause of the engine-miss. One spark plug had blown out of its hole and was dangling by a plug wire. I shut off the engine and pulled my work gloves out of the toolbox.

Expecting the worst, my guess was that the plug had blown out of the engine block threads and all. This would mean the end of our trip. Once I had hand threaded the plug back into the hole, Jay handed me a plug wrench. I slowly began tightening the plug and was surprised to find that the plug actually did tighten up in the hole. This could only mean one thing. I had somehow forgotten to tighten this particular plug while doing the tune-up last weekend. In order to avoid any further surprises I checked the torque on all of the other plugs. None of the remaining seven were loose.

"I'll drive," said Jay, rounding the driver side of the truck while I replaced the plug wrench and work gloves into the toolbox.

"OK," I said, making myself comfortable on the passenger side as Jay pulled out into the roadway. I reached for the big thermos and began pouring. "Like some coffee?"

"Not right now, thanks."

We drove along quietly for several miles. I was just listening to the big block engine purr. *How the hell could I have missed tightening that plug?* I asked myself silently.

We were now driving on highway 90 and are about half the way up to the summit elevation of 3022 feet on Snoqualmie Pass. The temperature is dropping steadily with each mile we ascended.

"How did you do with the heater?" Jay asked.

"Got it covered," I said, reaching behind the seat. I brought out a ten-inch radiant camp-heater attached to a one-quart propane bottle and proudly displayed it to Jay. "I'll have us warmed up in a couple of minutes."

"Well, then fire that rascal up, my fingers are freezing to the wheel."

I patted my pockets, then opened the glove compartment and dug around. "Jay, do you have any matches?"

Jay's hand went to his own shirt pocket as a reflex action from an ex-smoker. "No, I don't think so."

I didn't give up that easily. I was crawling up under the dash poking around.

"What the hell are you doing now?" Jay wanted to know.

Still reaching around under the dash, I answered. "The cigarette lighter doesn't work, but if I can just unhook this wire on the back of the lighter, I think that I can arc it against the heater and make a spark."

"Got it," I said, crawling out from under the dash holding the bare wire that I had removed from the cigarette lighter.

Jay watched in disbelief as I held the heater, grounded against the dash, then turned on the gas valve, and attempted to arc the bare wire on the metal screen heating element. *Whoosh,* the heater came to life. *I almost dropped the damn thing.* Once lit, the flame quickly died down and the sound became a gentle hiss. Our truck cab started warming up instantly.

Within about five miles, we both had our wind wings wide open and side windows rolled down a couple of inches.

"Can you turn that thing down a bit, H?" Jay complained.

"It's down as far as it can go without turning it completely off," I replied.

"Well, then turn it off for a while," Jay said as he unbuttoned his heavy wool hunting coat.

I did. Ten minutes later I was back to arcing the wire again. Climate control is becoming somewhat of a problem. We are nearing the summit and I am about to re-ignite the heater when Jay shouted, "WHAT THE HELL!"

I turned my attention away from the heater to see what Jay is hollering about and see that smoke rising from the dashboard. It seems to be coming from somewhere inside of the dash. The gauges are so cloudy that I can hardly make out the speedometer.

"PULL OVER!"

Jay wheeled into the wide shoulder lane and shut off the ignition. The transmission is still in gear but the truck wouldn't quite stop. We kept sort of bucking along. I thought the engine was still running.

"Push in the clutch," I said.

Once Jay pushed in the clutch pedal, we could hear the distinct sound of the starter motor whining. It had somehow become engaged. I reached behind the seat for some tools and got out of the truck.

"I'm going to disconnect the battery," I said. "Hold it as best you can." Once the battery cable was disconnected, all became silent and the smoke drifted away. I crawled under to have a look.

"Well, H, what do you think?"

"We have some badly burnt wires under there. I'm going to disconnect the starter motor cable and then see if we still have any ignition when I hook the battery cable back up."

"OK, but how will we get it started without a starter motor?" Jay asked.

I looked at the road behind us and smiled. "We're on a hill. She should bump start."

Disconnecting the starter motor cable was pretty easy. While I was under the truck, I could see a mass of melted wires just above the starter. I didn't have any idea how much damage had been done just by looking. I reattached the cable to the battery and cautiously waited for more smoke. When nothing happened, I asked Jay to turn on the ignition switch and look for activity on the gauges.

"Yeah, the temp gauge and oil gauge are both moving."

"OK, I'll drive. Let's see if I can remember how to do this."

I turned on the ignition switch, put the gearshift into reverse, pushed in the clutch and eased off of the brake pedal. The truck began rolling backward along the shoulder.

"Now!" shouted Jay.

I popped the clutch and the engine immediately came to life. I pushed in the clutch and stomped on the brake pedal, stopping our backward descent. I set the emergency brake and let the engine idle for a couple of minutes, studying the gauges. Everything seemed normal. Then I put the truck in gear and slowly released the emergency brake as I eased up the clutch pedal. We are back in traffic.

The first opportunity to get off of the freeway was approaching.

"Well, Jay, what do you think, Idaho or back to Renton?"

"It's only about fifty miles back to Renton, H, but we are pointed towards Idaho. That's where I would prefer to go."

We had crested the summit when Jay said, "So, do you plan to find us a hill each time we stop?"

"No, I was thinking more along the lines of not turning off the engine."

"For the whole weekend?" Jay asked.

"Well, maybe we can have a look at the damage this afternoon when we get to Al's house. At least he'll have some kind of rig at his place that can give us a tow. Do you want to take a swing at lighting that heater?"

"Hell, no, I'm not messing with that wire. There's a quick-stop at the next off ramp. They'll have matches."

I smiled to myself. Jay hated just about anything that had to do with electricity.

I waited in the running truck while Jay went in for matches. He returned a couple of minutes later carrying a big brown bag.

"Did you buy all the matches they had?" I asked laughing as I eased the truck into gear.

"Nope, just a couple of butane lighters, oh, and this," he said, pressing a cold beer against the side of my hand.

"Jay, you are just about the best copilot I've ever had."

The miles melted away. We stopped once for burgers, and then once again for a nature call. The old truck was running pretty good and very soon we were leaving the State of Washington and turning off of the interstate, heading northeast toward my old neighborhood, Sandpoint, Idaho.

We found my buddy, Al, working on a big pile of cordwood as we drove up his driveway and rounded the house. Al looked up and gave us a welcoming nod, not taking his eye completely off of the chainsaw. I positioned the truck for an easy exit, just in case we would need to be towed.

I left the truck running and set the hand brake. We had three beers left in the cab, and Jay remembered to grab them as he stepped out of the truck.

"Hi, Al, glad to see that the bears haven't eaten you yet."

Al turned his serious look on me and said, "When it comes to bears, it's usually me that does the eating." Then he smiled and laughed his big laugh.

"Hell, you would probably be too hard to chew anyhow," I said. "Have you got another saw? We'll help you finish up this little pile of wood."

Al accepted a beer from Jay and handed me the saw. "Here you go, work on the wood Jay and I will get dinner going." Al placed an arm on Jay's shoulder as they walked around the corner of the house.

I checked the gas and oil in the old Husqvarna and saw that it was almost full, then started it up. About one hour later, I was just making my last cut when Jay walked back around the house.

"Dinner's ready, H."

Good smells met me at the back door. Using my hat to swat at my clothes, I removed most of the sawdust, hung my hat and jacket on an empty peg in the cluttered mud room and walked into Al's kitchen.

"Man something smells good, need any help?" I asked.

"Yeah, we need help eating this bear," said Al. "Sit down."

The food was good and there was a lot of it. Once we all had a couple of helpings, Al told us about the bow-hunt that had earned him the bear we were currently consuming. Our conversation gradually moved to more hunting stories, and then we got into small talk about the early cold weather and all the news about local happenings around town. I started to say something about my truck, but Al stopped me, like he just remembered something.

"Oh, yeah, Jay told me about your starter motor. I shut off the engine while you were cutting wood. We can get it started later, no sense in wasting gas."

"Thanks, Al. I was actually thinking about trying to fix it tomorrow morning. If the starter motor isn't messed up, hooking up a few new wires shouldn't be a big deal."

"OK, you can use my car to run into town and get parts. How about some dessert?" Al asked.

"You cooked us a pie?" I joked.

"Better," said Al, standing from the table and walking over to the oak stained cabinets behind us; he returned with a fifth of Makers Mark and three fresh glasses. We each poured our own drink, and then did a glass touch.

"To good friends," Al said. "Glad to have you here."

The following morning, Al had beaten us into the kitchen. He was in the process of cooking eggs when I walked into the room. The bacon was already cooked and a big pile of toast was on the table.

"Thought I'd let you guys sleep," Al said, with a big smile. "You boys have work to do, not me."

"What are you up to today, Al?" I asked, filling a coffee cup.

"You mean besides watching football?" he asked.

"Stupid question," I said. "Breakfast looks great."

"Morning, Jay."

"Yeah, morning," Jay answered from the hall.

Jay is never at his best this time of day so I added, "Did you sleep OK?"

"Shut up."

A cold north wind greeted us as I opened the back door. Jay is wearing his heavy red plaid wool coat, gloves and an ugly brown hat with earflaps. I am just wearing my Levi's jacket because I know that I won't be able to roll around under the truck with a heavy coat. My work gloves are still in the truck.

Without much ceremony, I put on my work gloves and climbed under the truck. Jay is standing in front of my protruding feet ready to hand in tools at my request.

"Nine sixteenths open end," I said, extending my gloved hand.

"Screwdriver; .... Side-cutters."

The temperature must be somewhere in the twenties. Add the wind chill and it is damn cold. My fingers are freezing. I am sure glad that Jay is here to help pass tools back and forth. I extracted the starter motor and rested it on my chest before passing it out from under the truck into Jay's waiting hands.

"What do you think, H?" Jay asked.

"Well, a pile of wire is fried but we can work around that. I'm just hoping that the starter motor still works. They can check it out at the auto parts store."

Jay carried the starter back toward the house and I walked along side, mulling over what would be needed in town.

The counter man at Napa Auto Parts mounted my starter motor into a big impressive looking yellow test stand. He ran some preliminary checks for open circuits then attached the heavy cables and pushed a button labeled 12 V Test.

The motor whirred to life.

"It checks out fine," he announced.

"That's great, now I have a small shopping list for you."

After looking at the mess of melted wire that was once the electrical wire loom for my starter motor, I had decided that I would simply bypass the old system and make up a new remote starter switch. I figured that this would be the quickest way to get the truck back into commission.

My list included a remote push-button starter switch, some heavy braided wire, assorted wire crimp ends, tie wraps, and three rolls of black electrical tape.

Jay looked over my shoulder at the little schematic that I was working on but didn't comment. He really tried to avoid anything that involved electricity, and I smiled at the thought of him holding the propane heater yesterday.

We left the auto parts store, made a stop at the market for a fresh supply of beer, and then hit the fast-food drive through to buy lunch for the three of us.

Back at the house, we found Al just about finished stacking the firewood that we bucked up the day before. Jay and I walked over and helped with the last few pieces of wood.

"We brought lunch," I said. "Are you hungry?"

"Always," Al answered. "Let's get on inside and warm up."

We ate our lunch in the living room while Al channel surfed, finally settling on a pre-game show for the football game that he intended to watch. I pulled out my crude schematic and flattened it on the coffee table.

"Is your starter OK?" Al asked.

"Yeah, the motor itself is fine, just the control wires that run from the ignition switch are burned out. I'm going to build a new circuit. I think it will work OK." I got up to go outside. Jay stood as well and reached for his heavy plaid coat resting on the back of a kitchen chair.

Jay and I worked together and quickly replaced the starter motor. Then I climbed into the cab of the truck to see if I could find a good mounting location for the remote starter button. I was in luck. The truck had a couple of accessory knock out plugs on the left-hand side of the dashboard. After punching one of them out, I tested my push-button switch for a fit.

"Perfect," I said. "Jay, I can handle the rest of this by myself; why don't you go on in and help Al with the football game?"

"No, I'll hang here with you, H. No sense letting you have all the fun."

"OK, thanks. Let's get that heater going," I smiled and was glad for the company.

It took about an hour to make all of the terminal connections.

I didn't want to zip tie, or wrap any wiring until I actually checked out the operation.

It is all looking pretty good. I slid behind the wheel, checking to make sure that we were in neutral. "Here goes," I said, pushing in the new starter button. This action brought an instant whirring sound as the starter motor began turning. I smiled over at Jay. "Now for the real test," I said, as I turned on the ignition switch, and then pushed the starter button once again. This time the starter motor engaged, followed by a roar from the engine.

We grinned at each other like kids. "Well, I guess we won't need another hill," I said. "Let's wrap this mess up."

It took us another half-hour to zip tie the loose wiring, and tape some of the connections. After gathering up the last of our tools, we headed back into the house. Jay and I made a bee line for the wood stove and just stood there for a couple of minutes warming up before pulling up beers and joining Al to watch the game.

"Get it working?" Al asked, not taking his eyes from the set.

"Yeah, my patch job should hold up OK," I answered. "Damn, it's cold out there."

Al turned and laughed at that. "You are really getting soft, Howard. How long you been gone? It's not even winter yet."

It took about one more beer for me to get in my football quota. I stood up and walked towards the wood stove.

"Jay, I think that I better go have a look at the dump truck before it gets too dark. Want to come?"

"OK," Jay said, standing. He put on his coat and pulled the ugly brown hat from his pocket as he started toward the door.

"Al, would you like to do dinner in town tonight?" I asked.

"Sure," Al answered, not turning.

The sun never made an appearance today. Gray sky promised rain or maybe even snow. I was silently hoping that it would hold off just one more day as I thought of what tomorrow might be like.

My property is only about one mile away from Al's house. I have rented the place to a man named Randal who works at the same wood processing plant that Al does. I drove slowly on the familiar county road and can see smoke is coming from the chimney at my place. That means that Randal is probably home. As I drive up the driveway I see the front door open. Randal looked out and then waved recognizing my truck as we neared the house. He crossed the porch and walked over to my truck window. We talked for a couple of minutes and I told him that we were after the old dump truck and a couple more things. Randal seemed to be OK with that, and went back into the house as Jay and I walked around back to have a look at the dump truck.

I let my eyes wander around the property that had been my home just a short time before. Randal and I were working out details for him to buy the place. It was already taking on a cluttered, run-down appearance and I was not feeling too good about Randal. Jay and I continued our walk to the old Chevy dump truck.

"She looks a lot better than I remembered," said Jay.

"Oh, yeah, she is a real beauty," I said, letting my eyes rest on the only new thing that had been added to the truck, which was a solid two-by-twelve wooden dump bed that I had built a few years before. In truth, this was just an old worn-out truck and it was pretty much in the same condition as Jay had last seen it.

I walked past the truck to have a look at the homemade loading dock that was about twenty yards farther into the field. Jay walked up beside me and admired the loading dock.

"I didn't know that you built this ramp," he said. "It will make life real easy for us to load up the truck."

"Yeah, I built this loading dock about five years ago. I've loaded up the John Deere tractor several times. The truck should be a piece of cake."

We walked back around the other side of the house, and I tried my best to ignore the mess that Randal had scattered around. I stopped at the front door and knocked, then told Randal that we would be back in the morning.

"No problem," he said. "I'll probably be at work."

It was almost dark when Jay and I got back to Al's place. He is standing near the big corral gate with several horses milling near him on the opposite side of the fence. We joined Al at the corral.

"Plan on riding to town?" I asked.

"No, I was just thinking that riding is about over for the year," Al answered seriously, completely ignoring my attempt at humor. "These girls are already getting long coats. It might be a pretty cold winter this year."

"Damn, Al, it's pretty cold every winter. In fact it's getting pretty cold right now. Why don't you have a coat on?"

Al smiled back at me. "Just like I said before, it isn't even close to winter yet. You city boys are all the same; come back in a couple of months and we'll talk about cold weather."

I knew that he was right—not the city boy part, but that it would be at least two more months before the real cold weather set in. This was just a nice brisk evening in North Idaho. Maybe I was getting spoiled living on the west side of the mountains.

"You about ready for town?"

"Sure, whenever you guys are ready," Al answered as he turned toward the house.

"Your car or mine?" I joked.

Al fished a set of keys out of his pocket and tossed them to me.

"My car, you drive."

Sandpoint is not lacking for choices when it came to places to eat. If you counted the fast food joints and bars that served hot meals, there were probably thirty or forty possibilities.

"Where are we going, Al? This will be my treat," I said as we got within a mile or so of town.

"Well, if you put it that way, how about Connie's?" he asked.

I glanced over at Jay knowing that Connie's Cafe is his favorite place to eat in Sandpoint. "OK with me; how about you, Jay?"

"Perfect," said Jay. "I'm starving."

Connie's was busy but several booths were open. We walked up to the first empty one and seated ourselves without any discussion. Al swiveled in his seat and waved to a friend he had spotted across the room. A waitress that I didn't know came to our table with menus and a coffeepot.

"Hi, Al, she said. Coffee?"

"Evening, Sue, sure, coffee for all of us," Al said in a voice reserved for polite conversation. "Kind of slow tonight, isn't it?"

"Yeah, typical Sunday, I'll probably only work until around six or six thirty tonight. What would you boys like for dinner?"

"Sirloin steak," Al said. "You know how I like it."

"Yeah, Sirloin for me too," I said. "Medium rare."

Jay consulted the menu for another second. "I'll have the prime rib, medium, baked potato."

"OK," Sue said, "just a couple of minutes." She retrieved our menus and left us all warming our hands against the large white coffee mugs.

"She's cute," I said to Al.

"Yeah, married and three kids cute," he answered.

"That marriage thing sure seems to be going around," I said. "You and Jay are about the only single friends that I have left."

Jay looked over at me and smiled. "Tried it once and didn't like it," he said.

"My sentiments exactly," Al said, extending his coffee mug toward Jay for a mock toast.

Huge salads arrived, accompanied with a half loaf of warm, homemade French bread and refills of coffee all around. Conversation came to a stop as the three of us attacked our plates.

After dinner, we stepped from the warm cocoon of Connie's Restaurant into a strong wind-driven cold sleet.

"See," said Al, "the horses always know how to dress."

"So do I," said Jay, pulling the ugly brown hat out of the pocket of his heavy hunting coat.

"Let's go find some place warm," I offered, as I adjusted the collar of my Levi's jacket.

"Murphy's?" said Al.

"Perfect," I answered, turning left and starting across the street. Murphy's Bar was just half a block away.

Murphy's is warm and comfortable. A crackling fire is blazing in the big stone fireplace. We each removed our coats and hats; then started walking toward a conversation-pit area near the fire. The owner Paul Murphy is working behind the small but well-appointed red-oak bar. He walked over and greeted us, offering a large bowl of pretzels, then took our drink orders as we seated ourselves.

The fire is nice and the conversation easy. None of us are in a big hurry to call it a night but eventually we find ourselves back outside. The weather has not improved and once behind the wheel, I find the road is pretty slick. The only good news is that most of the folks in this part of the country are accustomed to the poor driving conditions and will typically drive slowly and carefully. Accidents are actually very rare in Sandpoint even during severe winter conditions.

Morning caught me kind of disoriented. The room is still very dark with only weak moonlight making its way through the window. It is one of those unsettling moments when I wake up in strange surroundings and have to try and figure out where I am, and what I'm doing here. As the cobwebs in my head began to clear I can hear voices in the next room. The smell of coffee brought me back into the present and I soon join Al and Jay in the small kitchen where breakfast is well underway.

"Morning, Al, morning, Jay. Sorry I slept in."

"You didn't sleep in," Al said. "I just got up early. I have to go to work today but I didn't want to send you boys off without a good breakfast."

"Well, this sure looks like a good breakfast to me," I answered, admiring the fresh biscuits, gravy, ham and eggs with farm style potatoes.

After breakfast the three of us made short work of cleaning up the kitchen. Jay poured the remainder of the coffee in our thermos, and then made a fresh pot for Al as he packed his lunch.

"Al, thank you for the hospitality," I said.

"Yeah, Al thanks for everything," added Jay.

"Not a problem, it's always good to see you guys."

"Well, I ate better than I have for a month. Would you consider adopting me?" I asked.

"Sure," said Al, "I'll consider it" he laughed.

"OK, I'll see you this summer for our annual fishing trip," I said, clasping him on the shoulder.

Jay and I said our good-byes to Al and headed outside.

When we reached my old place, the lights were on, indicating that Randal was still at home. We drove around back and began preparations for moving the dump truck. I knew that the battery would be dead so we lined up the big truck with the dump truck to attach a tow chain.

"Which one do you want, Jay?" I asked.

"I'll take the dump truck," he answered, already walking toward the vehicle.

"OK, just don't get in a big hurry. The brakes don't work very good, but the emergency brake will hold you if you're going slow."

Jay nodded and opened the dump truck door. I started my truck and pulled forward until I felt a familiar clank from the chain. Glancing in the rearview mirror I chuckled as Jay blinked on his small flashlight, *déjà vu*. I began a steady pull. Within the first ten feet I can see that the dump truck is running. I continued forward a couple more feet to give Jay a chance to get his vehicle under control. The small flashlight blinked on once more, and I stopped. I walked back to Jay and leaned into the window.

"I'll back around to the loading dock and then you can drive right onto the truck."

"OK."

I unhooked the chain from both vehicles; then threw it into the wooden box that was strapped down near the front of the flatbed. It is good and light now so backing up to the loading dock is pretty easy. I get my truck centered up, then backed slowly until I feel contact with the big timbers on the dock. Leaving the truck running with the emergency brake set, I stepped out and waved for Jay to come on. Jay is being careful with the unfamiliar vehicle. He kept it moving slowly but is giving her plenty of gas to prevent stalling. The loading ramp is steep and I know that Jay would lose sight of the big truck once he starts up the ramp. It could actually be kind of scary when you couldn't see anything but sky through the front window. The trick is to keep moving. Jay is doing just fine and within a couple of minutes he has the dump truck nicely centered on my big flatbed. I placed chocks under all four wheels of the dump truck, and then ask Jay to shut her off. We are ready to chain up.

Climbing back up on the flatbed, I went over to the wooden box and began removing lengths of chain and chain binders. Jay and I worked on the same side of the truck setting the chains, and then we both moved to the other side and fastened the chains and binders as well. We each walked from binder to binder making final adjustments.

"What do you think?" I asked.

Jay smiled, "Hell, we could haul this load to New York."

"Well, I'll settle for Renton" I laughed, as I climbed back up on the bed. I located a small ball of bail twine that was in the wooden box and began tying off the handles on each of the chain binders.

"I know," I said before Jay could say anything. He has told me on several occasions that the chain binders would hold without tying them, but I have seen binders lying along the highway and preferred to keep mine.

We each check the load and are satisfied with our job. Jay climbed into the passenger seat and I got in on the driver's side. I began to drive around the house.

"Damn," I said.

"What?" Jay asked, swiveling in his seat.

"No, it's not the dump truck. It's the damn trees."

"What trees?"

"Oh, those stupid trees," I said pointing to a spindly pine tree that was planted in a one-half wooden wine barrel just outside of Jay's window. "There are two of them. The other one is at the far end of the house. I promised Susie that I would bring them home. I completely forgot until now."

Jay got out and gave the barrel a tentative tug. "Damn, H, this thing is heavy. I sure hope you wife appreciates the back strain that this will cause."

"I know. The last time I moved that box of dirt I had a tractor with a front loader."

"I don't see your tractor H. How the hell are we going to get them up there today?" Jay asked, eyeing the flatbed, which was at least four feet above the ground.

"Well, maybe we can make a ramp," I said, not at all sure of this idea. I began walking toward my old shop to see if there was anything we might be able to use. On the far side of the shed I found an old two-by-twelve about ten feet long. "This should work," I said as I began freeing the board from the weeds.

I carried the board back to the truck and placed one end on the bed. The other end was only about one foot from the potted tree. Jay and I both grabbed the wine barrel and began wrestling it toward the wood ramp. We gained one inch, then another, then one more.

"Damn, this thing is heavy," said Jay, pulling off his coat.

"You know, I could easily forget about the trees," I offered.

Jay looked at me for a second to see if I was serious. "No, we can get it, H. Maybe it will be easier once we get the barrel up on the wood ramp."

It wasn't. Once on the ramp we were trying to push the barrel uphill. It took us ten minutes to gain three inches. "This sucks," I said, sweating in spite of the chilly morning. "Let's have a cup of coffee and think about this."

Jay brought out the big thermos and two cups. He set the cups on the running board and filled them with the fresh hot coffee.

"Thanks," I said, picking up one cup and setting my Levi's-clad butt in the spot the coffee cup had occupied. We drank our coffee, not talking, not looking at the tree. I considered simply walking around to the other side of the truck, starting it up and driving away.

"OK, I got it," I said.

"What's the plan, H?"

"I'm going to drive forward about five feet. You'll have to slide the board along as I move. I want to get the ramp about even with the front of the dump truck bumper. Then we can rig the come-along and pull the damn thing up."

"This can work," Jay said, tossing what was left of his coffee. "Let's do it."

We secured a small length of chain around the bottom of the wine barrel, and then hooked the come-along to the front bumper of the dump truck. I worked the come-along while Jay guided the pot up the ramp. Once we had the barrel even with the truck bed, Jay lifted the bottom end of the two-by-twelve and helped me position the barrel. This only took us about twenty minutes.

"One down and one to go," Jay smiled over at me.

When both trees were loaded, we lashed the wine barrels against the truck bumper, and then used bale twine to tie the tree branches themselves to the dump truck. I surveyed our load, which looked like the Junk Yard Exhibit for a Fourth of July parade.

My arms ache from cranking on the come-along, and I am sure that Jay is equally worn out.

"To New York?" I asked.

Climbing once more into the passenger seat, Jay reached for the big stainless steel thermos.

"Renton," he said.

If I Had a Camera

*C*arol and I were still laughing as we took turns digging through the well worn cardboard box. My wife and I have been looking at pictures of mountains, trees, open landscapes and clear blue lakes that included many shots of old boats and young people. I was doing my best to assign names or locations to the old pictures.

"What about this one?" Carol asked, holding up a picture of a decrepit old barn.

It only took me a second to remember.

"I found that one in Montana. We actually stopped the car and I walked into a muddy pasture to get a good close shot. I took lots of old barn pictures."

"What's special about barns?" Carol asked, puzzled.

"Oh, nothing really, I was just on an old barn kick for a while. I always had a camera in the car. We took pictures of everything. I got the kids in some of the shots, including most of their cats and one or two dogs. We also took a lot of these road pictures. I remember driving along snapping pictures from our car window. Now that we are sitting here looking at these pictures of highways and fields and I can't even match them up with a state. There isn't any sense to how some things stay with you. When I look at this old barn picture, I can remember exactly where it was, like it was yesterday. The barn was about fifty yards off of the road, just before we left Montana, driving toward Idaho. It was somewhere near Libby.

"I always wanted to make up a book with pictures of old barns. I just couldn't imagine that I was the only one that liked looking at them. About five or six years ago I found *The Barn Book* in one of the bookstores. Someone had beaten me to it. I wasn't mad or even disappointed. I bought the book and love it.

"You know what's funny? The things that I would really have liked to catch on film were the launching ramp incidents; but I couldn't."

"I thought you said you always have a camera with you."

"That is true, I usually do, but the kind of incidents I'm thinking about probably wouldn't look like anything on film, unless you were there. It would be hard to explain, but I don't think anyone will ever make a photo book about all the crazy things I've seen happen around boat launching ramps."

"I guess it started with my love for water skiing. My dad got me into skiing when I was only twelve. My first boat was given to me at sixteen, and I've had a boat of some kind parked around the house ever since. The thing about small boats is that you can't use them without the occasional need for a trailer. Once you own a boat and a trailer you get the quick driving course at backing up. That doesn't mean very much to anyone who hasn't had the occasion to do it. But there are a lot of people who know exactly what I am talking about. My theory is that there are just two kinds of drivers—those who know how to back up trailers, and those who don't."

The first time I took my boat out, my best friend, David, and I were using his mom's car. Neither of us knew how to backup a trailer so fortunately for us we arrived at the launching ramp on a very quiet day. This particular ramp was made to accommodate twenty or thirty vehicles at one time. Being new to boat launching David used the whole ramp to backup and launch our boat. I am not kidding when I say he needed all of it. Once the boat was in the water we discovered that the stern of the boat was still attached to the trailer. We forgot about the tie-down straps, and swamped the boat right there on the ramp. We did manage to pull our boat out of the water. Once it was untied and bailed out we spent a wonderful day of water skiing without giving another thought to our close call. If I had tried to take a picture of our first backing up and boat launching experience, my pal, David, and I may not have stayed friends. As it worked out, Dave and I did remain friends, and now when I tell this story we both get a laugh out of it. Since that maiden voyage, David and I have both owned and enjoyed several boats. Over the years we have become so confident at backing, launching, and general boating safety that we both took the opportunity to observe what everyone else was doing. I refer to these close calls as *the boat ramp incidents*. We would seldom get around a launching ramp without witnessing at least one potential disaster.

Some of the typical incidents go like this. Fred backs his nice new inboard down the ramp. His girlfriend and best friend push the boat into the water. Fred lays rubber hauling his new trailer up the ramp toward the parking lot. His girlfriend and best friend jump out of the way to keep from getting run over by the trailer. A couple of minutes later the best-friend is running up the ramp. He is yelling and waving his arms, leaving the girlfriend holding the bow of the boat. Soon Fred and his friend are running back down the ramp just in time to see water flowing into the boat over the transom. Someone left the plug out! This is pretty funny if your name isn't Fred. If you are quick enough to take a picture, he might break your nose.

The trailer-camper-rig starts backing a small boat down the boat ramp.

Everything looks good, and then slowly the trailer begins turning left. Suddenly it catches itself and goes to the right, then further to the right, not quite a jackknife.

All stop!! The passenger door opens and someone gets out. Now the camper pulls back up the ramp. As the camper backs down the ramp a second and third time, the passenger, possibly the driver's wife was now standing on the ramp directly behind the boat. She is waving her arms and yelling. After a while the driver is leaning out of the camper window. He is yelling also.

At this point a stranger comes to the rescue. For an unknown reason, the driver always gets out of his brand-new camper-rig. He lets the stranger climb into the cab, then watches while the stranger backs the boat into the water for him. For another unknown reason, the stranger always does a magnificent job of launching the boat. You know it would be hard to take a picture of that.

We launched our boat at Golden Avenue, Long Beach, California. This is a big ramp, steep and wide. On a typical weekend you will see twenty boats launching at the same time. All of the launching spaces are painted with lines much like you would expect in a grocery store parking lot. Golden Avenue is only twenty minutes from my house in Torrance, so we come here quite often. My friend Dave has just launched our boat, a white sixteen-foot outboard. It is a beautiful warm Sunday morning. I am sitting on the edge of the deck with my bare feet in the water waiting for Dave to return from the parking area. Our two skiing partners Billy and Brian are in the boat messing with their gear and getting ready for a day of water skiing.

Almost all of the lanes on the ramp are full. Cars and trucks are staging along the top of the ramp at the north end waiting for an opening to launch. I notice a pickup with an empty trailer pull up the ramp a couple of slots south of us, then casually watch as a big fancy truck pulling an equally fancy flat bottom ski boat takes his place on the ramp. The driver swooped low across the ramp, jockeying for position in this vacated spot. The boat was at least twenty feet long with one of those great looking engines—all chrome and pipes. This boat is riding on a beautiful pinstriped tandem axle trailer that probably cost more than my car. The now common, telescope receiver style trailer hitch was new to the industry at that time, and this rig has one.

At the precise moment that the fancy truck and trailer are squared up with the open launching spot, the four-inch receiver hitch pin that secured the trailer ball assembly fell out of the receiver tube. The pin must have lost its safety clip and was just barely hanging in the hole. But at any rate, the pin picked this exact moment to let go allowing the slide assembly to slip freely out of the receiver socket. Gravity took over as the boat and trailer, unhampered by the truck, raced down the ramp toward the water. The speeding trailer rolled out of control over fifty feet down the ramp. People are milling everywhere, most of them unaware of any danger. I am looking right at this accident in the making and can't react fast enough to do anything to help.

One of the guys with that group is riding in the back of the truck. He leaped out of the pickup and helplessly chased the runaway boat and trailer. The man almost caught up to the front of the trailer as it reaches the bottom of the ramp.

The boat hit the water. There is a small splash. The water actually stopped the boat and trailer, which has managed to park perfectly centered in the white painted lane.

The beautiful ski boat has launched itself and was bobbing peacefully, unattended. A shaken crew caught up with their runaway. No damage was done to any property or person. I could see a small shiny object lying almost directly under the bumper of the nice pickup, idling motionless on the ramp. The driver cautiously backed his truck down to the trailer. He then walked up the ramp and retrieved the hitch pin. His buddies helped him put the receiver hitch back together. I don't know what they used for a safety clip that day but my guess is that they checked on that particular piece of hardware from that day forward. How lucky can you be?

One evening I was preparing to haul-out. I am in the process of getting my boat straightened up prior to going for the trailer as I glance casually over at my neighbor's rig. He has a big fishing boat, maybe twenty-five feet long. It looks pretty old but in fair shape, probably wood. The cabin is enclosed and I guess you could overnight in it pretty comfortably. Over the top of the ramp crested a Hillman car. It is pulling a big tandem axle trailer. It takes a couple of seconds for me to realize that this little car intends to haul the big fishing boat out of the water. Launching is one thing, but hauling out, especially on this slippery ramp, could be something else entirely. I don't have a camera with me, or I would love to take a picture of this for sure.

The Hillman squared up its trailer and backed down to the big fishing boat. I am thinking that the boat must draw a lot of water because it was still pretty far back from dry land. After perfectly centering the trailer, the driver set his hand brake and walked back to the trailer winch. He spooled off some cable and tossed the hook up to his partner on the deck of the fishing boat. Once the hook is fastened into the bow eye, the driver now standing on the front of the trailer started cranking. I watch as he cranks the winch and soon see that the boat isn't exactly coming up the ramp. But it is getting closer to the car. I called out in alarm when I realize that the driver has cranked the trailer and car backward, and now the boat is drifting away from the ramp, deeper into the water, taking the car with it. Apparently the rear engine Hillman only has rear wheel emergency brakes. Once the car is pulled backward, the rear wheels have come off the ground. Now a combination of the slight offshore breeze and gravity are causing the car to roll down the ramp, and the whole works is beginning to moving into deeper water. The light wind is taking the boat out to sea, car, trailer and all.

Suddenly both of the guys on the fishing boat realize what is happening. They both jump into the water and try to hold back nature. The men are trying to get a grip on the side of the boat and swim at the same time. Unfortunately there is really nothing to grab on to. The ramp is very slippery and the boat is slick. I tied my boat off as best I could and rushed over to help them hold it.

The big boat is slowly moving backward. Now the front wheels of the car are in the water. Amazingly, the rear of the Hillman is still out of the water, suspended near the front of the boat, hanging by the trailer ball. The heavy trailer is following the ramp down and the winch cable is still attached to the eye of the boat. The trailer tongue has actually lifted the back end of the car way above the water. A third citizen arrives in the nick of time. He materialized with a decent truck and a long chain. Without asking, the man hooked up to the front of the Hillman and pulled the whole mess up the ramp and out of harm's way.

When I cleaned up and was and heading for home I drove past the group. All of them are sitting in the parking lot drinking a beer. Now that it is on dry ground, the Hillman-fishing-boat combo looks like a motor home pulling a small car, only backward. It would take a lot more than a couple of beers to make me drive off with that rig.

My friend Kenny is an aerospace toolmaker. He can run any type of conventional machine shop tool or computerized equipment. Kenny enjoys contract work and maintains a resume that boasts over thirty places of previous employment. The trade nickname for contract workers is "job shopper." He travels to the job and stays for the duration. Kenny's real home is in Texas. He has lived near Dallas for several years but when the job in Los Angeles opened up last July, he went. The money was good, and the job lasted almost a year. Several times Kenny bought a plane ticket for a weekend visit home, but this time the job had ended and he sat in his favorite bar saying goodbye to his friends. Tomorrow he would start the fourteen-hundred-mile drive home to Dallas.

The bar is warm and sticky, but somehow comfortable. A big old-fashioned jukebox leaned against a metal post in the center of the room. Country music was on continuous play. Pool shooters circled round and round the four tables like they were dancing. Gray smoke hung layered and suspended in the room, some of it was from Kenny, who preferred cigars. Kenny reached forward and filled his glass from the community pitcher. *This was nice.*

Bob Kelly, a fellow toolmaker and longtime friend, started talking about the boat that he had bought six months ago, and how he should sell it before leaving town. Kenny leaned forward in his chair and rolled the tip of his cigar against the empty book of matches in the ashtray.

"Another pitcher?" Someone asked.

Kenny looked once again into the rearview mirror and still couldn't quite believe that he had actually bought the boat. It didn't look like a bad boat from what he could see in the mirror—the *fact that it is a boat* was bad enough. He could already hear the hell that his wife Lavada would raise about this. They had planned for some new furniture and maybe a couple weeks of vacation after this gig was over.

And now we have a boat. Shit. Kenny flashed an angry look at the mirror; it was still back there.

Sometime near midnight the road got pretty rough. Even as he slowed down to fifty, it was still shaking his truck. *Goddamn, it must be the boat.* It didn't take much of an inspection to see that the left rear tire on the tandem trailer had come completely unraveled. Kenny took another look but there wasn't a spare anywhere on the trailer. Nothing to do now but to jack it up and go find a garage, Kenny thought, unhappily looking at the deserted highway. It took some time to dig out the tire tools, and then locate the jack under all of the other luggage and equipment piled behind the seat of his truck.

The ruined tire gave off a nasty smell. Kenny rolled it up against the rear tire on his pickup and stretched his back. It must be close to two a.m. Kenny thought as he guessed at how far it might be to the next town. *What did that last sign say? Twelve miles, whatever?* He should have stopped for sleep a couple of hours ago but was still too mad about the boat to get any rest. Now he had this flat tire to deal with. Without another thought Kenny stuck out his thumb and hitched to Gallup. *What the hell, something should be open.*

There wasn't much traffic on the highway at this time in the morning, but Kenny didn't have many options. It was exactly four a.m. when his ride dropped him in the café parking lot.

Kenny sat on the front walk of the small café. His back rested against the brick wall just under the handwritten cardboard

CLOSED sign. He must have fallen asleep for a while because now there were cars parked around him, and he could hear noises coming from inside the little restaurant. A couple of cups of coffee later and some directions had him back on the highway, carrying/rolling the tire six blocks to Hal's Garage that should be open by now. Hal had a used tire that would match his rim. Twenty minutes and sixty dollars later, Kenny was back on the highway. It was already getting hot. Two hours later he was back at his rig and an hour after that he was once again in Gallup, New Mexico, having his first real meal in twelve hours. It was close to noon.

Now that I'm awake and have had breakfast, I might as well drive. It's too damn hot to sleep anyhow. Fourteen hours later, road weary, eyes bloodshot, tired and thirsty, Kenny pulled into his own driveway, and turned off the ignition. He leaned his head against the padded headrest and unconsciously glanced once more at the boat in his rearview mirror. *Shit.*

A soft tapping sound, then another still soft but persistent sound wakes him up. Kenny opens his eyes to see Lavada, wearing her nightgown, looking through the side window at him. *What is she doing up so early? She's probably pissed about the boat.* He opens the truck door and walks past her, heading for the house. Lavada must have put the towel over the shower door because he didn't remember seeing it before washing his face.

"Come on, let's go," said Kenny.

"Go? Where?" Lavada asked, confused.

"We're going boating. Don't you go boating when you have a boat?"

"OK, Kenny, let me call Judy first."

"What the hell for?"

"Judy and Jerry will want to go with us. They love boats."

Kenny just looked at her. *Like I really want to visit with my brother-in-law.*

"Have we got a cold beer in here?" Kenny asked, opening the fridge. "Lavada, you take your car; pick up Jerry and Judy. My truck is still loaded with tools."

"OK, we'll meet you at the lake."

I've pulled this pig for two days, and now it's going to pull me. Kenny says to no one as he backs down into the water and sets his hand brake, leaving the big Ford truck in gear.

Jerry is standing at the water's edge. Kenny made a quick decision to warm up the engine. He walked past Jerry to climb over the deck and into the driver's seat to start the engine before backing all the way in and unhooking the boat. He is still tired but the fresh air should wake him up soon enough. People are already skiing. As he turned the ignition key Kenny thought he heard the engine start a split second before the explosion.

It didn't really hurt him, just kind of pushed him forward against the wheel and then tossed him over the side like a rag doll. *What the Hell?* The initial intake of air burned his lungs as Kenny caught his first breath after coming to the surface of the water. Still spitting out lake water and trying to swim, he realized the water was shallow. Half crawling, Kenny pushed himself uphill toward the Ford.

Three or four men have run over and are cupping handfuls of water to throw at the boat; which is now totally engulfed in flames. Kenny reaches the big Ford; opens the door then using the steering wheel as a handle he pulls himself into the driver's seat, and starts it up.

"Get the hell out of the way!" Kenny yells at the men around his boat, as he slams the Ford into reverse and backs another fifteen feet down the ramp, driving the burning boat under water. He wades out of his truck and walks up the launching ramp. Even with shallow breathing the burning is still there; deep down in his throat and lungs.

One of the boat ramp spectators has a bright red ice chest in the back of his pickup. Kenny marches up to the truck and without a word for permission or a sideways glance he opens the ice chest, reaches in and pulls out a beer. Kenny presses the can to his lips and drinks rapidly until the can is empty. Then he pulls a second beer from the cooler and drinks it as well. Dropping the empty can into the bed of the pickup; he shoved his hand into the cooler once again grasping for a third beer. This time he was rewarded with four cans of Coors, three dangling from the one held firmly in his right hand, all of them hooked together with a clear plastic band.

"Go ahead man, take it. You need it more than I do."

Kenny sets the beer cans down in the truck bed and carefully peels the plastic band. He pops the tabs, opening each of the four beers, and leans against the pickup fender. He picks up the closest can and starts drinking, a little slower this time.

Cautiously the stranger asks Kenny what he is going to do with the boat.

"Hell, I'm going to unhook it and leave it there."

"In the water?"

"Where else?"

"Do you have a title?"

"Sure I do," Kenny answers without really thinking about the question.

"Would you take fifty bucks?"

Kenny pokes the three dry bills into his wet shirt pocket and digs the title out of his wallet, mildly surprised that the registration certificate is still dry.

There is no need to sign; Bob Kelly already did that back in LA. Kenny walks down the ramp into the water, then slowly crosses behind the Ford, reaches down and unlatches the hitch. He leans into the water again, deeper this time, and unhooks both safety chains.

Two or three people are still standing on the ramp looking at the burnt boat. They turn and quietly watch Kenny work.

An occasional bubble rises in the water above the submerged boat. Each cloudy looking bubble belches out a small curl of gray smoke as it pops open on the surface.

Kenny stands up straight and forces his shoulders back; stretching his stiff muscles as he rotates his neck, then slowly walks to the door of his pickup. The Ford starts, pulls up about ten feet then stops. He put the Ford in reverse, backs once again into the water and slams on his brakes. As he pulls forward the second time, Kenny is satisfied that the boat and trailer have stayed put.

There are three cigars left in the pack on the dash. Kenny pushes in the lighter and sits quietly while it heats up. The pop of the lighter seems to be a signal for movement; gently he starts the big Ford up the ramp. Kenny draws on the cigar as he takes a long look into the side-view mirror.

"—I'm outta' here."

Family Album

*G*andpa Harris was reputed to be the meanest man that was ever born in the city of Wheatland. In his younger years he was known as Tom Harris and his reputation as a fighter, and a "hard man to whip" was seldom disputed by anyone who lived in Yuba County. Tom had earned this intimidating status by pulverizing his classmates through the six grades that he attended in a small one-room schoolhouse in Wheatland. Then as a young adult he honed his skills with bar fights that extended to the neighboring counties as well. At the age of twenty-five Tom married a tall, thin girl named Tildy. She was about fifteen at the time, a quiet, shy girl from Lincoln. Nobody thought that Tildy would survive Tom, but they both seemed happy on their little farm, and promptly produced two children, Little-Bob first, then Kathy. Tom continued to enjoy his status as a tough guy until the age of twenty-nine when the tractor that he was driving found a boggy spot of ground and rolled over, crushing Tom and breaking almost every bone in his body.

The farm accident left Tom crippled to the point that he could only walk for a short distance with the help of a cane, but for the most part he still spent a lot of time in one of the two town bars. Tom would roll his way around Wheatland in an old wicker wheelchair that must have been an antique long before he started using it. The accident had aged Tom considerably, causing his hair to turn prematurely gray. It was then the locals began referring to him as Old Tom, or Old Tom Harris.

Fisticuffs from his early years blurred into almost a pleasant memory as Tom rolled his chair through town. He had indeed turned into a mean and hateful old man. The walking cane was always on his lap to be used as a weapon when anyone dared to get into his path. Men, women and children were all allowed equal shares of his wrath. He would lash out the cane without warning, following the initial assault with violent cursing. Very few people would share the same side of the street with Old Tom and his wheel chair. Children were terrified and would flee at the sight of him. Some folks think that it was the accident that made Tom bitter, but others say that with or without the accident Tom was always just plain mean.

During one long muddy spring, the roads were rutted and almost impossible to navigate by car, truck, or foot. Old Tom made a couple of attempts to travel outside but soon retreated back into his house to wait out the weather. Tildy and the children went to church almost every Sunday, but they had missed the past couple of weeks because of the roads. Three women from Willow Church put together a basket for Tildy and the kids. The ladies shifted uneasily, blowing into their gloves on this chilly Sunday morning as they waited on the front porch. None of the women had ever actually been inside the house. The door opened slowly and they were face to face with Little-Bob, now seven years old. Tildy soon joined Little-Bob at the door and invited the women inside.

"Tom's asleep," she said quietly, almost as an encouragement for them to enter.

It was quite dark inside the front room of this small two-room house with a single curtain covered window providing the only source of light. Old Tom was asleep on a floor pallet in one corner of the room. His left arm draped protectively across their daughter Kathy who was wrapped snugly in blankets and wedged against his side. The three church ladies, Tildy, and Little-Bob moved into the kitchen space, which was much lighter and thankfully for the ladies, well away from Old Tom. Four kitchen chairs were lined up along one wall. The women seated themselves as Tildy went to the stove and began to prepare coffee for her guests.

Remembering the basket that she had brought, one of the women stood up and walked to the kitchen table.

"Oh, thank you, let me take that," said Tildy, reaching for the basket and then placing it on the sideboard. "I try not to put anything on the table. The pig," she said, by way of explanation.

Three heads nodded, not really understanding. Then three sets of eyes took a closer look at the table. Wire mesh had been wrapped around the four table legs. Suddenly the table moved several inches across the floor.

"WHAT'S UNDER THAR?" shouted one of the church ladies, jumping to her feet.

"It's just the pig," said Tildy calmly. "Tom can't get outside in this weather, so he has been raising it under the table; we just throw's the leftovers to him. The pig is getting pretty big and can move the table around so I don't put anything on top. We will have to butcher him pretty soon."

Little-Bob didn't stay little for very long. By the time he was in the third grade Little-Bob was as tall as anyone who attended Wheatland elementary school. His only real friends were his dog, Speck, and his sister Kathy, whom he seemed to adore. Little-Bob, Kathy and Speck were inseparable. Speck would go to school with the children and then wait outside by the big birch tree until class was over. After school, they would often walk into town, which was out of the way for them on their way home. The children didn't get into any mischief and Speck was well behaved in a "don't mess with us" kind of way. Nobody in town could blame the kids for not rushing directly home, as Old Tom wasn't even begining to mellow out.

Trouble didn't really start for Little-Bob until Kathy got a bit older and a lot prettier. Now Bob's protection of his little sister took on a whole new meaning. Once in high school, Kathy tended to attract boys that were much older than she or Little-Bob. To make matters worse, the boys that Kathy liked all seemed to run on the large size. Even though Little-Bob was tall, he hadn't really filled out yet but that didn't stop him from standing up for his sister. Maybe he got some of the toughness from his dad. During these teen years Little-Bob had pretty much whipped all of the boys that had enough gumption to come calling on his little sister, so it was kind of understandable when Kathy up and married a man from out of town and moved away to Lincoln before she finished high school. The following year Tildy caught a bad fever that was going around. She took to her bed and died within a week.

Little-Bob finished school and went into farm work. He was never one to complain about the long hours, hard jobs or short pay. He became kind of quiet and sullen after Kathy left and there was no telling what his home life was like now that his mother Tildy was gone. Bob never took the time to make any real friends and was still living at home on the little farm with his dad Tom, who was now generally referred to as Grandpa Harris.

The nickname Little-Bob didn't fit too well anymore so as an adult he was simply known as Bob Harris. On Friday nights, Bob would spend a good piece of his paycheck at the tavern. Following in his father's footsteps, he would sit alone drinking beer until he got stupid drunk, then often ended the evening in a fight. Bob didn't lose very many of those fights. It got so that the only people who would actually fight with him were either from out of town or way too drunk themselves to realize just who the heck they were messing with. Bob had a reputation as a mean drunk and was often referred to as "the toughest man in Wheatland." Then the war started in Europe and Bob joined the Seabees.

Soon after, the Japanese attacked Pearl Harbor and fortified a good share of the islands in the South Pacific. Word came back that Bob Harris and his Seabee outfit had been working on Wake Island when war was declared. The Seabees were made prisoners of war. After turning the big world globe in the lobby of the Public Works Department and finding out where Wake Island was actually located, the local citizens of Wheatland just shook their heads and guessed that they had probably seen the last of Little-Bob, Bob Harris.

Grandpa Harris woke up early one Saturday morning, loaded a box of twelve chickens onto his lap and pointed the wheelchair toward Lincoln. It was his intent to sell the chickens to Le Wa, the owner of Lincoln's only Chinese restaurant. At least two locals slowed their vehicles as they rounded his wheelchair to ask where he was going, and then offered him a ride. Grandpa Harris just cussed at them and tried to unleash his cane so they each drove away leaving him to continue the twelve-mile journey smack down the middle of Highway 65. Once in Lincoln, Grandpa Harris banged his cane against the window of Le Wa's restaurant. Le Wa was not happy to see Grandpa Harris and did not have any idea that he was expected to buy chickens from him that day. A loud lengthy quarrel ended with Le Wa marching back into his restaurant and slamming the heavy oak front door. Grandpa Harris was red-faced mad. He opened the box of chickens and began pulling them out, killing them one after another by wringing their necks, then throwing the dead carcasses into the street in front of Le Wa's restaurant. Once this deed was done he rolled his wheelchair into the roadway and began the long trip back to Wheatland.

The state trooper tried again to get the old farmer to tell him what had happened. The farmer, a man of about sixty clad in worn brown coveralls, was sitting on the ground in the shade of his truck. The truck was flipped up on its side, straddling two fence poles about thirty yards away from the highway. A woman, possibly the farmer's wife, was sitting beside the farmer. She was dabbing at her eyes with a beautiful white lace handkerchief.

"Sir, please try to tell me what happened here," said the officer very calmly.

"He come right at me," sobbed the farmer. "I try to swerve out of his way but he hit me with the stick when I pass. I think the stick get hooked on the truck and drag him and his chair under the wheels. I'm so sorry, it not my fault. I try to miss him."

The unfortunate death of Grandpa, Tom Harris, rated a four line obituary on the fifth page of the *Weekly Reporter*. The front-page news was all about the Allied Forces winning a major battle on Wake Island.

On a warm mid-June day, about two months after Grandpa Harris was laid to rest, a thin faced, pale skeleton of a man seated himself at the bar known then as Wally's Tavern. The man ordered and quietly drank one beer, then left the bar. It took about fifteen minutes before someone asked Wally, "Could that have been Bob Harris?"

The news of Bob's return was the talk of the town for the next couple of weeks, but was he really back? No one had seen him since that one appearance at Wally's. The old farm that belonged to Grandpa Harris didn't look occupied. Some of the

Harris family actually stopped by and looked around, but no Bob.

A full six months later Bob Harris did return to town. This time he was driving a brand-new Chrysler sedan and was with a female companion. He escorted the young woman into the tavern and was greeted with a hero's welcome. Bob's complexion was better but the thin, gaunt look still remained.

Bob introduced Sue to the crowd at Wally's. This was the first time that any of them had ever seen Bob Harris with a lady friend. Sue was from Menlo, a neighboring town. It turned out that Sue and Bob had been dating for a few months just prior to his joining the Seabees. They had written to each other for the first four months of his enlistment but of course all correspondence came to a halt once Bob became a prisoner of war. Bob and Sue had decided to get married.

I met Bob for the first time years later. Our initial encounter at his home was rather strange. My friend, Ben, and I drove to his house. It was located in a small tract of homes on the outskirts of Wheatland.

"Have you ever been to Bob and Sue's before?" My friend asked as we parked in front of the light gray house with a nicely manicured lawn.

"No, why?"

"It's just kind of different," Ben said nonchalantly as we walked toward the front porch.

Young Bobby answered the door. He was a good looking kid, tall and clean cut, about fifteen, Bob and Sue's only child. We walked directly into the living room. Different it was. Several days or weeks worth of discarded fast food drink containers, and food wrappers littered every square inch of the room. Chairs and tabletops were piled high with books and newspapers. Sue was lounging in a big beige recliner watching a daytime soap and Bob was stretched out on a full-length couch covered in blankets, though it was a warm day.

"Hi, Ben, hello, Howard, good to see you again," he said, not rising from his prone position. "How are you boys doing?"

"We're good Bob, heard you were sick so Mary sent us over with some of her goose pie to cure you." Ben said, offering the package that he was carrying.

Bob laughed at that. "Mary is very kind, thank you, Ben. I really think the fever broke this morning. I'm feeling a lot better now."

He tossed off the blankets to prove that he was feeling better and I was very surprised to see six or seven baby chicks snuggled at his side.

"What have you got there, Bob?" I asked in my, *this is no big deal* voice.

"Oh, I raise pheasants in pens out back," Bob answered casually. "One of the hens isn't much of a mom. She won't set her eggs. So being as I was pretty hot with my fever I figured I could do a better job of setting them than she would. It worked pretty well; they all hatched out about two hours ago."

Later that day Ben told me about some of Bob's life as a POW. He said that the Japanese captured thirty-five men in his Seabee outfit. When they were rescued three years later only nine of them were still alive. Bob told Ben that most of the men just seemed to lose interest in life and quietly passed away. The prisoners were worked as slave labor and fed very little. Bob decided early on that this was going to be a long war and if he was going to survive he would need to find more than the meager rations of rice and water. Almost every day Bob would eat about half of his nightly meal. Then he placed the remainder of his rice ration near the edge of his pen as bait and waited until something tried to get it. Some nights it was a mouse, sometimes a rat or a little bird. Bob would capture whatever critter came for his rice, and then add the meat to his meal. He often forced his arm through small openings in his cage to pick grass and bamboo shoots or any weeds that happened to grow within his reach. When out on work parties Bob always attempted to snag a leaf or anything green from the bushes he passed. Life wasn't easy but somehow he and his eight comrades managed to survive.

One clear bluebird morning, Bill, Young Bobby and I were duck hunting. Or I should say bird watching, as we hadn't seen anything but dickey birds for more than an hour. A red-tail hawk was soaring low over the field near our blind.

"Shoot that damn bird, Bobby," Bill said. "He'll run off any ducks that try to work our decoys."

"No, I don't think so, Uncle Bill," Bobby answered in a clear soft voice.

"Why not, don't you think you can hit it?"

"Oh, I can hit it easy enough, Uncle Bill, but I really don't care much for hawk stew."

"Damn, Bobby, I didn't ask you to eat it, I just asked you to shoot it."

"Well, Uncle Bill, if I shoot that hawk my dad would be awful mad if I didn't bring it home and eat it," Bobby answered as if everyone knew that as a fact.

Bob Harris died from a heart attack at the age of seventy-eight. He had survived Sue by ten years. I can't say that Bob was ever completely a well man after the war years. He had many lifelong hang-ups when it came to food, and his social skills were slim to none, but Bob was a good friend, a good husband and father. As far as I am concerned his battles have definitely earned him a life time title as "The Toughest Man in Wheatland."

ABOUT THE AUTHOR

Howard Blinder and his wife Carol are long time residents of Kent, Washington. They enjoy bicycle riding, camping and fishing in the Pacific Northwest. Howard and Carol are pictured on the front cover with their granddaughter Christina Lynch. The *Snapshot* short story collection is his first book, soon to be followed by a second book in this series which will be named *Fall Colors*.
www.howardblinder.com

CPSIA information can be obtained at www.ICGtesting.com
Printed in the USA
LVOW091731220212

269959LV00012B/151/P

9 781456 764999